D1079469

MAMMA MIA!
HOW CAN I RESIST YOU?

MAMMA MIA!
HOW CAN I RESIST YOU?

THE INSIDE STORY OF MAMMA MIA! AND THE SONGS OF ABBA

BENNY ANDERSSON BJÖRN ULVAEUS JUDY CRAYMER
INTERVIEWS CONDUCTED BY PHILIP DODD

PHOENIX
ILLUSTRATED

CONTENTS

128 THE SHOW

1

THE SPIRIT

Nonchalantly propped up against one of the walls in Benny Andersson's office is a piece of artwork by Bruce Nauman, an American artist. It's a simple concept: a rectangle split into halves, one white, the other black. On the white half is the single word 'AH'; reversed out of the black is the word 'HA'. Benny appreciates its simplicity, and chuckles at the reminder that he and Björn Ulvaeus, his co-conspirator in ABBA, created – in 'Knowing Me, Knowing You' – one of the most famous 'ah ha's in music history.

Alan Partridge, the splendidly insensitive alter ego of Steve Coogan, used *Knowing Me, Knowing You* as the title of his shambolic chat show, a series Björn has watched and enjoyed. Benny would like to see Rowan Atkinson and co's famous 'Super Duper' spoof from *Not The Nine O'Clock News* ('One of us is ugly/One of us is cute/One of us you'd like to see in her birthday suit'). There is an agreeable lack of pomposity about these two Swedes; they wear their fame lightly and have an ability to laugh at both themselves and the ABBA years. But they are also fiercely protective of what they achieved as songwriters, producers, performers and musicians – which is why to hear them talk about their music is something special.

The office where Benny works, every day when he's in Stockholm, is in a building owned by Mono Music, his record company, on Skeppsholmen, one of the cluster of islands that make up Stockholm's city centre, a leafy former naval base that is now home to modern art and architecture museums, and where the annual jazz festival takes place. Mono Music's long single-storey building, an old nautical stores, looks out across waters criss-crossed by ferries and antiquated steamers.

Inside there is little that would tell you this is ABBA territory, even though Benny and Björn's long-time manager, Görel Hanser, also has her office at the other end of the building; her chocolate-coloured dog, Bruno, patters and potters across the wood floors. Her logo, Göööööööööörel, created by Rune Söderqvist – who also designed the ABBA logo – reflects the way Stig Anderson, ABBA's first manager, would yell to attract her attention back in the days when she was his assistant. 'I was very good at shouting back,' she says. There are no ABBA gold discs on the walls, no photos of the group, only traces of Benny and Björn's music-making after ABBA stopped recording: posters for *Chess*, the musical they wrote with Tim Rice, and for *Kristina Från Duvemåla*, their own musical based on one of the most famous works in Swedish literature. There are photos of other Mono Music acts, and of the Benny Anderssons Orkester, Benny's gathering of folk-inspired musicians, which is a return to one of his great loves. A double-bass sits in one corner of the office. The message is loud and clear. ABBA is in the past.

But there is memorabilia from *MAMMA MIA!*, the musical that gave the songs of ABBA a whole new lease of life. The Skeppsholmen office was where, on one short-lit November Saturday in 1997, Benny and Björn had a meeting with their old friend Judy Craymer, who had been nurturing the idea for a show

Björn (top) and Benny (bottom). Every day that Benny is in Stockholm he goes to his office on Skeppsholmen, in the heart of the city, to write music – because 'I don't know what else to do.' Living and working in Sweden has always given them a different perspective on the music and entertainment business and has informed not only their attitudes but even Björn's lyric writing. He says, 'There is a sadness which is special for the Nordic people. I'm not saying they are sad all the time or dull or boring, just that there is something different from the rest of the continent.'

based on their songs for more than ten years, with Catherine Johnson, the writer they all felt could create an uplifting narrative around the songs, and with Phyllida Lloyd, the freshly appointed and greatly respected theatre director. It was a meeting that propelled the musical, until then really only a notion, a concept, a dab of development money, a treatment and a draft script, towards reality.

The evening before, they had all gathered for dinner at Björn's home, on a small island just offshore from one of Stockholm's northern suburbs, to mark the occasion. Across the waters of the sound is Lidingö, where both Björn and Agnetha and Benny and Frida owned houses. The heart of ABBA's creativity and philosophy is rooted in Sweden, and particularly in Stockholm. The city is dotted with ABBA locations – from Stig and the boys' original turreted offices to their Polar recording studio (now a gym) high up over a gorge mid-town.

Stockholm explains so much about Benny and Björn's clear-eyed view of the music industry, about the particular brand of listening they grew up with, open to music from Germany, France and Italy as well as American and UK pop and their own country's folk tradition. It explains their measured, calm world view, their insistence on working 9 to 5, just as Benny still does, and their sense of self-deprecating fun.

Their canon of songs twist and turn, musically never predictable, and – as Björn started flexing his wordsmith's muscles – with increasingly dramatic lyrics: a husband walking through a family house being packed up, a father watching his daughter go off to school on her own for the first time, a woman lying in a psychiatrist's chair. It was that inherent theatrical quality that Judy Craymer and Catherine Johnson mined so cleverly to create the plotline of *MAMMA MIA!*

So this is the story of how Benny and Björn joined forces with three dynamos – a determined, problem-solving producer, a cheeky fringe theatre writer, and a renowned theatre and opera director – who had all been 16 going on 17 when ABBA stormed the bastions of Eurovision at Brighton in April 1974. For the numerologists out there, all three – Judy, Catherine and Phyllida – were born in 1957, as were many other key players in the *MAMMA MIA!* saga, whose voices are in this book: the production designer Mark Thompson; musical supervisor Martin Koch, Siobhán McCarthy, the original Donna; Louise Pitre, the first Donna in Toronto and on Broadway; Michael Simkins, the second Sam in London. They all come from a generation for whom ABBA was part of the soundtrack of growing up. They all have in common the same cultural reference points, an attitude, a spirit – what they call 'the *MAMMA MIA!* factor'. And they share a sense of humour that not only meshes with Benny and Björn's, but helped them overcome the inevitable challenges of putting on a musical in the West End, on Broadway and around the world.

But first the two master craftsmen who fashioned the songs that made that musical possible, these two songwriters who rarely open up about their past, talk about how each of those songs emerged, with flashes of insight into the notoriously *in*explicable creative process, and that instant when something magical occurs – the 'ah ha' moment.

Philip Dodd

Left: Judy Craymer poses with the *MAMMA MIA!* bride.
Above: Catherine Johnson (top), who wrote the script, and Phyllida Lloyd, the director.
In Benny's view, 'I don't think the show could have been done by three guys. The element of strong women on stage is a reflection of what real life is about – and maybe three blokes wouldn't have gotten that.'

2

THE SONGS

THE STORY OF ABBA

WATERLOO

Life before Eurovision. Above: Agnetha, Björn, Benny and Anni-Frid out sailing in the Stockholm archipelago in the summer of 1973. Opposite: A 1972 photo session in the Gardet area of Stockholm, within sight of the city's landmark radio and TV tower, the Kaknästornet.

6 April 1974. The Eurovision Song Contest is being held in the Brighton Dome, England because Luxembourg has won twice running and can't afford the cost of putting the show on in back-to-back years. Sweden's entry is 'Waterloo' by ABBA: four performers, two couples, all well-known in Scandinavia as solo artists, in chart-topping groups and in their current combination. To virtually everyone outside Scandinavia they are an unknown quantity.

Benny Andersson: Some people might have thought that entering the Eurovision Song Contest was a corny thing to do, but for us as Swedes it was almost the only way we could reach an audience outside Sweden and make people aware that there was this group called ABBA who thought they were good songwriters. Björn and I had previously written a song for the 1972 Eurovision contest, a ballad for a singer called Lena Andersson, and then as ABBA we had entered in 1973 with 'Ring Ring' – a song that I still like. We had only come third in the preliminary competition to find the Swedish entry, so we hadn't made it through to the finals. For 1974 we wanted to be more prepared. We recorded an album with two new songs that might be suitable, because we wanted the record to be available as soon as the competition happened.

Björn Ulvaeus: When the prospect of Eurovision began to loom in early 1974, we had to make a critical decision, to choose which of the two new songs that we had written and recorded would be our actual entry. One of the songs was 'Hasta Mañana' and the other was 'Waterloo'. We hadn't set out in any kind of a clinical way to write a song for Eurovision. We certainly knew that we were going to be entering, but we didn't sit there thinking, 'This song will be good for Eurovision.' How could that be, because 'Waterloo' was completely different from anything else that had been done in the contest before. It was a more contemporary song, much more rock'n'roll – it fitted into the era of glam rock, of Roy Wood and Wizzard, and the Glitter Band. It also marked a break for us. I don't think we had ever done anything like that before.

Benny: 'Hasta Mañana' was more of a tra-la-la thing and I think Stig Anderson, our manager, thought, 'Oh, that feels more like Eurovision.' But Björn and I said, 'We don't care about that. We want to do what we think is good for us as a band. If we win, that would be wonderful, but whatever happens this is a chance to present ourselves performing our own music, and this is the song that we feel is most representative of what we want to do.'

I thought, 'Let's make a mark, let's be as different as possible so that at least, even if we end up ninth, people will still remember us.' Björn Ulvaeus

Björn: I just thought that for us to perform 'Waterloo' would be much more fun, and it would stand out from the rest of the songs in the contest, certainly more strongly than 'Hasta Mañana' would have done. I didn't think we'd win, anyway. Although I felt very confident about ABBA as a group with a future, as a group with something to give, as far as winning the Eurovision went, I simply didn't know. Eurovision is so fickle, you can never know for sure, especially when the different regions gang up to vote for each other.

Benny: Stig wrote the original lyrics for 'Waterloo'. As far as I was concerned, I hated lyric-writing. I can't write lyrics anyway, apart from the odd birthday lyric. It's tricky, writing lyrics – it's not just putting words together. Björn is a true lyricist, although he didn't know it then, and he didn't enjoy it any more than I did. Stig, on the other hand, was a music publisher and had written thousands of Swedish lyrics for songs that he had bought the rights to, and he could do it just like *that*. He also had the kind of brain that could listen to a melody and say, 'I think this is where the title should fall.' He had some sense of form. He was always happy to have a go at writing the lyrics and we were equally happy that we didn't have to. But Björn would always then fix the English lyrics. Stig would write 'Waterloo', for example, and Björn would take a look at it and say, 'Maybe we'll change that' and help to make it better. He did that more and more over the years until the day came when he decided, 'Well, I might as well do it myself.'

Björn: Stig was much the more accomplished lyricist between the two of us. I hadn't written that many lyrics at that point, and was really only starting out, but I did work on the English version of 'Waterloo' and changed it around a bit. I learned a lot from Stig during that first couple of years.

Benny: We hadn't heard any of the other songs that were going to be in the competition, but it didn't matter because there we were in the finals, people were going to see us as a Swedish band called ABBA and we were going to be performing a song that we liked… Once you find yourself in a competition you might as well go for it, so there was lots of excitement, people running around like mad rats all over the place, but we felt good. There had been a change to the rules that year which meant we could perform to the backing track, provided we brought over the musicians who had actually played on the recording so they could mime to it: a typical piece of BBC administration, as I was to learn. So that was a bonus. We knew that the music was going to sound OK, we just had to sing it right.

We moved into the Grand Hotel on the sea front at Brighton. The firehoses all over the hotel were labelled 'Waterloo', which we thought was a good omen, and when we arrived there I actually went out and placed a bet of a hundred quid on 'Waterloo' to win – we didn't have betting in Sweden at the time. The odds were pretty good, 12–1 or so, because we were up against some good songs. The Italians had a ballad called 'Si'; the Dutch entry, 'I See A Star', was being performed by Mouth and MacNeal who were already internationally famous. And Olivia Newton-John was there for the UK, although she didn't have such a good song in 'Long Live Love'.

ABBA's 'Waterloo' effect. Clockwise from top left: fans besiege the group when they visit Waterloo in Belgium; performing the song in the Eurovision finals with Rutger Gunnarsson on bass and Ola Brunkert on drums; the Waterloo police check all is in order; the group pose with Stig Anderson (middle back) and conductor Sven-Olof Walldoff in his full Napoleonic outfit.

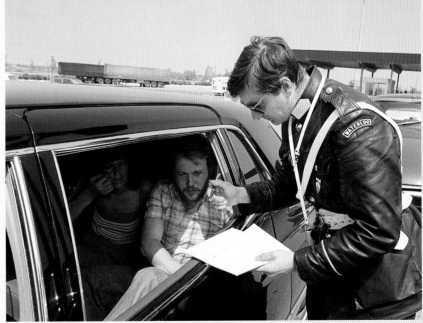

Overleaf: Celebrating for the press the next day in the spring sunshine on Brighton beach after a Champagne breakfast. The celebrations the night before had gone on until 4 am.

Working on costumes. 'We were a pop act,' says Björn. 'I firmly believed that we had to be as outrageous as possible visually in order to get noticed, especially during Eurovision. But we did only wear those costumes for about two or three years into our career. People forget that after that we became very sophisticated.'

In those days, the technology wasn't yet available for all the juries around Europe to be able to vote on the night, so they listened to a tape recording of the song taken from the dress rehearsal. That's all they had to vote on; they didn't see the live act like they do now, so the rehearsal was in fact the moment where we needed to be really accurate. Even so, we couldn't really relax on the actual night. You are always going to be tense entering a competition like that, realising there are hundreds of millions of people watching.

I knew exactly the moment we had won. We were standing in the green room, watching the votes coming in, and there came a point when I realised that even if we didn't get any more points and somebody else got all the twelves on offer we were still going to win. That happened with three or four countries left to vote. I said to myself, 'OK, we're home. This is ours.' For the prize-giving, the security guards tried to stop Björn and me going on stage. We said, 'Come on, we are the songwriters.' I managed to get past them and Björn had to struggle a little more; I'm not sure he ever managed to escape. But I remember Stig was very fast up on that stage.

From the moment we had won we realised, 'Now everybody knows who we are. We can start working. Now we'll start writing good stuff and we can release those records all over the world, or at least in Europe.' So we were extremely, immensely happy. It was wonderful. And then there were celebrations later on, at the Grosvenor House Hotel up in London, with a lot of press attention. So in many respects it was very good for us that the contest was held in England that year.

Björn: We were lucky – it could have been held in Ljubljana or somewhere rather far-flung. And events might have been different if it had been. I think ABBA could still have had as big a career as we did, but winning in the UK was certainly one hell of a springboard and it meant that things took off like a rocket.

During the build-up I had been very tense and nervous, and everything had been a bit of a blur. But I remember distinctly when I went to bed the night after 'Waterloo' had won – or rather early the morning after; the evening had been so frantic. When we finally got back to the hotel room and I lay my head on the pillow, I thought to myself, 'Oh, what is this?' I knew that something had happened that was such a turning point in my life it's almost impossible to imagine. I thought, 'We have the world at our feet almost. We have every possibility in the world.'

Then it was back to work. The very next day we had this brainstorming session, a real pow-wow with Stig, asking, 'Where do we go from here?' It was a wonderful feeling to be able to talk about this, looking at all the letters and telegrams that had come in from around the world, discussing this and that offer, which was much more exhilarating – but also daunting – than going off on a binge to celebrate. We also knew this would have an impact on our family life. Agnetha's and my daughter had only been born the year before, so we knew that extensive tours were not on the cards. We were talking about limiting ourselves to one-day trips to do TV shows. And we also knew that songwriting was much more important. Besides, I don't think people made much money touring in those days. That came later with the big arena tours put on by bands like the Stones and Pink Floyd. So it didn't even make economic sense.

Life after Eurovision. Above: A photo session in Stockholm with Wolfgang 'Bubi' Heilemann for *Bravo* magazine. Left: Plotting and planning.

HONEY, HONEY

Benny: 'Waterloo' had been Number One in a number of countries around Europe, and most importantly for us, in the UK. To follow up on that success as swiftly as possible we wanted to put out another track from the *Waterloo* album that we had already recorded at the end of 1973. 'Hasta Mañana' was a possible, but the song that we really wanted to have as our second single was 'Honey, Honey'.

We were on a variety of record labels at that time – Epic in London and Deutsche Grammophon in Germany – so we needed to talk to everybody about every decision. And Epic didn't want to go with 'Honey, Honey', because they wanted something that was more like 'Waterloo'. Typical. The record companies never learn, you know. In the UK the follow-up was 'Ring Ring', which didn't do that well. And then there was an English duo called Sweet Dreams who recorded a version of 'Honey, Honey' when we didn't release it as a single; they had a Top Ten hit with it, which kind of proved that we were right and the A&R guys were wrong.

We have always liked to do things differently. But I remember so well thinking to myself at one point, 'Why do we have to go against the grain *all* the time?!' Björn Ulvaeus

Björn: I know that 'Honey, Honey' was being discussed as a follow-up, which would have been a very wise decision, but then it was thought that 'Honey, Honey' was much more middle-of-the-road than we wanted to be. The fact of the matter is that we had not yet found ourselves; we didn't really know where we were. So we hadn't really started off on the right foot, and subsequently this English group made a cover version and had a bit of a hit with it, whereas we had a major flop with our follow-up.

Benny: It taught us a lesson about taking advice from other people who thought they knew what we should do. We always wanted to do exactly what we wanted to do. All the time. If a record company said to us, 'Well, guys, you can't do this, you need to keep in this little box here, we don't want you in this other box', they were welcome to say that, but we didn't care because we still did it the way we wanted. And it turned out to be quite healthy that we happened to be Swedish, being apart from what was going on in other countries. We always tried to keep away from what we had done before, and this we learned – at least I feel this – from the Beatles. Now they were still a tight band, they were within their own framework all the time, but their songs were definitely all over the place.

We were happy with 'Honey, Honey'. It is really very bubblegum-ish, but it isn't a pastiche, because to write a pastiche, you have to intend to create one, and

this was not a conscious attempt on our part to copy that style. It was what emerged, a song in that vein that popped up in our consciousness.

I think it is a smooth-sounding recording. It is something of a strange song because it has no end really. Normally a song would have a beginning, a middle and an end or it would have a verse, chorus, verse, chorus and so on. The structure that 80 per cent of songs follow. 'Honey, Honey' doesn't do either of those things. It just starts and goes on but it has no ending. It heads into this intricate middle section – which I always thought was really nice, because it doesn't really belong in that song, and it stopped the song being too straightforward – and then comes back and there's a fade out. We didn't write many songs like that. 'The Winner Takes It All' has no ending either; that's the only other one that comes to mind.

Björn: I have to confess that the lyrics for 'Honey, Honey' are a little stupid! They do make me cringe a bit. Stig and I wrote the words – it was about half and half between us – so I'm afraid I do have to take my share of the responsibility… But it does have a strong and catchy title, which was something Stig in particular was very good at coming up with. And because we were foreigners writing songs in English, I think we paid much more attention to creating a hook, to finding a title that would stand out and be very, very catchy, perhaps more so at the time than a British or American songwriter, because they didn't need to think along those lines. We felt that we had to be catchy because a song had to go

ABBA walk through the streets of Hamburg on their way to accept their gold discs for selling two million copies of the 'Honey, Honey' single in Germany.

Above and opposite: Life goes on as normal. Björn says, 'Even during our heyday we could walk the streets of Stockholm with people recognising us but not bothering us, which I think is unique for the Scandinavian countries. I remember being mobbed in London and other places, but in Stockholm there was a sort of sanity, a feet on the ground thing, which was very, very good.'

down well in France or Spain, whereas a songwriter whose first language was English could be much more introvert and didn't have to pay so much attention. They could be confident that because they were writing in English it was going to become a hit in the rest of the world anyway. For example, a song title like 'I Want To Know What Love Is', that is a great title in English, in the Anglo-Saxon market, wonderful, no doubt about that. But it's not very catchy in France or Germany – it's simply a collection of English words, even though there's the word 'love' in there, which people would recognise. Whereas 'Waterloo' or 'Mamma Mia' or something like that is much more a signal.

Benny: There's a bit of autoharp in 'Honey, Honey'. An autoharp is quite easy to play; you don't need any special skills: you press down the chord bars, strum the harp and it plays all the right notes for that chord. When there is a hole somewhere in the recording you need to fill it with something and it shouldn't just be ad libbed. If you listen, I think that if there is something significant in our arrangements it is that there is never any strumming along stuff, at least not in the good recordings; everything knows exactly why it is there. So if there was a gap somewhere we needed to put something in there, not just wait for the next line. For example, on 'Waterloo' we had added a saxophone fill. It could have been anything, but it happened to be the saxophone. And on 'Honey, Honey' it happened to be an autoharp.

We were always looking around the studios to see what instruments might be lying around and whether we could use them, see what kind of a sound we might be able to get out of them. We were recording in Metronome Studio in Stockholm at the time, a studio that had been built in 1959, and they had a whole range of instruments available: timpani drums, marimbas, vibraphones. In those days there weren't so many sounds you could work with. Nowadays you can call up anything at any moment. You have all the sound effects and sound samples, everything you need, in your computer. All these sounds are at your fingertips. And you have a sequencer, which can correct anything that is not in rhythm, and you can adjust bad singers so that they are in tune, and you can snip things up into quavers. You can make anything sound pretty good. That's why there are so many bad records out there nowadays. Back then, we had to be inventive and innovative. And Michael Tretow, our sound engineer, never gave up. He was constantly trying new ideas, which was very inspiring. And we were also trying to use the girls' voices as best we could. Although I sing a little – my voice is OK doing harmonies for a record and I'm able to sing in tune – I have an ugly voice, I think, so I'm not a singer. Björn is sort of a singer, but nowhere near what the girls are. So we decided that we should write pop music and let the girls sing it. That was a good decision.

After their triumph in the Eurovision Song Contest, the remainder of 1974 had been an extremely busy year for ABBA – so busy that they had to cancel a tour of the Swedish folkparks to concentrate on songwriting and producing during the summer, and (working around the constraints of a European tour that autumn) recording the next album, simply called ABBA.

I DO, I DO, I DO, I DO, I DO

Benny takes a break, May 1974. ABBA were appearing on the *Chansons á la Carte* TV show in Brussels, performing 'Ring Ring' and 'Waterloo'. Benny describes the costume seen here as 'absolutely horrendous' – but he loves the coloured snakeskin shoes, which he bought in London.

Benny: The whole feel of 'I Do, I Do, I Do, I Do, I Do' is inspired by the sound of Billy Vaughn. He was an American bandleader who had a number of big hits in Europe through the 1950s, numbers like 'Sail Along Silv'ry Moon' and 'Twilight Time'. And one of Billy Vaughn's trademark sounds was using two saxes playing in harmony. So the two saxes on 'I Do, I Do, I Do, I Do, I Do' are a deliberate homage to his music. I remember listening to those tunes when I was in my teens. I really liked the Billy Vaughn numbers, everybody did; they'd be on the jukebox in the local café. This was at the end of the 1950s and the jukebox would also have had a selection of Elvis Presley, Tommy Steele, maybe Cliff Richard, certainly the Shadows: the first single I ever bought was Elvis's 'Jailhouse Rock'; and the first album I bought, later on, was Mantovani's *Film Encores*! I was raised on that kind of music. We didn't have commercial radio in Sweden in the 1950s and 1960s. There was one radio station, which broadcast perhaps one or two programmes of music – an hour or two each day – and those programmes contained a complete mixture of everything from classical to folk and pop. It was actually a very good musical education. And of course that becomes part of the music you know.

Björn: Billy Vaughn was a big influence on both of us, although I wouldn't necessarily say I was a fan; he was quite popular for a while. I think he was based in Germany, and perhaps not so well known outside Europe. He was a large presence in my mind as a sound, which we were both very aware of, especially that sound with the two saxes. I was aware of him more because they would play him at parties – he was the only one who had that sound and that way of playing. Where I lived there were no jukeboxes in town. So the records I most remember when I was a teenager are the ones that were being played when I started to go to parties and dance with girls, songs like Bill Haley's 'Rock Around The Clock' or 'Rip It Up'; one of those would have been the first record I bought. The first song I remember from the first party I went to was 'Zambesi', by the Stargazers, an instrumental which was a huge hit on the Continent.

Benny: There is a lot of *schlager* influence in a song like 'I Do, I Do, I Do, I Do, I Do'. The word '*schlager*' is the German word for 'hit' and when anyone who was growing up in Sweden at the same time as Björn and I did talks about *schlager* music, we mean a hit song that is not Anglo-Saxon in origin. It's much more like the kind of songs that were being recorded in Italy, Germany or France during the 1940s, 1950s and 1960s. Some of those songs, like 'Volare', which Dean Martin covered, had a much wider international success, and 'Volare' is a good example of *schlager*. It has a particular melodic style, it is

catchy and sometimes the songs had an extra touch of humour. It's easy listening in a way, not pop music. If you take a song like 'We'll Meet Again', that's typical *schlager*, even though it's an English song. It's a wonderful song, and Vera Lynn is a great singer.

Björn: There were German songs that were hits outside continental Europe in the 1950s – like 'Seeman' by Lolita – very, very sentimental melodies, related to Italian ballads. I imagine that our contemporaries in the UK did not necessarily grow up listening to those songs. I don't think much of that music was played on British radio – I suspect much more American music and jazz was being broadcast rather than continental European music. And that was even more true in America, which is why I think it was so difficult for us in the 1970s. Whereas now they take it to their hearts like mad because it is very European. ABBA is European. It's a definite hybrid between Anglo-Saxon and European musical traditions.

Benny: I act as my own musical filter for whatever comes into my head. I love the accordion, I love fiddles from Sweden and I also love the Beach Boys, Johann Sebastian Bach, Italian *schmaltz*, you name it... There's so much wonderful stuff in there, a wealth to draw on. Now, in the 2000s, I can write a song that sounds as if it could have been written in the 1940s or even earlier. But I've written it now because I like it now. A good song is a good song. It doesn't

Above: How to deliberately get noticed – hot pants, platform boots and snakeskin-a-gogo. The costumes were worn on the May 1974 short tour of Germany.
Below: Frida with the poster version.

In Stockholm, across the bay from the Stadshuset – the 1920s City Hall – venue for the annual Nobel Prize banquet.

matter where it is in history. And the same was true with ABBA. We would never say, 'Well, we can't record this stuff because this is too far out.' Something like 'I Do, I Do, I Do, I Do, I Do' would be within our framework even if it is a bit corny.

The recording of this song is very sharp; you can't play it loud because it has a lot of mid frequencies and goes straight into your ears, but the song is fun – and quite a good melody I think. There is a wedding feel to the lyrics, which was absolutely perfect later on for the ending of *MAMMA MIA!* of course. Stig had written that lyric 'I Do, I Do, I Do, I Do, I Do', and what else does that suggest but a wedding? That's why there are some tubular bells on the track. It fits into the song, and maybe we would have had it there anyway, but it goes so well with the lyrics.

Björn: 'I Do, I Do, I Do, I Do, I Do' is definitely a wedding song. It sounds jubilant. But it wasn't a deliberate marketing ploy.

We were always trying to achieve something special with every song. That didn't necessarily always happen, but that was our aim. Benny Andersson

Benny: When I am writing a song that I think is going to work, I have a particular sensation, something that makes me feel like I know what I'm doing, that makes me feel good and I can say, 'This is nice music, I like this.' It is

actually the only moment in the whole process where I feel connected to what I've been doing. If I go to see *MAMMA MIA!* or if I'm sitting in the middle of an orchestra doing a concert version of *Chess* or *Kristina*, it's like I'm in there, I know what everybody's doing and I can play along, but it doesn't belong to me any more. I don't feel, 'Wow, this is my music.' It's nothing like that. That sensation only happens when I am working at the piano, when a piece of music actually appears for the first time. Then it's mine. Once I have worked on it and given it to the band or to the singers and started to record, that original feeling goes out the window. I understand intellectually that I'm involved in all this, but emotionally I'm not.

Björn: There was a point a few singles into our career, following that initial success with 'Waterloo', when we'd had two or three flops, at least in the UK. We had had minor hits in the rest of the Europe with the other songs that we had released. But we were almost beginning to doubt ourselves – or at least I was. This was a period when we were definitely not at our best. We had been trying to be a rock band more than a pop band. We had released songs like 'So Long', trying to be just that, and then we found out that it was not us. So we said to ourselves, 'Let's write the songs we want to write and nothing but.' It is kind of fantastic that we were able to write new songs and record the *ABBA* album under those circumstances, because it actually felt as if we were on a downward trend at the time. And from then on we felt free to use all the styles we liked, from German *schlager* to Italian ballads, French *chanson* and Anglo-Saxon pop. We tried our hand at everything. Perhaps we ran out of ideas with ABBA in the end because we had tried almost everything.

Above: The Polar Music offices contained a dance studio where Agnetha and Frida could practise moves with their South African-born choreographer Graham Tainton. Originally Frida's jazz dance teacher, he went on to help both Frida and Agnetha with their stage routines.
Below: The Chicago gangster look. Costume changes quickly became an expected part of ABBA's performances.

SOS

Above and opposite: ABBA live at Gröna Lund in Stockholm, Sweden's oldest amusement park, in June 1975 – during their tour of the country's folkparks.

Björn: We hadn't been able to follow up on the success of 'Waterloo' as well as we would have liked. If the next single after 'I Do, I Do, I Do, I Do, I Do' had not worked we would not have known what to do. Luckily, our UK record company was very keen to release 'SOS', and we didn't mind at all, because we were very proud of that song. In fact, the single didn't reach Number One in the UK because I think there was still a problem with us being perceived as a Eurovision group. People didn't think we had any credibility. But 'SOS' reached Number Six, and that set us up for 'Mamma Mia', which *did* go to the top of the charts – and from then on we were flying.

Benny: 'SOS' was one of the songs we had written for the album called *ABBA*, which was the album that came out after *Waterloo*. We were benefiting from the burst of energy that came from winning Eurovision, and we were feeling good about our awareness that a lot of people now knew that we existed. Our attitude was, 'OK, now we can go for it. Now we'll do nothing else but sit down and write songs that are good enough for us to go out there and really compete.' So 'SOS' was probably our first really good song. It is quite intricate, even though it seems simple, and although the lyric is perhaps still not the best, the music and the actual recording are fine. The same applies to 'Mamma Mia', which was also on that *ABBA* album. They have different moods, but they're equally good songs.

We needed to have another big hit. 'SOS' was really the song that got us back on track in England, I would say. Björn Ulvaeus

Overleaf: Out-takes from the famous photo session for the cover of 1975's *Greatest Hits* album. A version of the park bench photograph showing Benny and Frida kissing was eventually used everywhere outside Sweden.

Björn: Agnetha sings 'SOS' solo, which was a change from previous singles where she and Frida had been singing the vocal together – and she later recorded her own version on her album *Eleven Women In One House*. Having her sing the song was not something that we had decided consciously to do. It was just that she *got* that song. Some critics have said they think Agnetha has a crying tone in this song. Certainly, when she wanted to, Agnetha could do a pretty good interpretation of the Connie Francis style of singing, where she always sounded like she was crying. But not on 'SOS'. I think she was pretty straightforward on that song.

I was still sharing the lyric-writing with Stig. And again we had managed to choose a very strong title that would work internationally, in all languages. It was always good to find a phrase that was universally known. Even on 'Waterloo' we had run into a problem when it came to producing the French version. I think that was the first foreign language we recorded 'Waterloo' in and it was being handled by Claude-Michel Schönberg and Alain Boublil – who later had such a phenomenal success writing and composing *Les Misérables*, *Miss Saigon* and *Martin Guerre*.

In 1974 they were working as producers, and Alain Boublil was also the French publisher for our music. They had written a French translation, which was still called 'Waterloo', but they were pronouncing it 'Vaterlow' and, more importantly, putting the emphasis on the second syllable, or at least that's how it sounded to me – like 'VaTERlow'. But it was impossible for us to sing it like that, because in English the stress falls on the first syllable of the word and that's how we'd written the song. It was quite difficult, and we had a lively discussion about that…

Benny: By the time of 'SOS', we were using synthesizers a little more. I had bought a Mini-Moog very early on, in 1972 or 1973: the album called *Switched On Bach* by Wendy Carlos had come out a few years earlier, and then Giorgio Moroder had produced a record using the Moog. I'd said, 'Whoa, what is *this*? How can I get one?', and heard that we could get hold of one in London. So Björn and I had gone over and bought a Mini-Moog, as well as this wonderfully quirky instrument called the Mellotron, which allowed you to play chords using tape loops of flutes, violins and voices. I still have both pieces of equipment. And now people often prefer to use those instruments because they are the genuine analogue article. We had used a synthesizer on 'Waterloo', but you could only play one note at a time, you couldn't play a whole chord. By 'SOS' we were recording on twenty-four tracks instead of eight, which meant that we could build up a much bigger sound, harmony by harmony, although it was quite painstaking work. On the early Mini-Moogs, the way the sound was created was by setting up a combination of different wave patterns, which meant that on any given day you would have a slightly different range of settings. The problem was that there was no way you could save those settings. There was no memory. It was like a Japanese ice sculpture. You could create a wonderful sound, but the next day it would have vanished, as people seem unable to resist turning Moog knobs.

Once we had recorded the backing track, the vocals and overdubs – all standard procedure – we would move into the mixing phase and when you start mixing, you will, all of a sudden, find that this is not so good or think, 'We missed something here, maybe we should try to do this.' This happened with 'SOS'. There's a guitar line – which is Björn playing because there was only Björn, me and Michael Tretow in the control room – and that's when we came up with the idea of doubling the guitar line with the Mini-Moog playing in unison. It was a question of trying to discover the full potential within the song. Sometimes it works, sometimes it doesn't. And then there would come a moment where we would say, 'This is it, we're happy now', a point when all three of us would be satisfied that we had done as much as we could. And that was usually that. It might have happened very occasionally that we would have everything in the can but then get cold feet and say, 'We need to bring this back. Let's put it up on the console again', but that was very rarely. Generally once we had decided 'That's it, we can't do anything more', we would be happy to leave the song as it was.

Björn: 'SOS' was one of the first songs where we brought in Lasse Hallström as the director of a promo film. I don't think that he had yet made any movies, but

he was working a lot in television and he was particularly well known for creating little inserts with pop groups for TV shows. Lasse had a great deal of experience working with bands – we knew him slightly, but in any case he was the obvious choice in Sweden at the time. The filming was all done very quickly. We would film maybe two or three songs in one day, miming along to someone holding a loudspeaker next to you, plugged into this big Swiss reel-to-reel tape recorder, a Nagra, which had to be lugged around. It was all very quick, as far as we were concerned: Camera. Sound. Let's go.

Performing 'SOS' on the German TV show *Disco* '75 in December 1975, in front of a studio audience.

From this point on we started to spend more time looking carefully at the actual arrangements, at what was really going on beneath the melody. Benny Andersson

Benny: Although studio work was taking up a lot of time, we were still doing some live performances. For me at the time playing live was just not as rewarding as writing and recording. But if you ask the girls they will say it's the other way round. It was a little difficult to transfer some of these more complex arrangements into a live show, but by using three keyboards, two guitarists, two drummers and three back-up vocalists, I think we got quite close to what was on the original records.

Björn: We were doing some touring at this time. In 1974, shortly after Eurovision, we had had to cancel a tour of the folkparks, in Sweden, that had already been booked. In the end, we just hadn't been able to do it, because suddenly there

were, to be honest, more important things for us to do. So we did the tour in 1975 instead. It was good to connect back to a Swedish audience, and of course, they were very proud of the fact that we had won Eurovision. Sweden had not really had any great international success – I mean there had been Ingmar Bergman and Greta Garbo, of course – but in music, really nothing. So it was a good feeling to be on tour around Sweden, and also it was easier for Agnetha and me, because we could go back home between shows to be with our daughter.

Benny: These folkparks were where people in each community could meet up in the forests during the summer months to listen to music and dance – in the winter the gatherings would move indoors to a *folkets hus* or 'folkhouse'. Nowadays there are perhaps only 10 per cent of the parks left – people's habits have changed, but at that time this was very much part of Swedish community life. And of course it was a wonderful opportunity for musicians, because there were hundreds of folkparks all over the country, all needing artists and bands to provide the music.

Top and above: ABBA's first major European tour in November 1974 allowed the group a chance to develop stage routines to complement the music.

Björn: The folkparks were fenced-in areas with – depending on which little town you were in – a variety of attractions, a bit like a funfair: a tombola, dart-throwing stalls and in the bigger ones merry-go-rounds, and, an absolute must, a hot-dog stand. There was an outside dance floor with a live band playing and a separate stage, which would feature acts by all kinds of artists playing 45-minute or one-hour sets; it was quite common to play at two, even three, parks in one day. The other attractions would stop, the dance band would take a break and all the people would sit down to watch this act who they had already paid to see as part of their entrance fee. I remember places where the manager would say, 'OK, lads, keep it down to twenty-five or thirty minutes', because he wasn't making any money while we were playing, and he wanted to get the money-spinning attractions back up and running. So each Saturday and Wednesday during the summer, and maybe Friday and Sunday too, artists like the Hootenanny Singers, the Hep Stars, Anni-Frid Lyngstad and Agnetha Fältskog would appear. And since we were all on the circuit individually in those days before ABBA, that was where we met. Benny and I first ran into each other at a kind of crossroads leading into one of the parks.

MAMMA MIA

Björn: The last song written for the *ABBA* album, but the one that ended up as the opening track, was 'Mamma Mia'. That turned out to be another distinctive and memorable title, and one that maybe a native English writer would have thought was too European – and very uncool. The saying 'mamma mia' is used very, very commonly in Swedish and is just as well known a phrase as it would be in English. And of course it was going to be very useful in a certain forthcoming musical!

In the lyric-writing I was definitely now into working with certain images in my mind, seeing little scenarios. 'Mamma Mia' was a very simple scene, of a woman confronting a man, but it was still an image rather than simply writing words. This was before I started to really understand that I could use this language almost as if it was my own; that came more rapidly to me later on.

Benny: The opening of 'Mamma Mia', that tick-tock, tick-tock, is played on a marimba, which is an instrument of wood blocks, like a larger version of a xylophone, really. Again, that came about because the marimba was sitting there in this little corner of the Metronome Studio. So when the song was going, and everybody was playing, we thought, 'Well that's OK, but it's not really a record is it? It's like four or five guys just trying to play something together.' And this was a time when we were starting to think, 'We need to get ourselves together and try to produce some good stuff.'

So there was the marimba, and I started playing on it. I just wanted to see what it sounded like. Now, I don't play the marimba, but I had an idea how to produce some kind of meaningful sound out if it. So that opening evolved from there, from this little idea that we were able to develop. And it changed the course of the song. Using the marimba could have gone in any direction. But it worked, and it made for a really catchy start on the song. But we also added a little twist. Instead of playing the line very straight, the chord change shifts slightly earlier than one might expect, not on the first beat of the bar. I like that, because it shows that we didn't just play this music and record it, we were thinking carefully about what we were doing.

Björn: On the chorus we stripped everything out. We had tried the chorus using the full band, with everybody playing, but it didn't work. For some reason, we felt, nothing was happening there. It was not convincing. So one of us said, 'Why not do it the other way around, take everything away on the chorus to see what happens', and of course that was wonderful. Suddenly the chorus stood right out, thanks to something as simple as that. If you listen to the song at the end on the third chorus, you can hear the full band playing, which is what it sounded

Top and left: 'Mamma Mia' takes
shape; Björn faking reading music
and playing the piano in his and
Agnetha's house.
Above: Agnetha with 'Superbjörn'.

like in the beginning. So we simply tried it the other way and it was such a revelation – one of those magical things that can happen in a studio: 'This is great, and we're doing it the wrong way round!' And we did it again, I have to confess, in 'Money, Money, Money'.

Stripping the chorus of 'Mamma Mia' back to just voices, keyboards and marimba was like a magician pulling a tablecloth out from under all the crockery. Benny Andersson

Benny: I think that with 'Mamma Mia' and 'SOS' this was the period when we started to try to do something that was us, rather than trying to interpret or impersonate somebody else's work – whether that was the Billy Vaughn sax sound, or a Phil Spector wall-of-sound production style. And that came from the kind of confidence you get when things are going well, when people are buying your singles and albums and you know they like them. That gives you a lot of extra buoyancy.

After we had finished overdubbing and mixing those two songs, 'SOS' and 'Mamma Mia', both Björn and I thought we had two very good songs. But we seemed to be the only people outside Scandinavia, Germany and Holland who thought that we had something. It felt like nobody else thought what we were doing was any good. When I say that I mean particularly the UK record company. One problem was that we were on different labels all over the world. Normal practice would be to sign up with one record company, who would be able to co-ordinate activity internationally. But we were on CBS in the UK, Atlantic in the States, Deutsche Grammophon in Germany and in Sweden with Polar Music, the company we owned 50:50 with Stig Anderson. So it was only when 'SOS' and then 'Mamma Mia' took off in Australia, where we were with RCA Records, that CBS sat up and took notice, and said, 'Let's work on this.' So we have always been grateful to the Australian audience, because that's when things started to happen.

Björn: We were working like mad in England but not getting anywhere. To keep ourselves in the public eye, I remember we would do whatever we could, appearing on as many television shows as possible in the UK and elsewhere, fighting to hold onto our profile. But it was the Australians who first started to play 'Mamma Mia'. And consequently that song became a huge hit in Australia, and that kicked off a very, very strong connection with the fans out there. So from down under comes this noise, and CBS in the UK must have been thinking, 'What the hell is this? There is still life in ABBA!'

We had gone down the typical route of a Eurovision winner: one huge hit and then a series of flops. And we were, of course, getting the usual bullshit, that everything was great, yeah, yeah, yeah, but the truth was that it was not until

Another German TV appearance, this time for the *Silvester Tanzparty*, aired on New Year's Eve 1975.

Australia started sending our singles to Number One that we got back on track. I have heard one explanation that the reason the Australians took to us was that like them we were exotic – way off the main map, us up north and them down south, and that this gave us a kind of affinity. But I think it is more likely that it was because Australian TV started showing the Lasse Hallström films for those songs. The possibility of us touring there must have seemed rather remote, so someone liked the music and decided to use the films to promote us and that gave us a huge amount of visibility **across Australia**.

*The success of 'Mamma Mia' and 'SOS' in Australia had restimulated interest in the UK, and 'SOS' finally made it into the Top Ten in September 1975. There then followed another busy phase, as Stig Anderson and ABBA moved offices, Frida and Agnetha both released solo albums (*Frida Alone *and* Eleven Women In One House *respectively) and to outward appearances ABBA was in abeyance, not making many public appearances. However, work was of course underway, and in particular two songs emerged from this period, 'Fernando' and 'Dancing Queen'. To follow 'Mamma Mia' it was decided to release the slower ballad 'Fernando' first and to hold back the release of 'Dancing Queen' until the summer of 1976.*

DANCING QUEEN

Benny: Björn had a little summer house on an island in the Stockholm archipelago called Viggsö. It's about an hour or so from the centre of Stockholm by ferry, thirty-five or forty minutes by speedboat. And that's where 'Dancing Queen' was written. Stig owned a house on the island and then Björn and Agnetha bought their house and then Frida and I bought a piece of land and built ourselves a log house. We would be staying there during the summer, all in the same spot. Björn had a little guest cabin, this tiny space, where we put in a small piano. That's where we sat and worked during the summers. Generally we didn't like to work in summertime, but out there it was fine. And for this song, it must have been a special occasion, because Björn never used to write on electric guitar on Viggsö. He used to play acoustic guitar, but this time we had brought in a little electric amplifier. That automatically creates a different style of playing, because using an electric guitar and amp allows you to experiment with different sounds.

'Dancing Queen' is a song that began in a nice place and stayed there. It wasn't like we were starting with a verse and then moving on to writing the chorus. As I remember it, the song always began with the chorus in some strange way. We liked what we had developed, we thought we had a really good song and it was solid pop music. Because sometimes I tend to drift along towards the Billy Vaughn style of playing, or to ragtime. Björn was much better at saying, 'We're a pop band so let's try to *be* a pop band.' Of course, some songs are good even if they're not pop, like 'I Do, I Do, I Do, I Do, I Do' or 'Money, Money, Money' or 'I Have A Dream'. You can do a lot of things. You should never be afraid of trying out weird stuff because that's when it becomes music and something worth listening to, rather than always following the mainstream. However, I think Björn was quite right, although I also think I'm right too… That's why we're a good team!

'Dancing Queen' was a song that came all in one go. Well, no song ever does really. You have to sit there for a couple of weeks before anything happens, but once it's started… Benny Andersson

Benny: While we were in the studio recording 'Dancing Queen', we had been listening to this song called 'Rock Your Baby' by George McRae over the studio sound system. It had a really nice groove and as we were listening we were saying, 'What are they doing here, what are they actually playing?' I know that Michael Tretow created a little repeat echo of the hi-hat, to give it a swing. It was something the drummer wouldn't play normally and I don't know exactly what it was that this little sound did, but it certainly added something. And it helped provide a real groove that we could stay with all the way through the song.

If you listen to 'Rock Your Baby' it doesn't sound anything like 'Dancing Queen' but they have the same speed, and almost the same kind of swing.

Björn: I do remember that we had, for the first time, a little repeat – I think it's called a Slapback Echo, the kind that Elvis Presley would use, where you have a distinct repeat to play along to. The whole rhythm and feel was very much inspired by 'Rock Your Baby'. We needed something to freshen up the monotonous way the song was going and 'Rock Your Baby' had been released in the summer of 1974 and had this fresh feeling about it. That feel makes 'Dancing Queen' fun to play. It's an extremely happy song and it even has a happy lyric – which is not common in ABBA! Nearly all the other lyrics are sad, aren't they, apart from 'I Do, I Do, I Do, I Do, I Do', 'Honey, Honey' perhaps and 'Dancing Queen'? But even with sad lyrics, you can set them with an uplifting melody and that creates an interesting tension of opposites.

Benny: If you listen to the ABBA records you can hardly find a track where there is no piano. I prefer working on a 'real' instrument ahead of the electronic equipment that exists. A piano is more real than most instruments, although it doesn't have the fine adjustment like with a violin where you can decide exactly where you want to put your finger to make the notes, but otherwise the piano has everything: it's a rhythmic instrument, it's melodic, and the grand piano in particular looks great. When we were developing the music and recording it, I needed to be on piano because I knew exactly where I was and what was going on all around me, and I would be able to change things around – and then the piano always stayed in the final mix. When we came out with 'Waterloo' in 1974 one of the first things that many people at the record companies said – when Stig was going round trying to get a deal for the record before the Eurovision show –

At this February 1976 photoshoot in Bubi Heilemann's Hamburg studio, the group were playing around with the letters of their name when Benny inadvertently swung his B through 180 degrees. The official ABBA logo with the inverted B was created by Rune Söderqvist (designer of most of the ABBA album and singles covers) in July of the same year. The name ABBA itself originally came from the shorthand Stig Anderson used on memos to Agnetha, Björn, Benny and Anni-Frid.
Overleaf: Summer 1976 on the island of Viggsö, where both couples owned summer homes, and where Benny and Björn had a small cabin where they could compose.

Above and opposite: ABBA's embroidered white kimonos, designed by Owe Sandström, were a feature of their live performances throughout 1975 and 1976.

was, 'We don't want that because, you know, piano is out, nobody uses piano any more.' I think that's funny. It just goes to prove my theory that you can do anything with music as long as it's good stuff, and it doesn't matter what style it is. And above all it proves that you should not listen to A&R people.

Björn: Something that strikes me as very strange is when people tell me that if the dance floor is empty or if a party is in danger of dying, all you have to do is put on 'Dancing Queen' and everyone is back out on the dance floor. I don't really understand that, because for me the song is too slow to be a disco number. 'Night fever, night fever' – that's the kind of tempo you need for the disco floor…

'Dancing Queen' not only gave us our first real hit in America, but it made it to Number One over there, which was wonderful, although maybe a little surprising because apart from some promotional trips we had not spent a lot of time out there. We knew what it would take to try and conquer America and perhaps if Agnetha and I had not had our small children, we might have given it a go, but as we did have our kids we never really tried.

Benny: Shortly before the single was released, we performed 'Dancing Queen' at a gala evening in the Royal Swedish Opera House, which was celebrating the marriage of King Carl XVI Gustaf to Queen Silvia. They had asked us if we would be prepared to perform there and we said, 'Yes'. The only thing was that we should be in period costume, so we said, 'Sure', and did the show in baroque outfits. And the song we had produced most recently happened to be 'Dancing Queen'. It was just a coincidence…

MONEY, MONEY, MONEY

Above and opposite: the group's 'Money, Money, Money' outfits were based on 1920s flapper styles.

Björn: After 'Dancing Queen', which had a disco feel, or certainly worked well whenever it was played in discos, we completely changed tack with 'Money, Money, Money'. This was Benny and me going back to our European roots. It is almost a tango. It has a very different mood, like something out of *Cabaret*. I created another title for the song – I was going to call it 'Gipsy Girl' – but it just didn't work. It didn't sound right. I had already written those words 'Money, money, money', but I really did not want to use them. I thought there were too many other songs out there already that used 'money' in the title, not least 'Money Makes The World Go Round', which was one of the songs from *Cabaret*. But those bloody words sounded so good when they were sung to the melody that in the end I gave up. I couldn't fight the power of the words any more. So from those three simple repeated words I built up the whole lyric. At this stage in our career I had more or less taken over all the lyric duties, although Stig might provide a title, which he was always so good at. It was a gradual process, which happened partly because my grasp of English was better than his, and it continued to improve as we were travelling more and more. And I consciously looked for books to read in English to become more fluent. Stig seemed to be happy with that – he certainly never complained. I was growing in confidence in my art.

The great thing about 'Money, Money, Money' was that because Frida was an alto, we could put her melody low, so that on the choruses Agnetha could sing a whole octave up. Björn Ulvaeus

Benny: There is an octave harmony in the background of the chorus; it is quite soft so you can't really hear it. Generally, we would set the songs in a key which would make the girls have to reach up for the notes. If you are trying to express a sense of energy, then it is difficult to do that in a low register. Although that low melody absolutely works for 'Money, Money, Money', it wouldn't be right at all for the chorus of 'Dancing Queen'. We wanted Agnetha and Frida to be pushing themselves to get something extra out of their bodies. It is a trick, which you cannot use every time – you couldn't do 'Slipping Through My Fingers' like that for example – but if possible it seemed to work when the girls were singing at the edge of what they could physically sing. That's easy for me to say; I didn't have to sing it. And with Frida and Agnetha we had two different voices, Frida's alto and Agnetha's soprano, so if we needed both of them to sing the melody, it was often really too high for Frida and she would have to sort of belt it out to make it happen.

Top: Working on *Arrival* in the Metronome Studio in Stockholm with (far right) Michael Tretow, ABBA's long-time recording and sound engineer and 'never-ending source of ideas'.
Above: The *Arrival* album cover featured Rune Söderqvist's new ABBA logo, with a shot of the group squashed into a Swedish police force, late model Bell 47G, helicopter at Barkarby airfield outside Stockholm.

She didn't like us much for asking her to do this, but she did it and the results were great because it created this metallic kind of sound, which is when I think the combination of the two girls is at its best, that mix between the two voices, especially when they're in the high ranges. I like that. I could spot that through a crowd. If somebody is playing an old ABBA song and there is some interference from other noise around, I might not be able to identify the song but I can always hear the sound of the girls. It's kinda nice.

Björn: We weren't convinced that 'Money, Money, Money' would work. I don't think we even dared to release it as a single at the time. It might have been a single some way down the line in various countries, but I know we were feeling quite cautious. There are several ABBA songs, like 'Thank You For The Music', and this one, that weren't really singles, but they received so much airplay that they became quite standard.

Benny: In general, Björn and I would agree when we thought a song had potential. We always tended to have the same emotions and would recognise a good song when we heard ourselves playing it, so it was always the good stuff we tried to keep – and if the song had really been too far out we would probably not have tried to record it with ABBA, since in general a pop band shouldn't stray too far from what people expect a pop band to do. 'Money, Money, Money', though, did seem to fall within what ABBA could release. It is a very European song. There's a little bit of violin in the mix, like the fiddle in a *klezmer* band. There's also a little bit of honky tonk piano, the kind

of thing they used to have in saloon bars – again one of the instruments that
was available to us in the Metronome Studio.

A little like we did on 'Mamma Mia', where we dropped most of the
arrangement out on the chorus, here we created a different feel. What is special
on 'Money, Money, Money' is that the bass line plays the melody, which is
unusual, but it works! And the phrase leading into the chorus is played twice,
but it is repeated with a little displaced variation the second time. The same as
we always did, we were trying to add a little twist.

Because of all the European flavour, we couldn't make the song something
that was really contemporary, we had to treat it as it was. So you need to treat
'Dancing Queen' one way, 'Money, Money, Money' another way, 'I Do, I Do, I Do,
I Do, I Do' a third way. If I play a song on the piano, I know instinctively that
this song needs one type of treatment and this one needs another type. Sometimes,
oh, you can make mistakes. There were a number of times when we thought we
had a good song from the beginning and we ended up not having a good song
because either we did something wrong along the way or the recording wasn't
good. Or maybe the song really wasn't good in the first place. What we tried to
do was to avoid writing too many songs. We wrote exactly as many as we needed
for a recording, which I now think is a good thing because there is not a vast
collection of rubbish and out-takes for people to track down and re-release.

Top: The 9 to 5 men at work in their
office, a model of Scandinavian chic.
Above: Recording vocals for *Arrival*.

I'm a 9 to 5 man. I come to my studio almost every day, and I'll sit down and try to write something. Benny Andersson

KNOWING ME, KNOWING YOU

Björn: As I developed my lyric-writing, I was starting to work on getting my little lyrical scenarios together. This was when all the imagery came into play. Now, people always talk about Agnetha's and my divorce influencing my writing. But 'Knowing Me, Knowing You', for example, which was released in the early part of 1977, and of course was written and recorded before then, was well before all those events. It's possible that I felt a premonition about something, but that was not what I was thinking about. It's as simple as me being able to imagine a house being emptied, with boxes standing against walls and all the furniture being taken away, just a few bits and pieces left behind, and the echoing steps of a man walking around those rooms and remembering the past. And that's a powerful image, that gives you a whole lyric. It's quite cinematic in a way. You have the image, you just write it down. That's always the best way. Sometimes there are songs that don't give you an image – 'Money, Money, Money', for example. That was driven by the three words that I couldn't manage to shake off. They dictated the lyric.

On our earlier songs, the lyrics Stig had written and Björn had polished had not been bad, and always had great hooklines. But with 'Knowing Me, Knowing You', Björn took the lyrics to a new level. Benny Andersson

Björn: 'Knowing Me, Knowing You' has the famous 'ah ha's. It is the most well-known instance – thanks in part to Steve Coogan's Alan Partridge – but not the first. In 'Honey, Honey' there's another 'ah ha'. That was probably the first. So 'Knowing Me, Knowing You' was most likely the second or third time we used that device. When we came to do the song in *MAMMA MIA!*, the 'ah ha's weren't included initially, and during the first previews the audience sang them. They just couldn't help themselves. It was a fun moment in a way, but terrible in another way. I thought, 'Is this what's going to happen from now on – they're going to sing along?'

Benny: I was there that night. The audience did it themselves, which was great. We had put the 'ah ha's in there originally because there was a hole to fill – without them it feels quite empty. It was something we used in many, many songs. I didn't realise this until somebody pointed it out to me. I had this piece of artwork with the words 'Ah' and 'Ha' hanging in my home, years ago, when we were doing *Chess*, and this guy said, 'Oh, you even have your "ah ha"s on the wall!' I said 'What do you mean? 'Well you have so many "ah ha"s in your songs'. I said, 'Do we?' and he mentioned 'Knowing Me, Knowing You' of course, and then named a number of songs that I had never even thought about. Blame it on the lyricist!

ABBA's first ever world tour opened in January 1977 in the Oslo Ekeberghallen.

Björn: When 'Knowing Me, Knowing You' came out, we were starting our first major tour in Europe, opening in Oslo, and later playing at the Royal Albert Hall in London. Benny and I were never really able to write when we were out on the road. I know a lot of other writers can do that, and may even be stimulated by the situation, but we couldn't. We did try a couple of times but nothing ever happened. It wasn't so much that we needed the studio environment, but we needed the *home* environment. It had to be a calm place where no one would bother us. We like peace and quiet. We like having our own space that we can return to every day.

Benny: I am extremely disciplined, because I have learnt that that is what works best for me. I have to sit at the piano or keyboard and wait for some good notes to come out of somewhere, and if I'm not sitting there they are not going to come. I think it was Robin Wagner who told me that being an artist, or being in any creative process, it's like there's a dragon in a cave. You know the dragon is in there, but it hardly ever comes out, so you have to sit outside and wait for it, and you know that if you sit there long enough, that dragon is going to come out. But if you go home and take a nap, you'll never see the dragon, because that

is precisely the time it will decide to come out. That's the way it works, sitting there waiting, putting in the time.

'Knowing Me, Knowing You' is a great recording – I really like it, and the verse is one of my favourites. We were still recording at the Metronome Studio when we recorded this song. We hadn't yet built our own studios at Polar. There had been a period when Michael Tretow left Metronome and moved to another studio, which was a small basement in a villa somewhere outside Stockholm. It wasn't such a good studio, but Michael was there and so we went there as well because of course we wanted to continue working with him – he contributed so much to the recording. And eventually we decided we needed our own studio, which we built in 1977 and into 1978.

Björn: This song has a fantastic and flexible bass line, which was played by Rutger Gunnarsson, who is a wonderful bass player and worked on so many of the ABBA songs with us. When *MAMMA MIA!* opened in Stockholm, Rutger became the bass player in the theatre orchestra. And that bass line was never the same on any night, he played it differently each time, allowing himself a certain amount of freedom. And of course all the young musicians playing in that band thought he was the best.

The 1977 tour line-up, including Francis Matthews (in white make-up, centre), the narrator of the mini-musical *The Girl With The Golden Hair.* Overleaf, main picture: Agnetha and Frida in identical outfits during *The Girl With The Golden Hair.*

THE NAME OF THE GAME

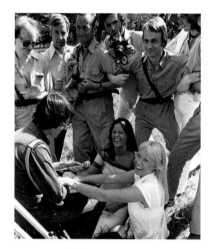

Above and opposite: *ABBA: The Movie*
featured the actor Robert Hughes
playing a hapless radio DJ, Ashley
Wallace (seen opposite picnicking with
the group), trying to obtain an exclusive
interview with ABBA during their 1977
tour of Australia. Subsequent scenes
were shot back in Stockholm in the
verdant, almost rural, setting of the
island of Djurgården in the city centre
– site of the Cirkus Teater, the venue
for both *Kristina* and *MAMMA MIA!*

Björn: The lyric for 'The Name Of The Game' was written for Lasse Hallström.
He needed a song for one of the scenes in *ABBA: The Movie*, which he was directing.
The storyline featured a reporter who was meant to be chasing us all around
Australia while we were on tour there, trying to get an interview with us. And in
the movie there's a short sequence where he has a dream that he is a psychiatrist
and is listening to Agnetha lying there, pouring out her feelings for him. Lasse
needed a song to accompany the section and so I wrote words to go with some
music which Benny and I had already written. I hadn't seen the film sequence at
that point; Lasse just told me what it had to be about. And it was very nice to
have that framework to work within. I thought it was a great experience: I could
not head off this way or that, the lyric had to go in this particular direction. And
that was very positive. It was the same when Benny and I started working on
Chess and *Kristina*, where I had to write something very specific to help develop
the storyline, to get from here to there. I like that. I guess if you don't happen to
be into psychiatry, you might have a different interpretation of the song.

Benny: I only found out in 2006 that Björn had written the lyric for Lasse's
movie! We met up with Lasse in New York to chat about *ABBA: The Movie* for
a DVD re-issue, and it came out in the conversation that Björn had specifically
written it for the scene Lasse had in mind. At the time I must have thought,
'Well, if that's the lyric that he wants to write!' That's how it works: a piece of
music might mean something particular to me, but once I have handed it over
to Björn he will find something in there that works for him.

'The Name Of The Game' is not that catchy a song, is it? There are some
good pieces of music put together within it, but the song was never a major hit
anywhere. It's a good recording, though. In fact it's a better recording than it is a
song, I think. The recording and the vocal arrangements lifted it. The way we
tended to record was that we would create the backing track with the other guys
in the band, with Rutger on bass, Ola on drums and Lasse on guitar. We would
work together a little on that and then record rough vocals, before adding any
fill-ins, the synthesizer lines and any guitar overdubs, or whatever arrangements
we wanted to do. We could work fairly quickly. The first question was, 'Who's
going to sing it, Frida or Agnetha?' That was vital for choosing the key because
the two of them had different ranges. So then I would write down the chords for
the guys, maybe suggesting a few bass notes and so on, so they would know
what to play, and we would start playing the song through. We would try to
work ourselves into some kind of groove or some sort of understanding: 'OK,
you do this, I'll do this, you do that and then maybe you can do that on the bass.'
They would all add their own marks to their sheets of paper. And there would be
a good moment in the whole of this process when I would sit down and say,

'Now, we're about to record this song, so what will I actually play?' I don't just want to go 'bang, bang, bang', playing the right chords, I want to play something that is good and adds to the song. It's not always easy. I am particularly pleased with what I am doing piano-wise on 'SOS', 'Thank You For The Music' and 'The Winner Takes It All', songs where I think the piano line is doing a good job.

Once you know that 'The Name Of The Game' was written about a woman in a psychiatrist's chair, the lyrics make sense – 'I've seen you twice... Every time I'm getting more open-hearted…' Björn Ulvaeus

Björn: When other people listen to our songs, they often find influences that we are unaware of. One critic said he thought there was a laid-back, Californian feel to this song because Benny and I had been spending time over in Los Angeles looking at equipment for our recording studio. But I don't agree. I think the sound of 'The Name Of The Game' came much more out of the *East* coast than the West. I don't know if I am right, but in my mind I think of Boston (the group, not the place) and their big hit 'More Than A Feeling'. It's much more of a guitar song than most ABBA songs: it's full of guitars, twelve-string guitars, all kinds of guitars. Another comparison that has been made is with Stevie Wonder's song 'I Wish'. Again, I don't personally make any connection with that song, but the guitars might be playing some little riff that has the same kind of feel. I suppose it might even have been inspired by his song, although 'I Wish' is not remotely like 'The Name Of The Game'.

Although the song was written for Lasse's film, I have only ever seen snippets of *ABBA: The Movie*. I don't really like watching myself on screen. But Benny says it's quite good, and of course it is also a record of our tour to Australia in 1977.

Benny: That tour was madness. Here was this country on the other side of the planet, with a Go West, frontier spirit, wonderful – and what's great is that it is mixed with some good old English humour. And it was so full of ABBA merchandising. ABBA pillows, ABBA dolls, ABBA everything. So much in the papers and on TV, that when we finally arrived there it was overkill. I think that for a couple of years afterwards we went stone cold there. We had been over-exposed. But luckily the fan base came back. The tour itself was an extraordinary, wonderful experience. I wish that everyone could experience something like that once in their life.

Björn: I remember coming into Sydney and Melbourne, with crowds of people all along the road waving flags. It was unreal. We were taken on excursions, but only in secret, and in fact I remember those more than the gigs. It was a little claustrophobic being stuck in a hotel room all day, so getting out was a relief. There was one absolutely wonderful boat trip round Sydney Harbour. They told me that there were sharks in the waters. We moored up somewhere and had something to eat. And then I insisted on going swimming. Agnetha was furious. It was only a short dip, but long enough for me to prove I had braved the sharks.

We recorded some of the shows on the tour for the movie: they weren't too bad. We were never really a performing group like the Stones, and although I'm not drawing a direct comparison, we were more like the Beatles, retreating more and more into the studio. On stage we were reproducing exactly what we had done on the record; there was no space for improvisation, because the music was as tightly constructed as it had been on the records.

Benny: Twenty years after 'The Name Of The Game' was released, the Fugees wanted to use the bass line of the verse for their song 'Rumble In The Jungle'. I don't really want people to sample what we have written, unless they ask us first. With the Fugees it was flattering that they wanted to use 'The Name Of The Game', because here was this incredibly hip American band wanting to use our track from the 1970s. I think they are a great band and Lauryn Hill is a fabulous singer. Once we had agreed to them using the bass line, they could use it however they wanted: I didn't feel any sense of possessiveness.

Björn: My attitude to sampling is essentially negative, especially if the people doing it are not really talented, but the Fugees version was very good, very interesting.

ABBA: The Movie *captured a very specific time in ABBA's career: their first and only tour in Australia, which at the time had gone completely ABBA-crazy. The visit was part of a longer tour, which had opened in January 1977 in Oslo before heading round Scandinavia, West Germany, the Netherlands, Belgium and the UK. This was the tour that marked the first fruits of a desire to produce longer works than the three-minute pop single.*

With the success of their world tour ABBA no longer needed to use outrageous costumes to be noticed – but audiences had begun to expect them. Here the band reject flamboyance for more comfortable, laid-back attire.

TAKE A CHANCE ON ME

With their legendary attention to detail, ABBA spent a lot of their time in the studio, recording and re-recording all the layers of the song to build up to the result they were looking for.

Björn: Ideas for the lyrics pop up in different ways. Often it's a little scenario that comes into my mind, but sometimes I start with a title. 'Take A Chance On Me' is a case in point. For this particular song there was no image, no scenario, there was only the title phrase, and I constructed the lyric around that. The phrase came out of the percussiveness that I felt the title would need to have, because of the way the melody happened to fall. I was an avid runner at that time – this would have been in 1977. I was running-mad in fact, and the words came to me while I was out running one day. I was thinking to myself, 'If the music sounds like "chuck-a chuck chuck chuck", which English words or what phrase might correspond with the percussive feel of the chorus?' The first notes in the chorus are very short and only the last note is long. And I found this phrase: 'Take a chance on *me*'.

It was wonderful to be inspired to come up with that title by running in the woods. We are always happiest working in Sweden: we seem to do our best work here. Benny and I were still working a lot on the island of Viggsö, where we both had houses. When our families were out there with us, we would go and write in a little cabin on my property which you can see if you watch *ABBA: The Movie*. It's a very, very nice shot, zooming out from where we used to work every day. And even when our families weren't in Viggsö, we still used to go out there anyway, but not all the time. Only towards the end of a period when we would have been working hard putting in office hours – in this disciplined way that Benny and I would apply to our writing, setting ourselves a specific time period each day to see what we could achieve, and then continuing the next day, same time, same place. It sounds very boring! We would do that for maybe three weeks or a month and then we would go away to Viggsö for three or four days for a change of scene. If I can I like to have a view of water while I'm working, but it's not essential. In fact, we've written some of our best stuff in smoky cellars.

Benny: That's a catchy song. I'm not quite sure how to describe it – not bubblegum pop. 'Honey, Honey' could be called bubblegum, perhaps, but 'Take A Chance On Me' is not. The guitar-playing is more country-music-like. The rest of the band sticks really quite strictly to the rhythmic pattern, but the guitar can do anything it likes. It really goes its own way there.

Björn: There is definitely a country-music feel to this song. We like all kinds of music. The only thing I'm not a huge fan of is jazz, but apart from that I like anything. And good country music is wonderful. Here you have a verse that is completely different from the chorus and that's what makes it interesting, for me. There's something of a disco feel to start with, and then the song

Above and opposite: While Benny and Björn preferred to spend their time perfecting recordings in the studio, Frida and Agnetha – who had less to do with the technical side of things – came into their own on stage.

becomes very square, almost like a German march crossed with country music. It's crazy if you think about it.

Benny: I like some country music, just as I tend to like a whole range of different kinds of music. I always liked Linda Ronstadt and Patsy Cline, and Dolly Parton and Willie Nelson are both brilliant songwriters. And I'm fond of a little bluegrass. So much music in America has come out of country music: bands like Crosby, Stills Nash & Young, who are not really country but not far away. And bands like the Eagles and Fleetwood Mac: I thought they were wonderful. *Rumours* would be one of my top ten best albums of all time; I know I played it hundreds of times after it came out.

Björn: It would actually be physically impossible to sing the 'Take a chance, take a chance, take a, take a chance' backing vocals without drawing breath, but I managed to convince Martin Koch, the musical supervisor on *MAMMA MIA!*, that Benny and I had sung the whole thing in one go. It took him a long time to work out that I was kidding… Nowadays you'd only need to sing the phrase once in the studio, because you could then sample it, repeat it as many times as you want and you'd have the whole backing vocal. But we had to build it up from individual pieces of tape, singing the phrase until we just couldn't sing it any more, and then starting all over again.

You can't sing that backing vocal in one go. That's impossible. No, no, no, no, you do have to breathe… Benny Andersson

THANK YOU FOR THE MUSIC

Opposite: ABBA's performances were physically very demanding, with maximum energy devoted to singing, playing and dancing.

Björn: For the ABBA tour at the start of 1977, Benny and I had decided to create a short musical, just four songs long, to form part of the stage show. We called this little musical *The Girl With The Golden Hair*, and 'Thank You For The Music' was the opening song. It's about this young girl who finds out, or it dawns on her, that she has a particular talent for singing. It's 'a wonderful thing', something that spreads joy, and she's very happy at that moment about this talent and the happiness that she can give to other people. There is a little story in the lyrics about how she grew up and discovered her talent. It is a very musical moment, a musical theatre moment – and that was a significant first step towards writing complete musicals, towards working on *Chess* and *Kristina*, and creating musical dramas on stage.

I remember very well the night I was writing that lyric – and exactly where I was. It was in one of the houses that Agnetha and I had, in a suburb of Stockholm, on a huge island called Lidingö, which is across the sound from where I live now. I think it was the second house we had together, and funnily enough it was below the house that my parents-in-law later bought. We only owned it for a year or so, and one night, in one of the rooms in that house, that's where I wrote 'Thank You For The Music'. It's really quite rare for me to be able to pinpoint the moment quite so precisely. One of the few other moments that I can remember was one night, lying on the dock of where my summer house is and looking up at the sky, a clear sky with all the stars, and 'there was something in the air that night'…

Benny: 'Thank You For The Music' is a deceptive song. Although it seems simple on the surface, there are a lot of chords in there. You don't realise this until you try to play it. This is a perfect song to play on the piano; it sits easily on the keyboard.

You can easily imagine a singer like Vera Lynn leading a singalong of 'Thank You For The Music' during the London Blitz. So it's no surprise to find that she has recorded the song. Björn Ulvaeus

Benny: I always liked to include something that is not strictly pop on our records; we thought this was a good song and we decided to record it. I always think that this song has a music-hall quality. I don't really know my music-hall history, but it's what I imagine it might be, maybe a singalong in a pub in the East End of London. And the piano has a little bit of chorus effect to give it the appropriate sound.

We were recording 'Thank You For The Music' in a studio where Michael Tretow was working which had been built in an old grocery store. We went in

Above: Frida and Agnetha mid-ballad, The energetic dance routines were reserved for the more high-octane songs.

there with the band and the girls, gave the band the chords and the girls the lyrics, and played the song through. Björn was at one end of the studio with his guitar, and I was at the other end at the piano. When we went into the chorus for the first time, we looked at each other and instantly we knew that this was something good, that this song was going to work.

Björn: When we decided to create *The Girl With The Golden Hair*, some of the songs or parts of them might have been in existence, but the piece is very theatrical, so I would think that most of it was completely new. We wanted to give the audience something more than an unconnected sequence of songs.

Benny: On the tour, this 25-minute 'mini-musical', as we called it, came at the end of the show. We tried to make it more dramatic by having the four songs linked together by a narrator, this British actor Francis Matthews, in white make-up, and the girls in their costumes and golden wigs. I suspect the whole thing was probably quite weird for the audiences: they just wanted to see ABBA. It's a problem if like us you are not out on the road all the time; you don't know how to behave. We weren't in tune with what audiences really wanted. So creating *The Girl With The Golden Hair* was not a wrong choice musically, as it led on to us working on full length-musicals in *Chess* and then *Kristina*, but it was not a good choice for a tour.

Björn: There must have been a small break in the show, maybe Benny played a short intermezzo to give the girls time to get changed. I think we might also have mentioned in the advance publicity that we were going to be doing something new, so the audience would have been expecting something a little different but not knowing exactly what it would be. The concept was completely untried and, as Benny says, I'm sure the audience would much rather have heard the usual ABBA songs.

Using a narrator to link the songs together must have been my idea, because I had written the lyrics and realised that I needed something more to tie this rather flimsy story together, and the device of bringing in a narrator was the easiest solution. We used a British actor because I was looking for somebody who was slightly Shakespearean and it was perfect for an English-speaking actor to add that tone. 'It's time for the show,' he said. 'And now if you please, we're about to begin.' There was Francis Matthews in his clown's outfit – the event must have been a total surprise for him.

Benny: The other songs in *The Girl With the Golden Hair* were of varying quality, but if we hadn't done the musical we would not have produced 'Thank You For The Music'. 'I Wonder (Departure)' was a ballad that Frida sang really well; 'I'm A Marionette' was quite nice and there's a slice of it in *ABBA: The Movie*, along with some of the final number, 'Get On The Carousel', which we performed but never released on record because we didn't think it was good enough. Instead we included the three other numbers together as one section on *ABBA – The Album*.

Björn: Benny and I had talked about the need to have a ballad in a musical and 'I Wonder (Departure)' was the one. We wanted a sad ballad and as always the melody came first. I felt that it would provide the vehicle for explaining this girl's trepidation, the worry that surrounds any departure, the feeling of what's going to happen to me. Much later on, the song was in the storyline for *MAMMA MIA!* for a long time, opening the second act, but in the end it did not fit with the story and we replaced it with 'Under Attack'.

'I'm A Marionette' I thought of as a typical musical song. This girl was in the big city and had made it, and now she was starting to feel that everyone wanted a piece of her, that events were outside her control. Although it had not been exactly like that for us, even though most of the song was fiction, there was still a little bit of truth about our own situation. And the closing song 'Get On The Carousel' was never released. We were not happy enough with the song, although it worked in the context of the shows. It strikes me now that 'I'm A Marionette' would have been a much better finish to the musical.

Above: Agnetha and Björn looking at *Bravo* magazine, which often published features on ABBA during their heyday in the 1970s.

CHIQUITITA

Björn: 'Chiquitita' is another one of those percussive phrases, like 'Take A Chance On Me'. I think 'Chiquitita' was the third title I had tried for the song. Never have I tried so many different complete lyrics, getting the girls to sing them, and still not being convinced. I do speak a bit of Spanish, so I must have heard the phrase somewhere.

Benny: It usually worked like that for us. Most of the time, Björn and I would have written a song with no lyrics. We would decide who was going to sing it and give it a nonsense lyric for the girls to try out, so we could set the right key and record the backing tracks, and maybe do some overdubs to give it the right flavour. And then after that Björn would take the backing track home to listen to it and see what it suggested to him. And in this case, there emerged a Spanish title. I don't think that it ever happened the other way round – I can't remember that we ever had an idea for the lyric content of the song and then wrote and recorded the music afterwards.

'Chiquitita' is, once again, a song that is really nothing to do with a pop group. But you have to stick to what you feel is good music. If you have something you think is a good song, you can't throw it away because it's not really in style. We had established that we could do anything with songs like 'Fernando' or 'Money, Money, Money' or 'I Do, I Do', so why not 'Chiquitita'? I think that was one of the good things about ABBA, that we were prepared to go off in different directions, that it always was a blend of styles. I believe that this is one of the reasons that we were so successful.

It's another simple-sounding song, but it's full of counter-melodies and vocal arrangements. And the verse is the same as the chorus. I don't know if people would realise that. Well, it's not *exactly* the same, but it is very nearly the same.

Björn: Although creating the words had definitely been a lyric hell, I don't remember any particular difficulties in recording the song. It was pretty clear that we would have wanted to use a Spanish-flavoured guitar and it might have needed time to get that flavour right.

Benny: Sometimes songs would take a while to get right. Although 'Chiquitita' by its very nature could not be treated in too many different ways, and the choice of treatments was narrowed down, it could still take a long time to get to the end result.

'Chiquitita' is a very friendly word. It's something you would say to a female friend, especially when you want to comfort her. I thought that was nice, and the lyric followed on from the title. Björn Ulvaeus

Björn: We performed 'Chiquitita' at a UNICEF benefit in the UN General Assembly Hall in New York at the start of 1979. The other acts included the Bee Gees and Donna Summer, and Rod Stewart was singing 'Do Ya Think I'm Sexy'. I remember thinking how 'Chiquitita' stood out as so different and so European. I was tremendously proud of the song, but I thought this was so unlike everybody else's material.

Benny: We gave the song to UNICEF and we're glad that the money from its sales still goes to them. It was fun to be part of that UNICEF TV show with the likes of Rod Stewart and the Bee Gees and Donna Summer. We felt we were in good company... Everyone had been asked to perform a new song and 'Chiquitita' was our new song of the moment. But we did realise it felt a little bit weird, that it didn't fit in with the American style of music.

Björn: Appearing on TV like that was how we thought we could achieve success in America, the same way we had originally in Europe, by appearing on huge TV shows, but that didn't quite work in the States. Bands were touring like mad, all the time, and we were constantly being told that this was what we would have to do. And in the 1970s I think that America was anti-European pop to a certain extent. Although that changed in the 1980s and 1990s, at the time it was darker rock'n'roll that worked and we obviously did not offer that. But nonetheless we did have fifteen Top Ten hits in the US.

Benny: We had mixed feelings about the US. Of course, like any act we wanted to be successful there, but the record company told us that to do that we would have to be over in the US, working there, touring heavily, and we said, 'No way, we want to be in Sweden.' Considering all that, I think we really didn't do too badly in America.

Top: In the recording studio. ABBA opened their own Polar Studios in a disused cinema by the waterside in Stockholm in 1978; producer Michael Tretow kitted it out with state-of-the-art equipment and the band went on to record three of their best-selling albums there.
Above: One of many press conferences.

Björn: 'Chiquitita' was also a huge hit in South America, with Spanish lyrics that were written by Buddy McCluskey, who worked for the record company out in Argentina, and his wife: 'Gracias Por La Música'. It was the first time, other than the foreign-language versions of 'Waterloo' and 'Ring Ring' that I had been involved in translating songs into foreign languages. I suspect somebody had said to us that if we wanted to have a hit in South America we would have to translate the song into Spanish. Buddy and his wife produced back-translations for me to check; I understood a certain amount of Spanish and when I sang it through I could see if it worked, even if I didn't understand every word. And when we recorded the song in Spanish – along with some of our other songs which had also been translated – we had a very frisky Spanish lady with us called Ana Martinez, who was in the studio to advise us on whether the translation worked. It was fun because the girls were singing something that quite often they and we absolutely did not understand, but for some reason – and we were told this – it is not hard to sound reasonably good in Spanish if you were a native Swedish speaker. There is something in the way we talk that lends itself to pronouncing Spanish, whereas apparently English speakers would have found it a much harder job. The Spanish versions of the songs would not have been such a huge hit otherwise.

When we put *MAMMA MIA!* on in Madrid, the songs were translated all over again. The theatre people told us we should redo them and they were right: in the show the translations need to be as literal as possible so they still work within the overall storyline, whereas Buddy and his wife could stray away from the original lyrics if they needed to.

Benny: 'Chiquitita' is one of the songs in *MAMMA MIA!* that works so well within the storyline. People who haven't seen the show before really don't know what's going to happen and which song is coming as Rosie is talking; it's such good humour. And even in the foreign-language productions it still works. It's as funny in Stockholm or Hamburg as it is in London or New York.

Björn: Apart from Scandinavia, America, the UK and Australia, the territories that were always strong for us were the Northern European countries, particularly Germany, the Netherlands and Belgium. We actually did well in France, too, which is a market that can sometimes be very choosy about the English-speaking acts it likes: perhaps the TV people there gave us a chance because they thought, 'They're Swedish, not those bloody English!' In Italy we did less well. We went on one early TV show, where the producers kept us waiting and waiting for such a long time, with absolutely no explanation, that we decided never to set foot in an Italian TV studio again, and that affected our profile there of course, which was a great shame. And then Japan gave Benny and me our first ever big hit outside Sweden, a song called 'She's My Kind Of Girl' by Benny & Björn and Svenska Flicka (the Swedish Girls). It just so happened that the two Swedish girls were able to sing better than Benny and me, because they were Agnetha and Frida!

Filming the BBC/European Television
Network show *Snowtime Special –
ABBA In Switzerland* at the winter
sports resort of Leysin.
Overleaf: Rehearsals for ABBA's 1979
tour of North America and Europe.

DOES YOUR MOTHER KNOW

Björn: As time went on, Benny and I started to spread our wings a little in terms of where we could write songs. We still preferred working in our home environment, but at the beginning of 1979 we responded to the same instinct that would make us get up and head over to the island of Viggsö in the middle of winter, and by helicopter if need be. However, this time we thought, 'Why don't we choose somewhere more exotic?' We must have read something about other bands going away to write and work in various exotic places and decided to follow their example. We picked the Bahamas as our destination, which seemed like a good idea, especially in the middle of January. We had fun in the Caribbean, although I think we came back early, as we usually do. And one of the songs that came out of that trip was 'Does Your Mother Know'.

Benny: We went over to the Caribbean twice; first we went to the Bahamas and later on we went to Barbados. We said, 'Let's go to the Bahamas, why not?' I mean, we'd been sitting in basements and attics for so many years trying to work. We had never had a genuinely good working place until we used the house where Stig and Polar Music had their offices: we had the whole of the top floor there, so all of a sudden we had a really decent place to sit and work, but that actually happened almost too late because by that stage Björn had moved to England. This particular decision to go to the Caribbean was made well before then. We said, 'Let's do this, let's go somewhere, let's find somewhere pleasant to stay, rent a nice set of instruments, bring in a grand piano, and we can work there for a week or two.' So we ended up in a villa in the Bahamas, quite small but rather nice, with a piano shipped in for me, and some extra bits of kit, but not any recording equipment. It was meant to be a space where we could sit down and do nothing else but write songs. And maybe have a few margaritas.

We recorded a couple of songs at Criteria Studios in Miami where the Bee Gees were recording. We thought, 'Since we're down in the region, why don't we go over to Miami?', and instead of going back to Stockholm we asked Michael Tretow to fly over. We worked with the great producer Tom Dowd, who seemed to be producing every major record of this time, from Rod Stewart to Eric Clapton, and had previously worked with Dusty Springfield, Otis Redding and Aretha Franklin.

In the Bahamas we were staying next door to the Rolling Stones – 'Sitting In The Palmtree', one of the songs I sang lead on, recently reminded me of Keith Richards in Fiji! Björn Ulvaeus

Benny: Tom was one of Michael Tretow's biggest idols. We hadn't asked him to be there, he just happened to be at the studios. I think it was Atlantic Records, our US record company, who had said, 'Do you want us to ask Tom Dowd to come down?' and we said, 'You bet, if *he* wants to be there.' So Tom came over just to be helpful; he said he didn't want any credit, but he was around. And he would contribute something like 'No, it's not 120 beats per minute any more, it's 123 bpm.' There was also another pair of producer/engineers, the Albert Brothers, who had worked with the Allman Brothers and Crosby, Stills & Nash, and who sat in for one day: maybe they were just interested in seeing what we were doing. Of course we would listen to what all these people had to say, but the fact was it was an environment that we didn't know, we didn't know anybody apart from Michael.

Björn: On nearly all our other recordings before then we had been working very closely with a tight-knit group of musicians, but it didn't make that much difference in the end, because most of the stuff that we recorded in Miami we re-recorded later anyway. It was a slightly more anonymous process than we were used to – these were very talented and extremely professional and proficient musicians who were used to coming straight into a recording session and playing whatever you could throw at them. They were always technically excellent, but they lacked what you'd call a real musical personality.

Benny: We could communicate and make ourselves understood and they would know in principle what we meant. But we had enormous problems trying to explain 'If It Wasn't For The Nights' to them. They did not get what it was. They were asking, 'What kind of song is this?' and we told them, 'It's more like a big band number,' and they said, 'Uhh?' In the end Björn picked up his guitar and

Opposite and above: Unusually, Björn takes the lead vocals in 'Does Your Mother Know', which is about an older man and a younger girl. Later, in *MAMMA MIA!*, the story was to be flipped on its head, with an older woman singing the song to a younger man.

Above and opposite: Working with the backing vocalists. According to Benny, the backing vocals were one of the most important elements of ABBA's songs: 'We tried to look for natural counterpoints and melodies; that came out of the whole American tradition of harmony singing.'

played what we wanted, and they said, 'Oh, OK, that's what you want.' Björn got this riff going and then they understood. When I had played it on the piano they had no clue, but when Björn played they got it.

That session produced the backing tracks for two songs, 'Voulez-Vous' and 'If It Wasn't For The Nights'. But in fact all we retained from those sessions was the drums and maybe a bit of bass and guitar. It was a good group with a great groove, so we kept that feel. The actual choice of studio did not make much difference. By this time, all the professional studios were equally good. The brass section, funnily enough, was not recorded in Miami, although they had some fantastic brass players around; that was recorded back in Stockholm.

Björn: I had read a newspaper article about relationships between men and young girls. I can't remember exactly what the original article was actually about – it was most likely about predatory older men using younger women – but it talked about older men and younger girls and I had the idea of reversing the situation and creating a song about a man who, instead of trying to pick up a girl, turns round and says, 'Oh, what are you doing out tonight, does your mother know that you're out?' And I also knew this phrase 'Does your mother know?', which I'd come across in a book or a magazine, and it fitted so well with the overall idea. I decided early on, when I looked at the shape of the chorus, that the title should not come at the start of the song. I thought, 'You could introduce the title straightaway at the beginning, but no, let's hold it back.' This is something that you have to analyse with every song. With a song like 'Take A Chance On Me',

'If you change your mind, dah dah da dah dah', the title could have come right there, but I thought it was much more effective to wait. And that is just a feeling. There's no theory involved. I couldn't tell anyone, if they showed me a song, 'The title should be there, because of this or that theory, or the hook should be there', but it is something that I can feel, by instinct, in my own songwriting.

Benny: When we were recording 'Does Your Mother Know', I had just bought this wonderful Yamaha, the last great analogue synthesizer, a huge dream machine, which I still own but which I store with this guy who has every keyboard ever made. He asked me, 'If it's just standing around in your studio, couldn't I have it here with me. I'll fix it up for you.' The first time I made music with this Yamaha, I discovered how bloody complicated it was to create a sound. It was a bit like the Mini-Moog where you had to set all the parameters by hand, but on the Yamaha you had an additional control board. So you would adjust the knobs on the synthesizer to create a sound and once you had found the sound you wanted you then had to plug in a little cassette. There were tiny knobs, numbered from 1 to 24, and you would take a miniature screwdriver, turn screw number 1 until a green light came on and then you knew that you had the right parameters. And you had to go through all those twenty-four tiny little knobs doing the same thing. It took forever, but all of a sudden you had this fantastic sound, if you turned the right knobs. When you'd finished this lengthy process, you then had to take another blank cassette and do exactly the same thing on the other side of the board, because you needed a slightly different effect for the stereo mix. It all took so long but it created great sounds if you had the time and the patience to work your way through all the mechanical operations. And one of the sounds that I created on the Yamaha was the one we used for the beginning of 'Does Your Mother Know', which is a very short, dark, distinctive, wet, wonderful sound. The keyboard was really expensive, it cost maybe 400,000 Swedish krone, which was a lot of money for a synthesizer, but I think it paid for itself just with that one sound, which was different from any other sound that had been heard before.

Björn: This song has me singing the lead – to be honest I don't know why. I really don't like listening to myself singing. I think that Agnetha and Frida were happy listening back to themselves, but I'm not. I'm not a singer as such but it can be an interesting exercise sometimes. My voice is not bad, and it's even a bit charming in a song like 'Does Your Mother Know', I think. It works very well in that context. Given the story behind the song I guess that the reason I sang it was because of the title, the nature of the song and the scenario that I had set up in the lyrics. Yes, it had to be.

I'm not keen on all the songs I sang: 'Watch Out', for example, which was on the *Waterloo* album, I don't particularly care for, because it was from the period when we still trying to find out what we were about. I prefer 'Two For The Price Of One' off *Visitors*. It's a nice little story about a guy who is a cleaner at a railway station who answers a lonely hearts ad from two girls looking for a blind date – the twist is that when they turn up it's a mother and daughter.

Benny: The songs Björn sang provided a different dynamic to the balance of each album. He could have done more, but we were blessed with two great singers in Agnetha and Frida, and as Björn and I had quickly discovered when we began as a duo, we were not such good singers. Although I can sing in tune, I do not really consider myself a singer.

Björn: I think that Benny is unfair on himself. He has recorded some really good vocals, particularly on a song like 'One Man, One Woman' on *ABBA – The Album*, where he does some stunning backing vocals.

Benny: The middle section of 'Does Your Mother Know', which has something of a ragtime feel about it, had been part of a previous song called 'Dream World' that we got as far as mixing. However, we decided at that point that we didn't really like the song, but that section was worth keeping, and it found a home in 'Does Your Mother Know'. It is so bloody difficult to create good musical ideas that it is a shame to waste them. The trick is to wait to see if there is a hole where using that idea will make a difference. It's part of the craftsmanship of songwriting: splicing a section in so that it sits naturally and doesn't feel forced or out of keeping with the rest of the song.

Björn: Benny and I always carried this battery of little ideas around in our heads, thinking of ways to combine the old and the new. I don't know if that is a technique other songwriters use, but it was certainly ours.

Above: For the 1979 tour, which opened in Edmonton, Alberta, designer Rune Söderqvist and costume designer Owe Sandström created a Nordic theme of icy whites with blues, indigos and violets.

Overleaf: This iconic shot of ABBA by Anders Hanser was used as the basis of a Swedish Post Office stamp honouring ABBA in 1983.

VOULEZ-VOUS

With Britt Ekland after the show in Los Angeles in September 1979. Ron Wood and Donna Summer also came to see the show.

Björn: I don't speak French, so the title 'Voulez-Vous' had to come from somewhere else, probably from the phrase, *'Voulez-vous coucher avec moi?'*. Maybe it was from the chorus of 'Lady Marmalade' by Labelle – but I think I was more aware of the Serge Gainsbourg/Jane Birkin song 'Je t'aime, moi non plus'; I expect there's a bit of 'voulez-vous' in there somewhere. To be frank, I didn't actually know whether you could use 'Voulez-vous' on its own like that. I didn't bloody care, I just did it. I thought, 'It's French; no one will know, apart from the French.' I thought the phrase sounded so nice. It was perfect. What I had in mind before I even had the title was a kind of a nightclub scene, with a certain amount of sexual tension and eyes looking at each other. I can see it now, exactly the kind of room in a club, so I only had to describe that room and what might be happening and then add that final touch, 'Voulez-vous?'

There's another 'ah ha' in 'Voulez-Vous'. It could have been a baritone saxophone, or another instrument, but it works so well as a vocal device. It's using voices as instruments. Benny Andersson

Benny: You rarely hear cymbals in our records, unless they're added on afterwards. We found out quite early that if the drummer was playing along and using his cymbals all over the place, you could never get rid of the sound because the cymbals would be over the whole recording; you were stuck with them. So we found it better not to use cymbals and then if we did want them, we could add them on afterwards, so we could have total control over the sound. One of the most important elements of the arrangements were the backing vocals, which we always spent a lot of time on. There was no secret. We just worked on them. First we had to decide what the vocal lines had to be. Every melody line in an arrangement needs to have somewhere to start and somewhere to go, in a natural way preferably. The same thing applies in an orchestra. If you are writing a bassoon part, you should ideally create a line that means something to the person playing that line, not just a series of notes that fit with the melody – and that's what we tried to do with the backing vocals, looking for natural counterpoints and melodies. That came out of the whole American tradition of harmony singing, whether that was barber-shop quartets or the Four Freshmen or the Beach Boys.

'Voulez-Vous' was one of the backing tracks we had recorded in Criteria Studios in Miami. The drummer, bassist and guitarist – Joe Galdo, Arnold Pasiero and Ish Ledesma – were part of Foxy, who had had a major US hit with 'Get Off'. It was odd because we had always worked with musicians who we knew well and who knew what we were trying to do. The guys from Foxy were

Opposite: Backstage on tour, with stylist Elisabeth Hofstedt (top right) and appearing on the BBC TV show *The Multicoloured Swap Shop* (top left).

Above: A press conference following the Edmonton show that opened the 1979 tour.
Opposite: The members of ABBA tried to fit a little time for relaxation into their gruelling schedule of sell-out concerts and press conferences.

professionals and like all American session musicians had a certain style of playing, which was not the same as ours, but that meant it was a useful experiment to see what emerged.

Björn: As the Bahamas is close to Florida, and Miami was then the recording capital of disco, it seemed like a good idea to ask Atlantic to find a backing band: we knew they would choose wisely for us, and the musicians from Foxy, who had worked with the Bee Gees, were the *crème de la crème*. Of course it was a strange situation for us. It was great fun, but it felt a little awkward and a bit scary because we were not only working with unfamiliar musicians but also in unfamiliar surroundings, and we probably finished it more quickly than we would have done at home. In any case when we got back to Stockholm we changed and added so much to the track, but way back you can hear the original backing track inside the song.

The *Voulez-Vous* album was one of the first to be completed at our own studios, Polar, in Stockholm. Previously, when we were recording at Metronome, we were having to compete with other people regarding time. But once we had got Polar Studios, that's when we became totally independent and could actually block out months at a time if we wanted to, which was the object of the exercise, of course.

Benny: We sold our share of Polar Music in the early 1980s and the studio was part of the package. However, we continued to record there – the Benny Anderssons Orkester was the last group to use it before it finally closed in 2004. What is nice is that the Metronome Studio, in Stockholm, where we did so much of our early recording, is still going strong, now called Atlantis Studio. The studio looks exactly the same as it did in the 1970s, so it is quite nostalgic going back in there.

During this period I was able to fit in some outside production work with Finn Kalvik, a friend who is a folksinger and composer; we did a couple of albums together which were good successes in Sweden and Norway. Right at the beginning of our ABBA career Björn and I had been hired by Polar Music as producers and worked with many different acts including Ted Gärdestad, a wonderful songwriter and singer, and Björn's old group the Hootenanny Singers. We carried on doing that even after winning Eurovision, but soon we really didn't have enough time; we had to concentrate on what we were doing with ABBA.

Björn: We recorded the *Voulez-Vous* album during the period when my and Agnetha's marriage was ending, through the autumn and winter of 1978. It was naturally a difficult time, but on the other hand, going into the studio was almost like closing off our private life and entering our professional life. We actually had no problem working together, other than the occasional irritation in the studio, but that had existed before! It must have been because we both felt that the work we were doing was so important and we still had so much to give, that we never considered ending the group. Stig thought it would be the end, but that never entered my mind and I think it was the same for Agnetha. Maybe if we'd been working together in some other business it would have been harder, but we were able to immerse ourselves in the music and to transform ourselves into civilised professionals.

BOX OFFICE HOURS 930.6 MON.
YOU WANNA FIGHT SEPT 10
MAX WEBSTER _ FM SEPT. 9
ABBA SEPT 13 SORRY FULL!
VAN HALEN SEPT 18
RODEO NOV\4.18

Entertainment

Bob Hope
in China
tonight

Slick ABBA struts for 17,000 in Coliseum

GIMME! GIMME! GIMME!

Björn: We were in the era of disco. And 'Gimme! Gimme! Gimme!' is very much a disco number. Very, very disco. I was reluctant to use the title because the word 'Gimme' had been used before – 'Gimme Shelter', of course – but in the end the combination of the melody and the 'Gimme! Gimme!'s defeated me completely, I had to give in. But then I thought it was a nice touch, 'a man after midnight' which added a little mystery – what's going on?

Those disco tempos gradually got faster and faster. Eventually they were frantic. Björn Ulvaeus

Below: Frida as a Gooner – in each city on the 1979 tour she would put on a local sports shirt for one number. Opposite: The view out from the cocoon at Wembley Arena. Backing vocalists for the tour were Tomas Ledin, Mats Ronander, Birgitta Wollgård and Liza Öhman, and the backing band included stalwarts Ola Brunkert, Lasse Wellander and Rutger Gunnarsson with Anders Eljas and Ake Sundqvist.

Benny: Yeah, disco. Boring! I thought it was no fun to try to hang on to whatever was going on in the music industry at the time. I preferred doing 'Chiquitita' and 'Money, Money, Money' and those odd kinds of songs instead of trying to be 'with it'. It's fine to listen to what other people are doing to see what's going on, whether the snare drum sound is thin this year or big this year. These things are nice to know – if you are aware of them you can adjust your arrangements and you know where you are in respect of what everybody else is doing. Disco was not the same as writing music that people could dance to, where you're having a party and want to buy a record to get your guests dancing. Disco was a trend, a formula. And it was good at the time to have a song that could fit into that trend, because 'Chiquitita' and 'Thank You For The Music' were definitely not disco. Even 'Dancing Queen', which ended up being played in discos, was really not a disco song; it was a much slower tempo.

Björn: Of the groups who were there at the start of disco, the Bee Gees really stood out. They were a fantastic group who had two, if not three, careers: they had been successful in the late 1960s and then come back with a vengeance in the 1970s, completely transformed. They are probably the most prolific songwriters there are; the Beatles catalogue has not been recorded a lot, but the Bee Gees songs always come around – they are timeless. When *Saturday Night Fever* came out, I didn't think the movie was that exciting, but the soundtrack, which also included Yvonne Elliman and Tavares, was so new, so special. It was like when Benny and I heard *Jesus Christ Superstar* for the first time; we thought, 'This is breaking new ground.' The tracks were meticulously produced; they must have spent days, even weeks, getting those vocals right. The Bee Gees were not credited as producers on the soundtrack album, but their influence is there.

Benny: I was a big fan of the Bee Gees, their production style and their singing: they made the vocals sound so easy. And the fact that they had been hanging in

Agnetha and Frida had the vocal talent and technique Benny and Björn needed to interpret their songs. Björn says, 'When I look for singers I look for real quality. I know very well I don't have that quality myself – the role I played in ABBA was fine, but as a solo singer I'm not good enough and as a writer I want my songs to be sung by the best.'

there all the way through since the late 1960s. Working with their producer, Arif Mardin, had given them a new lease of life, creating the music for *Saturday Night Fever* – I knew the music, of course, but I never saw the movie – and on the flow of that, writing songs for Dionne Warwick, Diana Ross and Barbara Streisand.

Björn: An album like the *Saturday Night Fever* soundtrack, anything that was really good in these years during the 1970s when we were active, would push us to try harder. We would feel very much that we then had to excel ourselves, not to imitate, but to reach a new level. Other bands at the time who we really admired were Fleetwood Mac and the Eagles. I remember going to California sometime in the mid-1970s, and listening on the radio for the first time to 'One Of These Nights', which was so good on the radio, 'Lyin' Eyes' and, of course, 'Hotel California'.

Benny: The only good thing with 'Gimme! Gimme! Gimme!' is the instrumental part. That's original and I'm not surprised that that was the part of the song Madonna wanted to sample. Somebody called the office one day and said, 'Madonna has done a sample of 'Gimme! Gimme! Gimme!', can she use it?' We replied, 'Well we should hear it first, just send us the recording and we'll listen to it.' They said, 'No way, but we'll send a person.' And so Madonna's manager, Angela Becker, came to Stockholm with the recording and a very nice letter from Madonna. Björn and I didn't need to hear more than half the record to know it was good, so we split the copyright 50:50. Madonna is a brilliant performer and she has hung in there for a long, long time, constantly recreating her image. And I'm happy for her that she had a good success with 'Hung Up'. As I now say, it's my favourite Madonna song!...

Björn: Madonna had gone ahead and completed the whole recording – it wasn't a demo – knowing that we might say, 'No'. She is a very brave woman. On the other hand it was absoutely the right strategy, because we were able to listen to the finished result, and the song was so well constructed and so cleverly done. There was no question of us refusing. In any case we would have been pre-disposed to agree, since Madonna is an incredibly talented lady. We were particularly pleased that 'Hung Up' went on to become one of the biggest singles of that year.

Benny: In the 1980s, 'Gimme! Gimme! Gimme!' was covered by Andy Bell and Erasure. They did us a huge favour – as did the movies *Muriel's Wedding* and *Priscilla, Queen Of The Desert* later on, because they made our back catalogue come alive in a period before Polygram bought Polar Music. It came at exactly the right time.

In the autumn of 1979, around the time that 'Gimme! Gimme! Gimme!' was released, ABBA embarked on their only tour of North America. It had originally been planned as part of a much larger world tour that would include Eastern Europe and the Far East, but since the recording of the Voulez-Vous *album had taken much longer than anticipated, the tour had been truncated to a three-and-a-half-week, eighteen-concert, tour of Canada and the US followed by a series of dates in Europe. ABBA opened the tour in Edmonton, Alberta – their first ever show in North America. Highlights included their performance at the legendary Radio City Music Hall in New York, and the low point was a terrifying flight in bad weather the following day that unnerved everybody on board, especially Agnetha.*

I HAVE A DREAM

Above and opposite: On the 1979 tour, ABBA arranged for a local children's choir in each city to join them on stage to sing 'I Have A Dream'.

Benny: When Björn wrote the lyric for 'I Have A Dream' I didn't make any connection with Martin Luther King at all, and in fact I still don't, because if you listen to the actual words it has nothing to do with his famous speech. The idea there might even be a connection didn't occur to me until somebody mentioned it much later; I don't think it was Björn's intention to do a rip-off of Martin Luther King.

Björn: The night I finished writing the lyric for 'I Have A Dream', Benny was hosting a party over at his place. I called him from my house and he said, 'Come over', so I did, and we ended up with everybody there at the party singing that song.

Benny: I told the guests, 'We have a new song.' I played it to them and they simply thought it was a great tune. It's a song which marks a bit of a move back towards the *schlager* tradition.

Björn: I think 'I Have A Dream' is a bit more folky. There is a sitar playing, which gives the song a very Greek feel, I think. It sounds like a bouzouki.

Benny: It's a sitar guitar, being played by Janne Schaffer, the guitarist who worked with us from the beginning. The electric sitar looks like a guitar but there is something about the way that the strings are mounted that gives it that distinctive biting noise. It's wonderful to have good instruments to hand because when it comes to creating sounds, you don't want to use the same sounds everybody else is using. If you are making pop music I think it's essential. I heard this story about Steely Dan, who also used an electric sitar on 'Do It Again', that they could sit for like six hours adjusting the sound of a hi-hat. You know, that's boring. We never did that. We had thirty-two tracks in the later years, and thirty-two tracks sounds a lot, but it isn't really. Michael always used to start off with eight tracks or so for the drums: separate hi-hat, cymbals and tomtoms but we always ended up having the drums mixed down onto two tracks for the final mix because we needed extra space for all the backing vocals and the synthesizer stuff that I wanted to add.

The release of 'I Have A Dream' happened to coincide with the International Year Of The Child in 1979, although the song hadn't been written specifically for it. We sang it on tour in the States that autumn. And since it was the Year Of The Child, we arranged for a children's choir to take part in the show in every city we performed in. They were sent the song in advance, they rehearsed and they came on stage singing it. It was just to break up the performance, something else happening, and quite nice.

Björn: Bringing on the choir might have been on the verge of camp, and of course it is traditionally dangerous to use children, but it did work somehow. The choirs were, of course, of varying qualities. And I've encountered a few people in America since, who come up and say, 'I was in that choir that year in that place.' 'Good,' I always say, 'I remember you…'

I had forgotten where we had found the children's choir for the recording of 'I Have A Dream', but many years later I sent my two youngest daughters, Emma and Anna, to the British International Primary School in Stockholm, where they could be taught in English, because we had been living in England and when we came back to Sweden they were virtually bilingual. However, the Primary School only catered for children up to the age of 11, so the girls then moved on to the International School of Stockholm. The first time I went into the school I saw a large picture on the wall of ABBA with a bunch of kids and it dawned on me that this school was where we had found the children's choir back in 1979. We had specifically wanted British and American children, so that they had the right enunciation, and Swedish kids that young would seldom be totally fluent in English. Of course, the choir had come into the studio to record their vocals and so I had never made the connection.

On the tour of the States Agnetha's and my daughter Linda came out to sing with the local choir when we played Las Vegas. And twenty years later she appeared in *Kristina Från Duvemåla*, the musical that Benny and I wrote based on the novels of Vilhelm Moberg. She had told me at some point in the 1990s that working in the theatre was the only thing she could contemplate doing, and although I knew it was a perilous profession, I could not discourage her. She was well aware that the unemployment rate in acting is high, but she went into it with open eyes. In the musical she took the role of Elin, a relatively small part as the daughter of one of the main characters, Ulrika, although she was on stage a lot; her biggest scene came with Robert, the younger brother of the male lead Karl Oskar. It was a little bit strange to see my daughter playing a daughter in a musical I had written, but she had been there all the way through rehearsals for the original production, living in Malmö for the duration, and so I had become used to her being part of the show.

Benny: I think it is quite wonderful to have children trying their hardest in the entertainment or music business, even though it is not easy. My elder son Peter has been a songwriter and producer for many years; he and his wife Nanne were part of One More Time, who came third for Sweden in the 1996 Eurovision Song Contest and had a big European hit with 'Highland'. My younger son Ludvig released a solo album in 2003 and now has a rock band called Ella Rouge, songwriting, singing and playing guitar. He met his wife Lisa when they were both in the Swedish production of *Chess*; she is a dancer and formed a trio with two of the other dancers, Sara and Anna. They later put on a show of their own, including five songs Lisa had written in English. I liked it and encouraged her to write more – and I produced an album called *Feel* which they released in May 2006 under the name Florence, after the heroine in *Chess*.

That tour of 1979 was the only real big tour we made – to America and Europe – and then we went over to Japan in 1980 with the same show. We were well taken care of: good promotion, good management on the tours. Somebody would tell us when to go and where to go and we just followed instructions. There had to be a lot of planning beforehand but when the organisation is in place, it's fairly easy. But on tour, everything is all the same; it doesn't matter if you're in Brussels or in Phoenix. It's not a good life. We once met AC/DC who had been out on the road for five years and we were told they had no homes, literally.

Björn: Agnetha finally decided that she wasn't going to travel any more right at the end of our American tour. After that I seem to recall she went to Japan because that had been planned before the American tour. But I would gladly have stopped touring anyway. Agnetha had a fear of flying, as indeed my present wife does. We had this terrible incident over Boston in a small jet, in terrible, terrible weather, a dreadful storm, circling and knowing that underneath us were ten other planes circling and waiting to land, with lightning going off all around us. It was awful. I think it was after that she became really scared of flying.

A good song should not consist of more notes than it really needs. 'I Have A Dream' and 'The Winner Takes It All' are both good examples. They are really, really, really simple. Benny Andersson

Agnetha and Björn's daughter Linda joined ABBA on the US leg of the tour, making her stage debut as part of the children's choir in Las Vegas.

THE WINNER TAKES IT ALL

Above: Filming the video for 'The Winner Takes It All' in the Society House on the island of Marstrand. Director Lasse Hallström, a long-time collaborator with ABBA, later found international success as a movie director with films including *My Life As A Dog*, *What's Eating Gilbert Grape*, *Chocolat* and *The Shipping News*.
Opposite: Portraits of the four band members by Anders Hanser.

Benny: 'The Winner Takes It All' is something special. The song didn't sound like that from the beginning. The same notes, the same chords, but not the same rhythm. The first backing track was rigid, it wasn't good at all. It was just an embryo of something, certainly catchy, but nothing worth keeping until a moment when we were writing away on Viggsö, the island where we went to work, playing guitar and piano. For some reason I divided the existing phrases into halves, and so introduced a lot more space between the phrases.

Björn: Suddenly, slowed down in this way, it became completely different, dramatic, something we could identify with, a song in the French *chanson* genre, with an Edith Piaf feel. In fact Mireille Mathieu did record the song in French later on. Discovering the song could work was such a revelation; we were so happy, just as we always were when we'd written something really good, because we could always feel when we had something good. And this was one of those moments.

Benny and I lived in the same place, two houses but the same area so we'd share the car journey back and forth. We always used to play backing tracks driving back home and this time we were so convinced, both of us, 'No, no, no, we have to redo this, it's worth it.'

I went home with the backing track to write the lyrics and played it loud on a big sound system, over and over, walking around, listening and listening. As usual the song did speak to me and say, 'This is what I'm about', though I know that sounds silly. And that night, with 'The Winner Takes It All' I did have a little help from a bottle of whisky, some Scotch – not a whole bottle, but definitely a couple of big snifters! I was trying it out to see whether writing with a drink helped. I had done that before and it never usually worked. In the morning the words would look dreadful. But this time it did. Don't ask me why or how. The words just came. I hardly had to change a word, which was fantastic. I am a ruthless editor of my own words. I keep nothing that I'm not absolutely convinced about.

The lyric is not to do with my and Agnetha's divorce, really. There is some element of someone writing this who has had an experience like that but other than that it's totally fiction. There was no 'winner' in our case, for instance, standing by the side and looking at this terrible thing happening. It wasn't like that.

I remember Björn coming in with the lyric for 'The Winner Takes It All' on the morning Agnetha was going to sing it. I thought it was a wonderful lyric, the best so far. **Benny Andersson**

Björn: We recorded the song a couple of days after I finished the lyrics. I remember writing out the words, going into the studio and giving them to the others, who hadn't seen them before. There were tears in some eyes. I would say that 85 or 90 per cent of our songs are sad… Of course, Benny and I both come from the north, so minor keys are natural for us. And there is a sadness which is special to the Nordic people. But I'm not the type who goes around opening my heart to everyone.

Benny: What I'm always aiming for is that the inner core of a song is as simple as possible. 'The Winner Takes It All' is made up of very little. It actually consists of very few notes. Two short phrases that go around and around. That's it, nothing more. But then a song as good as 'Da Doo Ron Ron' has really only three notes. And 'The Winner Takes It All' includes a lot of emotion, treated the right way, and there is a counterpoint thing going on with the vocals in the backing track. That's the Brian Wilson influence. Counterpoint harmony, that's what the Beach Boys did all the time and what I always liked a lot. There's a lot of that in the ABBA records, which I think is one of the reasons the songs work. It's intricate in a way and it adds value. Being in the studio is very special. Playing music on stage or with friends is a different – but equally wonderful – thing, because then the music happens in the instant that you play it, but in the studio you are in total control and you can do whatever you like, if you have the time. I always enjoy that very much.

I actually met Brian Wilson in the mid-1970s. He was not in particularly good shape, but he was nice and we went to his house, just to say hello and have a cup of coffee. And although he wasn't really feeling well he knew we were there and he knew who we were. I know that because I have a friend who played violin on one of his tours. Brian Wilson is my hero really, but it's sad when people burn out.

The counterpoint melody in 'The Winner Takes It All' runs throughout the verse and the chorus. Sometimes it's hummed, sometimes it's on piano or guitar, sometimes sung by the choir or played by the strings. That for me is the good thing about this song. People have tried to record cover versions and if they take that element away it doesn't sound right. Sometimes you just cannot take away one of the jigsaw pieces.

Björn: I am always interested in listening to cover versions of ABBA songs, where the artist is trying to create a new interpretation and not simply copy what we did on the original record. I very much enjoyed the Erasure EP *Abba-esque* because they did it absolutely their own way, and even if that was not always necessarily to my taste, I liked the fact that they had really gone for it. Kylie Minogue did a great version of 'Dancing Queen' for the closing ceremony of the 2000 Olympics in Sydney, and Westlife's 'I Have A Dream' was also very good.

Benny: I don't listen much to cover versions, I'm not particularly aware of them. But I was involved a little in an album recorded by the Swedish mezzo-soprano Anne Sofie von Otter called *I Let The Music Speak*, which includes a version of 'The Winner Takes It All'; the album is her choice of songs by Björn and me. We talked about her selection and I suggested a couple of songs, and I played piano on two songs. She included songs from *Chess*, like 'Heaven Help My Heart', and from *Kristina*: 'Ljussa Kvällar om Varen' and 'Ut Mot Ett Hav'. And there is one song never heard before in English – 'After The Rain', which Tommy Körberg and Karin Glenmark sang in Swedish on one of my solo albums, with new English lyrics by Mats Nörklit. And there are words to an instrumental I had written with the fiddle band Orsa Spelmän and my Synclavier for the album *November 1989*, called 'Stockholm By Night'. It's a nice tune and I sent it over to Björn to create a lyric: it's now called 'I Walk With You Mama'.

Björn: The video for 'The Winner Takes It All' was shot by Lasse Hallström up on the island of Marstrand, a very old Swedish fishing community, which is now a popular summer holiday resort on the West coast of Sweden, north-east of Gothenburg. Lasse was up there working on a film, and Benny and Frida were on a boating holiday, so it was very convenient for them to get there at that point. But although Marstrand is a beautiful place, making the video was, as always, a pain in the neck for me, just like doing photo sessions – and we must have done hundreds of those in our time. You stand there and pose, and then you have to change your clothes and pose again. And it all takes so much time, a lot of waiting around. The redeeming feature was that when I was at my most bored in these sessions I could remind myself that 'This is all worthwhile. There is at least a reason why we are doing this, for the good of the group.'

Above and opposite: Agnetha on location in Marstrand for the video of 'The Winner Takes It All'.

SUPER TROUPER

Above and opposite: It was a tradition that every Midsummer's Eve ABBA and the Polar Music staff would celebrate on the island of Viggsö, where Stig Anderson and the group had homes, dancing round the maypole and generally having a good time. Overleaf: Images from the photo shoot for the cover of the *Super Trouper* album cover, with circus performers and friends of the band, including (bottom, second from left) Anders Anderson, son of Stig, and (bottom, far right) backing vocalist Tomas Ledin.

Benny: We were finishing off a new album in the early autumn of 1980. We had recorded all the songs for it, but then we thought, 'Boy, we need one more good song for this album.' So Björn and I stayed in the studio one day to write a new song, which was a bit of a luxury. And just like that, 'Super Trouper' came.

Björn: It was uncanny. We had already decided to call the album *Super Trouper* because we'd been on tour and had used these huge colour spotlights called 'super troupers' which we thought would make a good name for the album. And then we listened to the album and thought, 'It needs something more, it needs another song.' So it was a song that we wrote in the studio, the only time that ever happened. It happened quite quickly, and for some reason the title of the album fitted completely with the chorus we had written. I think otherwise the song would not have been called 'Super Trouper' because it was very, very difficult to build a story around that title. To write a song about a spotlight was not easy...

I had met my wife Lena at that point and ABBA had been on tour earlier in the year, so I was inspired from that. I thought the only way here was to write something about someone who was on tour, obviously, since 'Super Trouper' is the title. And then I could only think of me out there on the road, longing for her, and what a difference it's going to make if she's in the audience and the spotlight hits me. Quite a clever way, actually, of getting out of that problem...

Benny: When the chorus of the song came we cleaned up the sound. There's a kind of tingling sound to the verses which disappears in the choruses, because we have the backing vocals and a more rhythmical feel. And in the background is this little tune that everyone who ever learns the piano knows how to play – Russ Conway once recorded it as 'Lesson One' – which was fun to add in, a touch of humour.

I even managed to get a rhyme out of 'Glasgow'. Tim Rice once told me it was probably the only time the word 'Glasgow' has been rhymed with in a pop song! Björn Ulvaeus

Benny: *Super Trouper* is an album I particularly like. That and *Arrival*, and there are some good songs on the *ABBA* album. But overall I'd say *Super Trouper* is the best. If there is a best. All of a sudden we had our own studio, we could be in there whenever we wanted, instead of having just Wednesday each week, we could record as much as possible. It's wonderful to have your own studio. You can take the time that you need, which is what I think you have to do.

Both pages: Portraits by Anders Hanser from the 'Super Trouper' video recording.

We came to the realisation that the more energy we put into any song the better it became. Since then I always do that; it doesn't matter if it takes too long. You just have to be in there until you're satisfied with the outcome of the work. So that wasn't the case for the first years. I think we did pretty well despite having no studio time in the beginning of our recording career. We always had limited time in the studios and we needed to be finished when the time was up. That's why there is a potential compilation you could call *ABBA Wood*. Instead of *ABBA Gold*, you could issue the Worst Of ABBA. Because there were often times when we were in a rush and had to finish songs off just in order to get records out at the right time. I like the idea of *ABBA Wood*, but unfortunately our record company doesn't!

Björn: I think the lyrics about the stresses and strains of touring were particularly relevant at that time. I did still get a buzz from performing at the beginning of each tour with ABBA, but it wore off quite quickly and then it became tedious, not so much from the constant moving on tour, although that is naturally difficult, but more because as a group we always had to do the same thing at the same time. If you are a solo artist you have a little more flexibility in the way you perform each show, but vocally and musically our songs were so tightly constructed and on stage we were trying to recreate the sound we had created in the studio, so we were really restricted.

In the studio we never really left any room for improvisation – it's not something that pop music lends itself to. In any case I am not a natural improviser, and I never really got into jazz, although when I was younger I had been in a trad jazz outfit. I was working in London one summer at the end of the 1950s, at the height of the trad jazz boom in the UK, when Acker Bilk and Chris Barber were playing at clubs like the 100 Club on Oxford Street, and when I got back to

Sweden I started to play banjo in a trad jazz band with my cousin Joen, who had already introduced me to skiffle.

The other reason touring had lost its appeal was because I had done so much of it when I was younger. When I was in the Hootenanny Singers we toured so much, because it was the only way of making some money. You hoped to have a hit, but knew that the level of record sales in a small country like Sweden were not going to generate very much income. For ten years, every bloody summer from 1964 up to 1974 – when we cancelled the tour of the folkparks because of the demands on our time after winning Eurovision – I was playing 100 to 140 gigs. So the novelty of playing live had definitely worn off. In the beginning I had loved performing. It was incredible to stand on stage and people would listen to you, wanting autographs, all that adulation. Somehow it got less and less interesting. I think you have to be born to be an entertainer, an exhibitionist, to want to go on and on, and I'm not like that. I've never felt the urge to go back on stage. I'm not a natural born performer. Benny is much more of a performer than I am, definitely.

Benny: Thank you, Björn! I certainly feel confident on stage. I like playing with other musicians – it doesn't matter if there's an audience or not. The best thing about being a musician is being able to share. Although touring was extremely boring, not being able to do anything you wanted, having to sit around for hours and hours on end, I maybe did not become as jaded as Björn. I still love to play music with other musicians, and most recently have been doing so with the Benny Anderssons Orkester. The others in that band perform all the time, but together we only appear eight or nine times a year. Because I spend a lot of time working in my own office, writing music every day, it is wonderful to get out and perform with them: it makes me feel as though I have been let out into a wide green field.

OUR LAST SUMMER

Opposite: Rehearsing and recording
'Our Last Summer' at the Polar Music
Studios in July 1980.

Björn: 'Our Last Summer' is a true story. It's about someone I went to visit in Paris. It was one of those bitter-sweet, young love stories. The version in the lyrics is not all true. It's half fiction but very much inspired by that experience and my memories of Paris. So that song was easy to write, no problem.

When I was a teenager my parents would send me abroad during the summer holidays. They thought it would do me good – and it did. In 1959 I had worked in London for a paper agency that sold paper around the globe for the paper mill which my Uncle Esbjörn owned, the summer when I discovered the trad jazz boom in the UK. The following summer I had worked in a brewery and on a building site in Heppenheim in Germany, on the Rhine, south of Frankfurt. And then this particular summer I went to Paris. A Swedish girl I knew from my hometown was working there and I decided to travel down there for a week, my first visit to the city. We had not been romantically involved in Sweden, but Paris tends to have that effect on people, and so it was with the two of us. She certainly took me to see the Quartier Latin, the Champs-Elysées and the Eiffel Tower, but to be honest I don't really remember much of Paris. I mostly remember her! And the rest is blotted out in my memory…

Something in the musical feel of the song triggered this memory and suggested a story to me, this idea of the last summer of innocence. But rather than leave the song simply as a romantic tale, I added a twist with the lines 'Now you're working in a bank, the family man, the football fan, and your name is Harry…' I liked the fact that this young romantic guy was now a bank clerk or a bank manager – when Catherine Johnson was working on the storyline for MAMMA MIA! it gave her the name and the character of one of the three dads straight away. But my wife Lena was mad at me for including that verse – she said, 'You've killed all the romance of the song with that last little bit!'

Benny: 'Our Last Summer' is a good song, I like it. It contains some sort of different sentiment than many of the others, I don't know quite how to describe it. There is a kind of nostalgic feel about the music as well as the lyric. There is something about its innocence that reminds me of when I started writing songs in the mid-1960s. I was in a band called the Hep Stars, a rock band, quite a wild band, sort of punkish in a way. We weren't very sophisticated but we had fun and the audience liked us a lot. Initially the Hep Stars only did cover versions – our first Number One was a song called 'Cadillac', written by an English group called the Renegades – but eventually we ran out of material. And because I was such a huge Beatles fan, I thought to myself, 'Well, Lennon and McCartney write their own stuff, maybe I should give it a try', and I wrote a song called 'No Response'. As a rock band in Sweden, you had to sing in English, but my English was really bad at the time… I started with the rhymes, wrote them down and filled in the lines backwards.

Above and opposite: At Polar Studios, the custom-built facility that finally allowed Benny, Björn and engineer Michael Tretow the time and space to work as long as they needed on recording and mixing.

To be honest they were terrible lyrics, but being in Sweden, nobody really cared – and it became a number two. The second song I wrote was called 'Sunny Girl', which I still think is a good song. It was a kind of minuet, soft, nice, a strange little thing for a rock band. Maybe that was one of the reasons why it worked well, because nobody else was doing anything like that. With 'Sunny Girl' I felt that I had got connected to something. All of a sudden, I felt like I knew what I was doing. I had felt something when I wrote the song and obviously the audience felt the same thing, so from the moment we became Number One with 'Sunny Girl', I was filled with the feeling, 'Now I know what I'm going to do with my life. I'm not going to go back to being an engineer', or whatever was going to happen to me after the Hep Stars. 'I'm going to write music because I think I can do that.'

I don't know where the music comes from, all I know is it takes a lot of time. The reason we did not go on tour with ABBA was that we understood that we needed time to write good songs. You don't write a good song in an hour; well you may appear to do so, but you need to have two months before that trying out ideas, before writing the good song in that hour. That's how it works for me. I don't know how it is for other people, but for me that's the way it is. If you don't sit there and if you don't work on it really hard, trying to achieve something and trying to make something good, it's not going to happen. It's not going to happen sitting in the car, thinking, 'Oh I have this good idea', nothing like that. I have to sit at a piano or a keyboard and play through the rubbish, and get rid of that, and sometimes things will pop out and I can say, 'This is good.' If there are two of you writing, like we

were in the ABBA days, it makes it a little easier because one of you can pick up when the other one is not really on it at the moment. But basically what comes out is not for me to understand.

We never went into the studio with a song that was not completed to a degree that we knew we already had the core of what we were going to record. That's why we don't have a lot of recordings lying around that were never released – maybe only one or two songs – because we always wrote the song first and we had the finished article that we could then adjust and treat once we were in the studio. Most of the time they came out all right, many times worse and a few times much better than we expected. Probably 10 per cent were better than we expected, 60 per cent as we expected and the rest worse. We were prepared to spend the time to try and make the songs work. Because if you feel you have a good song, you don't want to give up on it. Sometimes you learn to realise by experience that if you can't make the recording as good as you think it is then it's not a technical fault, it's just that the song is not good enough. You can work for ages and nothing's going to happen because it's simply not good enough. Whatever 'good' is.

It's a struggle to reach something I know I have a talent for – and for some reason I do have that talent – but I don't know how it works and I don't know why it works. Benny Andersson

LAY ALL YOUR LOVE ON ME

Benny soundchecking during the 1979 tour – his piano is at the musical heart of nearly every ABBA recording.

Björn: 'Lay All Your Love On Me' is like a hymn. Although it seems quite modern, and seems to some people that it has that early 1980s sequencer feel, we did actually use live drums. But they were played against a click track and sung over and over again to get a kind of congregation feel to the chorus. This was a song where the chorus and the verse existed separately and we didn't combine the two parts until some later point. There is a huge difference between the chorus and the verse.

The song was inspired in part by Supertramp, who wrote songs like 'The Logical Song' with lots of unusual words, rhyming on different, strange words that songwriters would not normally use. That's what I hear in that verse. It's the beauty of popular music that you can draw on what other people have done. John Lennon was quite open about where something in one of his own songs had come from. This is the way of pop. It's the way it has to be and the way it's always been. No one is ashamed that they've been inspired by someone else. As long as they don't nick something, to be inspired is nothing wrong. As far as our own music is concerned, I can't see stuff out there that has been directly inspired by us, but other people can probably see that.

The verse is definitely Supertramp-ish. And I'm particularly proud of the fact that I was able to include the word 'incomprehensible' to rhyme with 'sensible'. I enjoy the sound of the English language, its nuances and subtleties, its anomalies and the richness of its synonyms and rhymes. Swedish is not as flexible a language; someone once told me that it only has a third of the synonyms that there are in English. I even dream in English, whenever I am dreaming of British or American people; whereas if I am dreaming about Swedish people, it's in Swedish.

When I came to write the words for *Kristina*, it was the first time in a very long time that I had written in Swedish and I found that I could use many words in Swedish that I wouldn't have been able to do thirty years earlier. The subject was literary and the audience was literate, and that meant I could write the words that I wanted. The next stage was to translate it into English, working with Herbert Kretzmer, who was co-lyricist on *Les Misérables*, to see if the musical would work – especially for an American audience, since the story is directly concerned with Swedish immigrants to the States.

Benny: 'Lay All Your Love On Me' is definitely a hymn, but with 125 bpm. I wasn't involved in the church when I was younger, but the chorus really is a hymn. It's not even really a chorus, it's just one line repeated. A little different from the other songs in style. Although I had never been a church-goer, I was aware of the power of the music. And in both *Chess* and *Kristina*,

Opposite: Appearing on German TV's
Show Express, November 1980.

I used something of that choral effect. In *Chess*, the choir at the beginning of 'Endgame' recites all the names of the chess players, but that was created specifically to create a record initially, since Björn and I – and Tim Rice – felt most at home with that, and the musical was organised piece by piece. With *Kristina*, there was much more of an organic flow and instead of constructing a choral piece here or there I was able to use a symphonic approach throughout.

In fact, I do also have two hymns in the Swedish psalm book. In 1999 I wrote a hymn for the new millennium called 'Innan Gryningen' ('Before The Dawn') with words by Ylva Eggehorn. The second was the last song on the second Benny Anderssons Orkester album *BAO!*, 'Kärlekens Tid', also with lyrics by Ylva, which Bryn Terfel performed at a Trettondag, or Twelfth Night Concert, in Stockholm in January 2005.

Hymns are like folk music, part of the popular consciousness. I have always been close to folk music, all my life. This is why I now have the BAO – not that everything we do is folk music, but it is the base of what we do. It doesn't really matter to me if it is Swedish or Irish or Austrian, or the zither or the fiddle or the bagpipes, as long as it is communicating something, and as long as it comes from people, from folk. Something that is rock solid. And it is there in ABBA too, from time to time.

It may sound like it was, but 'Lay All Your Love On Me' was not sequenced. It's just well played! Benny Andersson

Benny: We never used sequencers. Only on one song, and that was the last one, which was 'The Day Before You Came'. We had some click tracks but never any sequencers. I couldn't handle that at the time, I didn't know how to do it, although I do now when I sit at my work station in my office. It's nicer, though, to play for real, together with the other band members. On 'Lay All Your Love On Me' there is a vocal line descending, which never came out quite the way we wanted it, although we spent a lot of time. We wanted it to sound a little different, but it was never really what it should have been.

The period from late 1980 to late 1981 was one of significant change for the members of ABBA. In January 1981 Björn married his second wife, Lena, in a top-secret, low-key wedding. A couple of weeks later the group helped celebrate Stig Anderson's fiftieth birthday by writing a special song about Stig, 'Hovas Vittne', and recording a promo film for his lavish party, all dressed in their original 'Waterloo' outfits. In February the formal announcement was made that Benny and Frida were getting divorced. Björn later said, 'We wrote some of our best stuff after the divorces. A thing like a divorce can be – for a songwriter – a new experience and something to use in lyrics.' By March that year, the group were in the studio working on 'When All Is Said And Done' and 'Slipping Through My Fingers'. Both songs saw Björn drawing heavily on recent events.

SLIPPING THROUGH MY FINGERS

The sombre cover shot by Lars Larsson for *The Visitors* album was shot in the studio of painter Julius Kronberg (1850–1921) in the Skansen park in Stockholm.

Björn: 'Slipping Through My Fingers' is another true story. We lived so close to my daughter's school that she was allowed to walk there by herself at some point, she might have been eight or nine, and she was very proud and sort of brave. That image is very clear to me, so backwards from that image I was trying to recreate what I must have felt at various moments and that classic feeling that any parent would have that they are not grabbing every moment, they are losing so much. Whatever we try, however hard we try, we're losing moments.

Benny: A good melody. And a great lyric too. The music is really a love song, isn't it? And so is the lyric, although obviously it's dealing with a different subject. It's really about a father and daughter, about Björn and his daughter, although it's sung through Agnetha's lips.

Björn: It's a very powerful emotion, for all parents. I've seen that in the audience at performances of *MAMMA MIA!* over the years, people getting very emotional about that particular song, especially because of the staging of the number in the show, which is so perfect for that song.

Björn has written a lot of lyrics that fit really well with women. It's like he has a sense of what it is like being a woman. And I hear this from women as well. Benny Andersson

Björn: I have never really talked to my children about how they relate to ABBA, but I have noticed some interesting reactions. Emma, my second youngest daughter, is very English about it. She has a very dry sense of humour. She says, with her tongue firmly in her cheek, that it is astonishing how much success ABBA has had, considering it's only crap… When she and my other children were younger, I would not consciously put on a tape or a CD of ABBA music, but of course they would hear the songs either when they were out and about, or while I was working.

I did try and protect my children from the excesses of the entertainment industry and I was able to do that because I was living in Sweden all through our heyday. And although, like all kids, they were somewhat spoiled, they have turned out to be extremely down to earth. Emma is very much a words woman; her younger sister Anna doesn't yet know what she wants to do; my son Christian is into computer programming; and my eldest, Linda, is pursuing her theatre career. She has a daughter, Tilda. I love being a grandad so much, taking Tilda out to Gröna Lund, the old funfair in Stockholm, where we performed as ABBA.

Images from the video shoot of 'When All Is Said And Done' from *The Visitors*, which was premiered on the *Dick Cavett Meets ABBA* TV special in April 1981.
Overleaf: For Stig Anderson's fiftieth birthday Benny and Björn wrote an affectionately mocking song called 'Hovas Vittne' ('Hova's Witness'), a play on words with the name of Stig's hometown – and ABBA made a video of it in their 'Waterloo' regalia to be shown at the party. On Benny's sign, 'Sticket' means 'bridge' (of a song).

Above and opposite: The group prepare to appear on *Dick Cavett Meets ABBA*, April 1981.

Children and grandchildren help keep your feet on the ground, although I was lucky to come from a small town in Sweden, and had an upbringing that made sure you never got too big a head, because there was always somebody who would say, 'Who are you to do this or say that?'

Benny: I have always led a normal life, and that made surviving easier. Being Swedish was one of the good things about ABBA. I have never lived for any length of time in London or New York or Los Angeles, so I don't know what I would have been like if I had, but I can never see the need to surround yourself with eight bodyguards, a driver and a hairdresser at all times. I like artists like Bruce Springsteen, who'll come to Stockholm with his guitar, jump in a taxi and turn up at the Swedish TV studios, saying, 'Hi, I'm Bruce, where should I go?' There is no need to let fame go to your head, although I think it is more difficult for solo artists to separate the image of themselves from their real selves. It's probably easier when you're in a group. Perhaps Björn, Agnetha, Frida and I were lucky, because we had all been working, recording and performing for so many years before ABBA. To the rest of the world it was as though we burst on the scene with 'Waterloo', but by then I was 28 and had been on the road since I was 18. It made success much easier to deal with.

ONE OF US

Above and opposite: Shooting the video for 'One Of Us' at the Filmbolaget Studios in Solna. The film featured Agnetha as a woman who had recently moved into a flat, and was shot in Lasse Hallström's apartment.

Björn: 'Slipping Through My Fingers' was on the album *The Visitors*, but it was never released as a single – 'One Of Us' was the first single to come from that album. At the time the song was released, at the end of 1981, Tim Rice was coming over to Stockholm to meet Benny and me and start talking about the show that later became *Chess*. So we might unconsciously have already been thinking about a natural end point for ABBA. Given the conversations we were having with Tim, we were maybe wandering away towards that instead. Although I think the whole album is very good. It's only afterwards that you can feel that something has happened.

Benny: *The Visitors* does have a little more drama in it. Looking back now I think that maybe we had became a little bit serious for a group who were a pop band; there was no 'Honey, Honey', 'I Do, I Do, I Do, I Do, I Do' or 'Thank You For The Music' on the record.

Björn: It is true that *The Visitors* is a little darker than anything we had done before. To a certain extent, we had modelled ourselves on the Beatles, in the respect that we were always trying to take another step forward whenever we recorded a new album – lyrically as well as musically. And becoming more mature sometimes meant becoming more sombre than we had been before.

People say that when they looked at the album sleeve of *The Visitors*, that they thought, 'Well, this is the end for ABBA', although we didn't see it ourselves at the time. Because though it is also true that there was probably an awareness that ABBA as a group was not going to last much longer, it was not a conscious decision on our part to make the cover design reflect that, for example. It may be that Rune Söderqvist, who had designed most of our album and singles covers, as someone who was a close friend but was also on the outside of the group, had picked up on something and that had steered him in this direction. As Benny and I had always done, we talked about the future of the group. These were conversations we had always had, whenever we found ourselves on trips and long plane flights, and although we were not quite meaning to give up the group, we were certainly thinking about other projects and considering solo projects, which most other groups at the time also saw as an option.

The cover of *The Visitors* has a sense of wrapping things up. In retrospect it certainly feels that this was when the energy started to run out. Björn Ulvaeus

Above and opposite: Lasse Hallström used mirror effects on the video of 'One Of Us', November 1981.

Benny: The decision to go and shoot the cover of *The Visitors* in this artist's studio was made by our art director Rune Söderqvist. It wasn't something that we would have questioned, we were just told to turn up and have the picture taken. We didn't, or I didn't, care very much about those ideas; we trusted Rune's taste and judgement, and we were happy for him to interpret what he felt when he listened to the album.

Björn: We only ever wrote ten or eleven songs in a year. There were no more than three or four songs that were unreleased, if that. That was all that was left. Virtually everything that we went into the studio with was recorded and released – which is a very different approach from what I hear other artists do, where they record twenty songs in the hope that they will end up with twelve good ones. We never entered the studio unless it was a good song. We tried to spot the rubbish before we got there.

Benny: There are three mandolins playing on 'One Of Us', which we credited on the album to 'The Three Boys' – the three boys being Rutger Gunnarsson, Lasse Wellander and Björn Ulvaeus. That's what they wanted to call themselves: we later hired them for *Chess* as well.

Björn: We weren't mandolin players, but we only had one little line to play followed by another. It was very effective because it's such an Italian beginning. I don't think anything we ever did was as Italian as that. But unexpectedly it's also the closest we ever got to a reggae kind of feeling, a semi-reggae song.

Benny: It's a nice start to the song, like a Portuguese woman going down to the well to do the washing – that's my image of the introduction, just to put a picture on what it sounds like. There's also an accordion on that recording. I didn't use accordion much on the ABBA records, but there's one there, playing the rhythmic pattern.

Björn: At that time we had, for two or three years, been using a particular method for finding the first single of an album. There were a few selected publishers and record people around the world whose judgement we trusted, so we used to send out the records to them – maybe not a whole album, but we would pre-release six or seven songs for them to listen to and compile a chart. And they would send back a chart, this song first choice, that one second and so on, and then in turn we would compile all those charts and see which song was the number one in their view. And then we would compare that with what the three of us – Stig, Benny and me – thought. And I had said my favourite on *Visitors* was 'One Of Us', but Stig and Benny didn't agree. I don't know which song they preferred from that album, I can't even imagine any other, but all the charts came back and were compiled and 'One Of Us' was top. What a victory!

Benny: 'One Of Us' should really have been a Christmas Number One in the UK. But that year they didn't have a chart over Christmas so we missed out on that.

UNDER ATTACK

Benny: We released *The Visitors* and then we recorded two more songs in the August of 1982: 'Under Attack' and 'The Day Before You Came'. I think 'The Day Before You Came' is the best lyric that Björn has written: it's a really good song, but not a good recording. Whereas 'Under Attack' is a wonderful recording, but not such a good song. It was good fun to record, and it has a lot of nice little elements within it, like a bass synth line that I worked on for ever.

Björn: The sound on the vocals of 'Under Attack' is very much of the 1980s, that Buggles' 'Video Killed The Radio Star' style. But the melody of the chorus is much more 1960s, even 1950s. And the counter-melody is very effective. I think it's a really good recording and had it been released a year earlier it would have been a Number One, I'm sure. But now, the 1980s had started and ABBA was uncool, you know. ABBA was *really* uncool in the 1980s. But the title of the song isn't about that. I wasn't feeling under attack personally. The title was just a good hook and dictated the rest of the lyric. I think it was very much the craftsman at work. Just doing my job.

Benny: Some people have suggested that there is a lack of warmth in this song, partly because of the way the vocals are treated and because things were moving to digital from analogue. But we had been working with digital technology for a while, and the Vocoder we used to treat the vocals was just for fun. I think people can read too much into these things.

Björn: By that summer of 1982 I am sure Benny and I already had our minds set on writing something with Tim Rice. I think we were even considering *Chess* specifically as an idea. But I also feel that we didn't do much to promote 'Under Attack', and this was a point where maybe people were starting to get fed up with this bloody group having Number One after Number One after Number One. There was definitely a degree of over-saturation. It was time to get out and it was so convenient that the girls wanted to do their own things because 'Under Attack' did not get to Number One. It was Number Ten or something. So we thought, right, now is the time to do something else.

The idea was for ABBA to take a break for a while and then get back together again. But it never happened. Björn Ulvaeus

Above and opposite: The 'Under Attack' promo was shot by a new directorial team, Kjell Sundvall and Kjell-Ake Andersson.

Benny: We said, 'Well, that's it then isn't it?' When we had recorded 'The Day Before You Came' we knew that was going to be our last ABBA song for a while. It was like drawing a line in the sand. But even though we were moving on to try something

Top and above: ABBA's final recording sessions, in the Polar Music Studios, August 1982.

new, there was still going to be some continuity. There were some pieces of music that had been with us all the time, like 'Anthem', which is in *Chess*. I had written that song in the basement of my house in 1976 or thereabouts, and I had tried to push it into ABBA but Björn said, 'This is not for ABBA' and the girls agreed. Which was lucky for us in the end, because we could save it up for *Chess*.

We intended to write the musical with Tim, to spend a year or two doing that and then go back to ABBA, but it all took longer than we thought and by the time we opened in the West End in Spring 1986, four years had passed. It had taken so long to get there, we just ran out of steam. And then we said, 'What's the point? It's been four years.' We talked to the girls and they said, 'No, we're fine. We think this is good.' They'd done their own albums and they were OK with it too.

Björn: When we made the decision to take an extended break, the record company did not try to dissuade us – after 1976 we never had anyone breathing down our necks trying to tell us what to do, or what not to do. It was solely up to us. And it was a decision made by the four of us, although I can't pinpoint a specific moment or a specific day when we came to that conclusion. It was a gradual realisation.

Benny: During the time that we were writing and recording 'Under Attack', we had been working on a number of songs that never saw the light of day as ABBA recordings. 'Just Like That' was a track that we did record, but we never liked what we had done, so it remained unreleased, and I know that for a while it was considered as a possible inclusion in *MAMMA MIA!*. We did actually produce a

version of the song in the mid-1980s, including a different verse, with Gemini, the brother-sister duo Karin and Anders Glenmark, who were the niece and nephew of the owner of Glen studios where we had recorded most of the *ABBA* album. Anders had actually played guitar on 'Money, Money, Money' and he sang the chorus vocals on 'One Night In Bangkok' from *Chess*.

Björn: The final recording we made was 'The Day Before You Came'. We were again heading into something more mature, more mysterious and more exciting. But this time it was one step too far for our audience. Tim Rice has told me this too, that although he really likes the song, it was beyond what our fans expected and consequently it was not a big hit.

Benny: On 'The Day Before You Came' no one played any instruments but me, and that had never happened before. We started off with a click track, and I was building up the music from that, but in retrospect that was probably not a good idea – although I think it's a good song.

After we had recorded the song, we had put out a kind of Greatest Hits album with that and 'Under Attack' on, called *ABBA The Singles: The First Ten Years,* which shows our intention was to go back and have another ten years, perhaps. We didn't know, but that's really telling that we didn't intend to quit. ABBA took a break and we're still in a break. It's just that the next ten years will never happen.

Top and above: ABBA's final TV appearance was on BBC TV's *The Late, Late Breakfast Show* in December 1982.
Overleaf: A shot taken during the recording of the promo film for 'The Day Before You Came', in the China Theatre, Stockholm.

I think the group that never came back is something mystical and wonderful. Björn Ulvaeus

3 THE SHOW

THE SAGA OF MAMMA MIA!

HAVE A DREAM

Previous page: *MAMMA MIA!*'s original Tokyo Dynamos, Izumi Mori, Chizu Hosaka and Yayoi Aoyama. Above and opposite: Agnetha and Anni-Frid donned matching wigs and identical costumes to perform the mini-musical *The Girl With The Golden Hair*, which formed part of the show ABBA took on tour to Europe and Australia in early 1977. This initial foray into the world of musical theatre included four songs. The opener, 'Thank You For The Music', was followed by 'I Wonder (Departure)', which for a long time Catherine Johnson had at the beginning of Act II in *MAMMA MIA!*, 'I'm A Marionette' and 'Get On The Carousel'. The whole 25-minute piece was linked together by a narrator, the British actor Francis Matthews, made up as a harlequin.

Björn Ulvaeus: We always knew there had to be a life after ABBA. There came a point around 1976 – when Benny and I had been writing pop songs, together and separately, for well over a decade – when we wanted to take our music up another step. We would have long conversations on planes and in the studio, long nights asking each other, 'What the hell can we do, where can we go from here?' We were both interested in marrying music with drama. It was something that struck both of us as stimulating, the grand scope of it all: I had been aware of musicals when I was younger, but I hadn't necessarily liked them at the time because I was into pop and rock, so musicals were not on the agenda.

Benny Andersson: I had never been a great fan of musicals either, but then I heard Tim Rice and Andrew Lloyd Webber's *Jesus Christ Superstar*. Stig Anderson, who was managing us and was one of the leading music publishers in Sweden, had been sent the record long before it actually came out. I got hold of a copy and thought it was astonishing, a wonderful record. I still think it is. I'm sure that was one of the triggers that set off this urge to explore. Writing a song which is three or four minutes long is fun and it can be tricky, but we wanted to see if we could build something that would hold together from A to Z, to try and do something that maybe was a little more difficult to achieve.

Björn: *Jesus Christ Superstar* certainly brought our understanding of musicals into focus. As it happened Agnetha had been in the Swedish version of the stage show, and although I never actually saw her perform in it, I had produced a single with her of 'I Don't Know How To Love Him'. This meant that when Benny and I were talking about how to stretch ourselves, the success of *Jesus Christ Superstar* was hovering in the background. We thought, 'This is fascinating. Why don't we try this, why don't we dabble in this for a while?'

Benny: We came up with the idea of including a little musical as part of our tour in 1977. We said, 'Maybe we shouldn't just play the songs, let's add in something more comprehensive, some little piece.' We didn't know what specifically, perhaps some sort of short musical, where the girls would wear wigs and with a narrator holding it all together.

Björn: This idea became *The Girl With The Golden Hair*, which ended up as a piece about twenty-five minutes long, based round four songs, opening with 'Thank You For The Music' and closing with 'Get On The Carousel'. There was a sketchy, vague storyline about the usual thing, about a girl wanting to get famous, becoming famous and then seeing the downside of it. It was nothing more than that – and in fact nothing more was needed at that point, just something simple.

Agnetha as Mary Magdalene in the first Swedish version of Tim Rice and Andrew Lloyd Webber's *Jesus Christ Superstar*, which had a short run in February 1972 at the Skandinarium in Gothenburg. Her version of 'I Don't Know How To Love Him', produced by Björn, went to Number One in the Swedish Svensktoppen charts.

At the time we were very pleased with and proud of *The Girl With The Golden Hair*. The result went down very well with audiences, it produced some songs which were quite good, and it had been great fun.

The logical sequence to this was to write a complete musical. The time had come when we felt that with ABBA we had had a very good run and it was now time to try something else. But we also realised that we would have to approach someone who was extremely experienced in making musicals, otherwise we'd end up making too many mistakes.

Benny: We had been discussing this with Thomas Johansson, our tour promoter in Sweden, who also helped us when we went out to Australia and America. Thomas knew we were keen on writing a musical and mentioned this to a Broadway producer who later met Tim Rice. Tim told him he was looking for some new collaborators, so this producer said, 'Well, I know two guys who are interested in working in musicals.'

Tim Rice: I had got a call from one of the big theatrical organisations in America asking if I was interested in doing a musical with Barry Manilow. That discussion didn't go anywhere. But the bloke said after coffee, 'Have you heard of Arbour?' I went 'Arbour..? No,' thinking of some trees. He said, 'I'm surprised, because I've heard they're big in England.' 'Oh, you mean ABBA!' 'Well, I understand that they're interested in writing a stage musical.' And it had never crossed my mind that they might be. I was a genuine fan. Even when ABBA were top of the charts they were being slagged off. All the intellectuals hated them, but one of the things I've been blessed with is a very commercial taste. I thought 'Waterloo' was all right, I thought 'SOS' and 'Mamma Mia' were pretty good, but after 'Fernando' and 'Dancing Queen' it was home runs nearly all the way. Because I knew Stig Anderson, I called him up, and he set up a meeting for me with Benny and Björn in Stockholm.

Björn: Tim had a couple of ideas but the one that caught our attention was *Chess*, especially the whole Cold War Spassky/Fischer theme. This intrigued us because we had been living so close to the Soviet Union and feeling the danger constantly. I certainly felt that it was a definite and omnipresent fear.

Benny: It ought to be impossible to write a musical about chess. It's a wonderful game, but it's a boring game to watch for anybody who's not playing. So we said, 'Yes, that's a challenge, let's do it.' Tim had a couple of pages of synopsis, that's all. We would write the music and then Björn would write some demo lyrics.

Tim Rice: We took each scene from my story and worked out the plotline. Benny and Björn – largely Benny – would write a tune inspired by the theme, whether it was a love song, an argument or a crowd scene. Björn would create what was usually a very interesting mock lyric, often with no particular meaning, but some lovely lines. He was the link between me and Benny: me at the lyric end, Björn in the middle and Benny at the musical end.

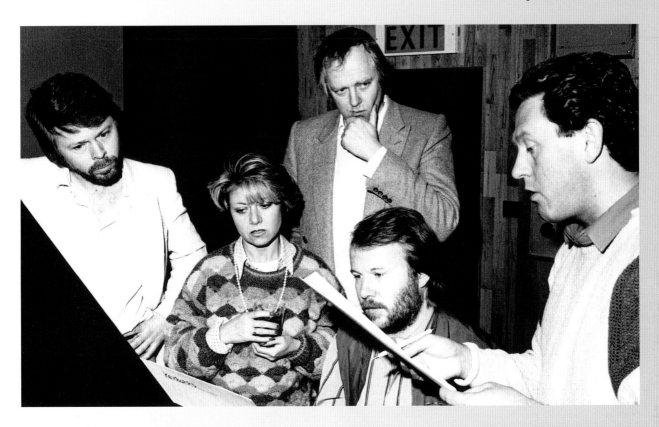

Björn: We spent hours and hours working together, advancing slowly. I had, of course, great respect for Tim's craft as by then he had written three enormously successful musicals. I would write dummy lyrics but with a lot of content which Tim could play around with. Or he would write something completely new, sometimes keeping my ideas or developing them, and then we'd try out the lyrics and see whether they worked when they were sung. Working with Tim taught me a lot and I discovered that, by intuition only, I had already been writing in a theatrical manner when I was writing the songs for ABBA.

From left: Björn, Elaine Paige, Tim Rice, Benny and Tommy Körberg rehearsing *Chess*. Björn and Benny credit Tim Rice and Andrew Lloyd Webber with increasing their understanding of what could be done with the musical form, while Tim remembers Björn as 'highly intellectual, a very clever words man' and Benny as 'a truly great composer, who in forty-five years' time will be up there with Grieg and Sibelius'.

Björn is a student of English. He writes more accurately, intelligently and logically than many pop writers who throw off a lyric and don't care what it means. In ABBA's songs there was the occasional giveaway that English was not his first language, but that was part of their charm. Tim Rice

Benny: For me it was like writing music for a concert with a context. Maybe that's why *Chess* works so well on record, because there was no script, no book, just those few pages of synopsis. Also I think that we, Björn and I, were basically records people and that's what we were best at. And it was during this period, while we were involved in writing and recording *Chess* that we first met Judy Craymer.

Judy Craymer: After I'd finished studying at the Guildhall School of Music and Drama, I had moved into stage management in the late 1970s, and been offered a job at the Leicester Haymarket. They thought I wanted to be an actress and I had

From left: ABBA's recording engineer Michael Tretow with Benny, Tim and Björn at the mixing console in Polar Studios, the group's custom-built recording studio in central Stockholm.

to persuade them that I genuinely wanted to work backstage, almost had to prove that I could change a plug. A little later I was asked to go to Andrew Lloyd Webber's Sydmonton Festival and stage manage a showcase performance of what turned out to be a show called *Cats*. I had no idea what *Cats* was: off I went and was told to put up a bit of set. I worked flat out for two or three days, sleeping on a lilo in Andrew's summer house, but it was all part of the learning curve. When *Cats* became a fully-fledged West End show, I was offered the job of assistant stage manager, partly because I'd done this workshop but also because I had previously worked closely with Wayne Sleep who was going to be playing Mr Mistoffelees. It was my first West End job – on the biggest show in the West End.

By this time I already had ambitions to produce. Elaine Paige was starring in *Cats* and she told me she thought Tim Rice was going to open a London office and wanted someone to support him in all the different projects he was involved in.

Working with Tim was perfect because you could be your own mini-entrepreneur. My first job for him was to throw a party for the *Guinness Book Of Hit Singles*, which he'd co-written with his brother Jo, Paul Gambaccini and Mike Read. Tim said, 'I want a rather fabulous party to launch the book, and I want you to invite everyone who's had a hit record between 1952 and 1982.' I said, 'Righty ho', but had no idea where to start. There were no computers then, I just had to go out and do the research, but it was incredibly rewarding because people *did* respond. Several hundred people turned up at the party in the main studio at Abbey Road. I'd never done any of this before and I thought, 'This is fabulous.'

Tim Rice: Judy was a very dynamic lady. I had recently set up Pavilion Books, and they shared the office with Judy and me. It was a time when I had this rather barmy idea that I would go into theatre production, maybe something along the lines of Andrew's Really Useful Group, though my heart was never in it. But Judy was very strong and virtually everyone else was bypassed as she shot to the top.

Judy: I knew that Tim was working on this project called *Chess* and that he was going to work with Benny and Björn. Soon after the book party Tim said, 'Oh, Judy, could you go to Heathrow and meet Björn, he's arriving with his wife Lena. Take the chauffeur-driven car and meet them at the airport.' I remember drawing in my breath because they were still so huge, even though they had disbanded as ABBA. Benny came in a few days later for a round of meetings. It was all very exciting because wherever you went with Björn and Benny, people would literally goggle. My initial impression was that Björn was very serious and Benny more flamboyant, but in fact Björn has an incredibly dry wit.

Tim and I went on a couple of visits to Sweden and work on *Chess* began in earnest. In their offices I was like a child in a sweetshop. These were the famous ABBA offices at Polar Music, their record company. I'd go up to the turret, which was Björn and Benny's studio cum office where all the white ABBA guitars and memorabilia were, and I thought this was the smartest office I had ever seen, very Scandinavian, ahead of its time. And from then on dealing with Benny and Björn became part of my life.

Judy has become much more serious and together, that's for sure! She was a very happy-go-lucky girl in those days. Björn Ulvaeus

Judy: The original intention had been for *Chess* to go straight to a stage show, but as Benny, Björn and Tim worked on the music and lyrics, the idea developed that they should produce a concept album and release some singles, which was very much in vogue in those days for catapulting a new musical into people's minds – in fact, Tim and Andrew Lloyd Webber had pioneered it. Another of my very first jobs was being asked, 'Could you book the London Symphony Orchestra?', 'Right, you know, how many musicians do you want?', 'Eighty-six', 'Marvellous. How many violins?' Somehow, by phoning Benny, who was very patient with me, we managed to get the LSO into the studios on time.

Benny: I have always loved the record of *Chess* but I never particularly liked the theatrical version as much. I don't really know why. Maybe the expectations we had from listening to the record were too high.

Björn: For one thing the Iron Curtain came down at an extremely inopportune time! We were the only people to curse that. It meant that the show immediately became something of an historical piece. In any case, the London production of *Chess* was never right. Sadly Michael Bennett, the original director, discovered he had AIDS while he was preparing the show, and had to leave. Michael had a vision of what the show would be but he had never shared that with anyone, at least not with us and not with Trevor Nunn, who came in to take over as director. Trevor inherited this set with sixty-four television sets, and he didn't know what Michael had been intending to do with them.

Benny: I only knew Michael for a year or so before he passed away, but in that time we became good friends. He was a very talented and artistic fellow with a great

Björn and Judy Craymer during the *Chess* years. Judy first met Benny and Björn when she was working for Tim Rice. Without that connection, *MAMMA MIA!* could never have happened. Judy says, 'I simply wouldn't have got through the door if I had been a complete outsider.'

Chess opened on 14th May 1986 at the Prince Edward Theatre in London's West End – the same venue where *MAMMA MIA!* would open thirteen years later. And the connections between the two shows do not end there. Siobhán McCarthy, pictured second left in the lower picture playing Svetlana in *Chess* (with Tommy Körberg, Elaine Paige and Murray Head), went on to become *MAMMA MIA!*'s original Donna, and North American general manager Nina Lannan and advertising director Nancy Coyne also both worked on *MAMMA MIA!* as well as *Chess*.

instinct, which I took to immediately. I really miss him, and am particularly sad that the musical theatre world was deprived of his talents; it needs people like him.

Tim Rice: I think the score of *Chess* is staggeringly good. The show itself got mixed reviews. The reason for that was 80 per cent down to Michael Bennett pulling out. Trevor Nunn did a pretty good job getting it onto the stage but he was hampered by having to work with people he hadn't chosen and he was slightly stuck with the set. When we opened in Broadway two years later, we changed the show so drastically we just wrecked it, which was a pity. Even the score suffered – because it is a very operatic score, which doesn't need interrupting too much.

Benny: Björn and I had been totally green about being in the theatre. In London, Trevor Nunn was running the show with Robert Fox, the producer. We were around simply to see if they wanted to take anything out or change something. By the time *Chess* went to Broadway we knew a little more. We stayed in New York for some months and were more involved. It was a better show, I think, on Broadway, but it still didn't work. And the critic Frank Rich didn't help.

Björn: Frank Rich killed *Chess* dead! Of course we didn't have the reputation that *Les Mis* or *Phantom* had brought from London when they came to Broadway. He couldn't kill those shows off, although he would have wanted to, I'm sure, because I think he thought Broadway was for the American musical, not these bloody European things. So with *Chess* he rubbed his hands and thought, 'Oh good, here comes one I can kill!'

Benny: Actually I read the Frank Rich review again recently. He wasn't that wrong – although he was a bit bitchy – and I don't think he was fair. He called the score 'a *smörgåsbord*', and in a way he was right because *Chess* is full of different things: pop songs like 'One Night In Bangkok', an operetta piece in 'Merano', and the symphonic material that belongs nowhere but the musical stage. He also called the show loud rock'n'roll stuff, which it isn't. It's symphonic and quite elaborate – and he just dismissed that.

Tim Rice: One of the problems with *Chess* was that the album was very successful and as a result we had everybody in New York wanting to do the show: it became a bit of a battleground for rival American producers to slug it out. Because of the album's success, the attitude of a lot of people – and maybe even ourselves – wasn't so much 'What can we put into this to make the show a hit?', it was 'If it's going to be a hit, what can we get out of it?'

Judy: It was during all the work on *Chess* that I became fascinated by the songs of ABBA. Because I had got to know Benny and Björn the songs meant a lot more to me. When the album for *Chess* was being recorded I spent some time in Polar Studios and ABBA's engineer Michael Tretow was there, which made a huge impression on me. In fact I became quite obsessive about playing ABBA records.

At the Polar offices I'd been given a copy of the singles collection on tape. Back in the UK I was staying in Tim Rice's London house. So there I was up in Tim's guest room with my portable cassette player, playing the songs over and over again, driving the neighbours mad. In the end the tape was so exhausted I had to rewind it with a pencil. The lyrics had a huge impact on me; I'd be listening and thinking, 'God, that's a lovely emotional moment Björn's written there' – but at the time I never really talked to him about it. It didn't seem cool to talk to ABBA about ABBA.

My mind started turning over what I might be able to do with these songs. There had already been a kind of musical using ABBA music. Before I really got to know them well, a show called *Abbacadabra* had been put on at the Lyric Hammersmith in London for a limited Christmas season in 1983. It was produced by Cameron Mackintosh, and created by Alain Boublil – this was before he brought *Les Misérables* and *Miss Saigon* to London – using ABBA songs but with brand new lyrics by Don Black. At the time Alain was ABBA's publisher in France, so he had an arrangement with Stig Anderson to use their music and change the lyrics. The show was very childlike, a fairytale, but I loved it – I've still got the album somewhere.

Judy and Björn in the late 1980s, at an agricultural show near Henley-on-Thames. Björn had moved to England in 1984 and lived in Assendene House, a couple of miles outside the town.

ABBA was part of the landscape. Although I was more interested in glam rock around the time they won Eurovision, obviously all those songs had been downloaded into my psyche. Judy Craymer

Benny: Alain had been listening to one of our songs, 'I Let The Music Speak', from *The Visitors*, and he said, 'This sounds like musical music. Can I do this pantomime?' It would only be on for one week or so, so we said, 'Yeah, sure, go ahead.'

Judy: A few years later, when I'd left Tim's empire and was working in film and television, I thought that I would like to produce *Abbacadabra* as a TV programme or a film with Jim Henson-style puppets. But I wanted it to be updated, to be less childlike and to have some more core strength to it. In fact I did talk to Cameron quite a lot about the idea, but it wasn't to be because I couldn't get permission from Alain Boublil. And of course if I had got those rights, I wouldn't be where I am now!

Not being able to pick up the rights was upsetting, but in the end I realised that it didn't matter because I still had a relationship with Björn and Benny and that it was their songs I was in love with, not their music with somebody else's lyrics. So I thought, 'I'm going to do my own show.' I would sit and make up tapes on a cassette player, stopping and starting and putting together different combinations and sequences of songs, stop, start, pause, all the time. But I couldn't do anything without permission, so I started talking to Björn directly, saying, 'I think that there's a story to be told from the lyrics in 'The Winner Takes It All'…' Björn was living in the UK at the time so I would see him reasonably regularly on social occasions, and I would mention, 'Oh yes, I've been thinking this and thinking that.'

Benny and Björn's musical, *Kristina Från Duvemåla*, was based on Vilhelm Moberg's *Emigrants* novels, which followed the huge diaspora of Swedes to North America in the late 19th century. The musical, which premiered in Malmö's Musikteater in October 1995, focuses on the tale of Kristina from Duvemåla, a village in southern Sweden. Far left: Helen Sjöholm as Kristina, with Anders Ekborg, on the right, as Karl Oskar. Third left: Peter Jöback as Robert with Björn and Agnetha's daughter Linda Ulvaeus, who played Elin in the Stockholm production of the late 1990s. *Kristina* has been the most successful musical ever in Sweden.

Every time there was another birthday do or an anniversary I felt I had to report something new. He also had a horse called Oskar in some nearby stables, so even when Björn wasn't around I'd be charging down the M4 to take Oskar out for a ride.

As I began to think of the show as a stage musical other people, who knew that I knew Benny and Björn, would contact me, and say, 'Wouldn't it be great if there was an ABBA musical telling the story of ABBA?' and I would tell them, 'No, they'd never agree to that.' I knew it couldn't be a biographical musical. Björn was my main link and he was the lyricist, so I was relying on his fascination that it was *his* lyrics that were going to be turned into a story.

Björn: Because I knew Judy it was quite easy for me to say, 'If you come up with a good script or a good scriptwriter, fine! We've got nothing against that.'

Judy: I'd already dissected the ABBA songs and I knew that 'Honey, Honey' or 'Take A Chance On Me' could be funny even though they weren't written as comedy songs. But I would never have wanted to write the show myself. It's all part of my love of steering something from behind the scenes. I worked with a number of writers on different ideas but they were never quite right, and Björn knew they weren't right.

Björn: Judy suggested some scriptwriters. There were several treatments created. One of the writers came out to my house and we looked at a script, but it wasn't really what we wanted. I had a clear idea of what a show should not be. I was happy for Judy to continue trying out ideas, but I didn't have much time to give her because Benny and I were now working on our next project, another musical of our own, five years after *Chess*.

Benny: When Björn was living in the UK I went over to see him one time and said, 'What do you think, shall we do another musical?' So we started looking for a good story because we knew that, whatever else, we needed a strong story. We read lots and lots but we couldn't find anything that could talk to us. And then one day we had some friends over for dinner at home and as I was going out with the lamb rack into the kitchen, I was thinking, 'Rather than looking for stories to like, what is the thing that I have already read in my life that I like the most?' And I knew in a split second what that was, the series of novels written by Vilhelm Moberg in the 1950s called *The Emigrants*, about the Swedes who emigrated to America in the 1850s: nearly a quarter of the population disappeared. Moberg is a Swedish national

treasure, his novels are some of the most popular books ever written in Sweden. But they are also four big, fat novels, not some little thin story. I called Björn immediately and said, 'What do you think?' He liked them too, so we started work.

Björn: When we read *The Emigrants* again I thought, 'This is a brick.' It's incredibly long, two thousand pages. How can you compress that? But we came back to it because there was something between the lines, some kind of musical feel to it. For a very long time I did my homework, reading and re-reading it, taking notes, learning to love those pages. So when I started writing I was very, very well prepared. When we premiered the show – *Kristina Från Duvemåla* – in 1995 I was very worried about what people would think. I had been working with and writing lyrics around text by maybe the biggest author we have in Sweden. I was afraid the critics would destroy me, saying, 'Who are you to do this?' So I was too nervous to see the whole show before the opening night and I proposed to my wife that although we would go to the first night, we should leave quietly through the backstage door and go to Rome where we wouldn't read the reviews at all. That's how nervous I was. Luckily the reviews were good!

During the time that Benny and I had been working on *Kristina*, things had been quiet with Judy on the musical front, although we spoke all the time. Then one day Judy called me and said, 'There's a writer I'd like you to meet', and that someone was Catherine Johnson.

Catherine Johnson: When I was pregnant with my second child in the late 1980s and my thirtieth birthday was looming, I thought, 'I've really got to sort myself out.' I remember having a conversation with my mum saying, 'I'm going to spend this year trying to do something with my writing, and if that doesn't work I'm going to go to college and train to be a probation officer.' Thank God the Bristol Old Vic had a playwriting competition in association with the local television channel. I thought, 'This is somewhere to start, something to aim for.' It wasn't about winning, it was about seeing whether I could write a script from start to finish, so I wrote a play and sent it in. Quite a lot of time passed. I was living in a small flat in Bristol with no telephone and a telegram arrived one morning saying could I phone this number, with no explanation. I panicked a bit and thought I was going to get into trouble about something or other, but in the end I discovered the number was for HTV, so I called them up from my parents' house. The secretary who answered said, 'I'm really not supposed to tell you, but you've won the HTV Bristol Old Vic

MAMMA MIA! would never have come about without the vision, drive and determination of Judy Craymer (opposite). The friendship she built up with Benny and Björn while working on Chess allowed her to approach them with the first spark of an idea: to create a musical based on the songs of ABBA by building on the inherent theatricality of songs like 'The Winner Takes It All'. Over the next ten years, the project went through various metamorphoses and a number of treatments that didn't work, but Judy persisted in her search for a storyline that would complement the songs. By the time she met Catherine Johnson in January 1997, she had in mind a clear framework of what the musical should be about: holidays, weddings, and the relationship between two generations.

Playwriting Award' and I screamed. I'd forgotten that there was money involved – two thousand pounds – so I bought my first computer, a good old Amstrad.

The play I'd written was called *Rag Doll*, and as part of the award it was put on at the Bristol Old Vic, directed by Terry Johnson – no relation to me. It was years later, when Judy was working on the film *Neville's Island*, which Terry was directing, that Judy said to him, 'I want to do this musical, do you know of any writers?' and Terry said, 'Well, what about Catherine Johnson?' and that's how it all came around.

Judy: *Neville's Island* had been a West End play and I was producing a TV movie version with Martin Clunes, Timothy Spall, Jeff Rawle and David Bamber. It's the story of four men on an Outward Bound course and so there we were, shooting this film in the remote Lake District. I had just had a new lease of energy on the ABBA project, because Björn had said to me, 'If you can find the right writer, if you can find the right story, then Benny and I will support you.' When he said those magic words 'If you can' and 'We will support', I had something to aim for. On one particular night shoot, I was talking to Terry Johnson and asked him if he fancied writing this musical, because as well as being a director he is a very good, award-winning writer. His plays have included *Insignificance*, which was made into the movie by Nicolas Roeg, *Dead Funny* and *Hysteria*.

But he wasn't interested. Maybe I didn't pitch it very well. A lot of people didn't share my passion for ABBA and I suspect Terry was probably one of them. So he said no, but had I thought of Catherine Johnson? I knew of Catherine's work because her agent had sent me some samples to read. I knew that she'd written a couple of very good, critically successful plays and that she'd written some of the BBC series *Love Hurts*. For some reason her name had stuck in my mind and when Terry mentioned her I thought, 'That's interesting.' I remember phoning Björn from some lakeshore where you could never get a decent signal on the mobile, telling him, 'I think I might have found the right writer' and him being very excited.

Catherine: By this time – towards the end of 1996 – I'd been trying to make a career in writing for television for nearly a decade. Things were kind of tough because I was writing constantly, always chasing the next commission. I always had about six or seven projects outstanding. I was by now bringing up two young children by myself, so my writing time was always limited. I'd stop at three o'clock to go and pick the kids up from school and that would be it for the rest of the day. Constantly exhausted.

Around Christmas that year, I was quite desperate for work. I called my agent, Bash (Sebastian Born), and said, 'I've got to have some work. I'll do anything, but you know me, make sure it's nice.' He set up two meetings for me. One was to write an episode for *Byker Grove* and I thought, 'Oh, that's perfect, I'd love to do that.' And then he said, 'Would you like to meet this woman called Judy Craymer who wants someone to write a musical based on the ABBA songs?' and we both laughed for about five minutes before I said, 'Yeah go on then, that sounds as if it might be fun.'

A few years before Bash had sent Judy the script of a musical play I'd written which included the songs of punk and new wave, though not in the way that *MAMMA MIA!* would, but I guess it showed Judy that I could do plot and music together. When he said, 'I'll give Judy your number,' I thought, 'Oh, it'll be another week' but I believe she phoned me later that afternoon, which was slightly off-putting, as was her voice. I imagined Judy was probably about 90 years old, a real theatrical producer you might have played by Maggie Smith. She sounded scary, and said she wanted this meeting almost immediately. I got really cold feet, but I agreed because I had to come up to London anyway for my *Byker Grove* meeting. We met at the Selfridge Hotel: I was walking up the stairs and saw this blonde lady about the same age as me having a cigarette. She said, 'I've just been on holiday and I haven't been smoking, so I've got to have about twenty cigarettes to catch up' and I thought, 'I'm going to get on with you.'

Judy: As soon as I met Catherine I had a very strong instinct that this was going to follow through. I wasn't thinking 'Oh right, I'll get several people with ideas and they all come in and submit.' It was 'I want to work with this woman.'

Catherine: Judy was clearly very fervent about her idea – it must have been her baby for so long – and it was very hard not to feel enthused back. She talked about what the ABBA songs sounded like, what they meant to people. And she said, right from the outset, 'I don't want this to be The ABBA Story. The songs have to be used in a very organic way, so the script and this brand new original story have to find a home for the songs which won't sound as if they've been shoehorned into it.'

It was very hard sitting there because although the ABBA songs were in my head, I didn't know them terribly well, and I couldn't really see what was going to be done with this. Nevertheless Judy's enthusiasm had made me really gung-ho for the project. We were talking about the fact that the songs seemed to fall into categories: the very light-hearted romantic ones and those that talk about the breakdown of a relationship. And the idea of telling the story via one character somehow didn't seem quite right. I don't know why I felt that, but it was probably because I felt that would have left the audience on a bit of a downbeat, since you would be following a young character whose early dreams of love ended in disaster.

There was an age factor as well. Judy and I had established that we were both 39 and looking at our forties and we knew that most musicals required young and beautiful leading characters. Yet we knew that the subject matter of the ABBA songs meant we'd have to write about a romance that would end in a break-up. If you have two young people breaking up – unless it's Romeo and Juliet, and one of them dies – the audience, especially the bitter 40-year-olds, will think, 'So what if they break up, they're only young, they'll meet someone else. Hah, you've got it all to come.' And that's when we decided the story had to be about two generations – a mother and a daughter. We had that and we had the whole sound of ABBA, which Judy described as 'holiday-ish' and summery, so again we knew the show had be set somewhere outside Britain, not on a rainy old housing estate.

We had been talking for two or three hours and it was time for me to go and get my train back. Judy was saying, 'Well this is great. I want you to call me when you get some ideas about what the story's going to be.' And I felt that if I left the room then, I'd have to stop thinking about ABBA and start thinking about what my script for *Byker Grove* was going to be like, what I was going to give the kids for tea, and that my life, my real life, would overtake everything and I would end up in a week's time having to say, 'I'm really sorry I haven't come up with anything.' It was something about that realisation that sent a little shaft of whatever it is into my head saying, 'Here's an idea for you.' I debated about whether or not to tell Judy because by this time we were both standing, in my memory. I think she was doing the old handshake and I said, 'What if the mother had slept with three men and she didn't know which one of them was the father?' And Judy said, 'Sit back down!'

Judy: Catherine had definitely 'got' the project. We had had such a laugh, sitting there with our sandwiches talking about weddings and holidays and ABBA and nostalgia. It was literally as we were ending the meeting that she gave me the idea about the mother and daughter, and I remember feeling very excited when she left.

Catherine Johnson in Bristol in the early 1990s with daughter Myfi and son Huw. By this time, she had gained a reputation as a playwright, with plays at the Bristol Old Vic and London's Bush Theatre, and was gaining TV writing commissions on series like the BBC's *Casualty* and *Love Hurts*. Looking back now she says, 'Before the *MAMMA MIA!* years there were the struggling, desperate years – but they were happy.'
Overleaf: Script notations and doodles by Catherine Johnson.

Without Catherine's brains, *MAMMA MIA!* would not have happened. The way she put the script together is so bloody brilliant, with a heart, with intelligence. With a great sense of humour. And with no respect at all for us. It's very unpretentious, and I think that's why it works. Benny Andersson

When I started working on the outline for the show, Björn told me, 'You can use any of our songs, but always remember that the story is more important than the songs.' Catherine Johnson

PROLOGUE

I Have A Dream: On an idyllic Greek island, Sophie Sheridan, 20, posts three envelopes. She is inviting Sam Carmichael, Bill Austin and Harry Bright to her wedding. She crosses her fingers, fervently hoping they will come.

ACT I

Three months later...
Sophie greets her bridesmaids, Ali and Lisa, and reveals that either Sam, Bill or Harry is her father. Sophie has discovered this shattering secret in her mother Donna's old diary. She reads the diary to Ali and Lisa: **Honey, Honey**.

Donna was in love with Sam, but when he went home to his fiancée, she had flings with Bill and Harry. The three men think Donna sent the invitations, but Donna has no idea they are arriving and Sophie has 24 hours to find her real father and ask him to walk her down the aisle. Aarrgh!

Meanwhile, at Donna's taverna...
Donna welcomes Tanya and Rosie – her 'one-time backing band', the Dynamos, and all-time best mates. Donna confides her concerns about her daughter marrying too young. We meet Sky, Sophie's intended, along with Pepper and Eddie, the 'help'. We learn that running the Taverna is All Work and No Play. Donna dreams of hitting the jackpot one day: **Money, Money, Money**. Pepper makes eyes at Tanya.

The courtyard empties and Sam, Bill and Harry arrive. As they swap stories, they are surprised to learn that they all last saw Donna twenty-one years ago. Is this significant?

Sophie comes out of the taverna and is thrown into confusion. Which one is her father? She tells the men she sent the invitations as a secret surprise for her mother. Bill and Harry are pleased to play along, but Sam remembers that Donna told him she never wants to see him again. Sophie persuades Sam to stay: **Thank You For The Music**.

Donna arrives and Sophie makes a smart exit as Donna confronts her three living nightmares: **Mamma Mia**. The men honour their pact with Sophie and don't tell Donna why they are on the island. Sparks fly between Donna and Sam.

Tanya and Rosie console a badly shaken Donna: **Chiquitita**. She tells them her secret and Tanya and Rosie promise they'll help keep the men away from Sophie. And will she stop beating herself up? She hasn't done anything to be ashamed of! A rousing chorus of **Dancing Queen** lifts Donna's spirits.

Sophie wants to confess all to Sky, but their moment of intimacy is interrupted by the stag party: **Lay All Your Love On Me**.

Donna and The Dynamos make a surprise appearance at Sophie's hen party: **Super Trouper**.

Sam, Bill and Harry arrive. Rosie orders them to leave, but is thwarted by Sophie, who uses the opportunity to question each man: **Gimme! Gimme! Gimme!**.

Bill has questions for Sophie, too. How did Donna end up running a taverna? Sophie explains that her mother was left some money by an old Greek lady, Sophia. Bill realises this must be his Great Aunt Sophia. But he'd always heard her money went to family. When Bill learns Sophie is 20, he abruptly leaves the party.

Sophie confronts Bill on the jetty: **The Name Of The Game**. He admits he is her father. Sophie begs him to give her away at the wedding, still keeping the secret from Donna, and Bill reluctantly agrees.

Overjoyed, Sophie reoins the party. Sky and the Stags are returning: **Voulez-Vous**. Sophie's happiness sours as first Sam, then Harry declare themselves her father. She can't divulge her mother's guilty secret, and now all three dads think they are walking her down the aisle!

ACT II

Sophie's nightmare: **Under Attack**, featuring her mother, her dads, her bridegroom and a Chorus of Under-Water Dancers. She wakes screaming and finds herself...

...in the Courtyard, at the break of day. Donna, misinterpreting Sophie's anxiety, suggests calling off the wedding. This provokes a heated exchange, with Sophie revealing she hates not knowing her father. Donna is left alone to digest this: **One Of Us**. Sam walks in. Their exchange is loaded with meaning, but Donna will never forgive him for leaving her: **SOS**.

Harry asks Tanya what fathers do at weddings. 'Pay,' Tanya advises him. When Harry beats a hasty retreat, Pepper wants Tanya to 'catch up from last night'. Tanya tells him 'last night never happened'.

Bill, Rosie and the Fishing Party arrive and we see Bill and Rosie are getting closer. Rosie invites Bill to 'pepper her snapper' – he can't refuse!

Pepper won't take 'no' for an answer, so Tanya puts him straight: **Does Your Mother Know**.

Sophie confesses to Sky. He is upset – is she marrying him because she loves him or as an excuse to find out who her father is? He leaves, and an eavesdropping Sam intervenes. Sophie shouldn't assume marriage means happy ever after. It didn't for him: **Knowing Me, Knowing You**.

Harry gives Donna a cheque. She won't accept it, but she opens up to Harry and they remember **Our Last Summer** in Paris. The mood is broken when Sophie arrives with her wedding dress. Harry leaves mother and daughter – and the cheque.

As a reconciliatory gesture, Sophie asks Donna to help her get ready. Donna looks back over the years. Is she losing her little girl forever: **Slipping Through My Fingers**? Sophie is worried she is letting her mother down. Donna reveals that her own mother disowned her when Sophie was born. With a new bond between them, Sophie asks Donna to give her away.

Alone, Donna chokes down painful memories. Sam enters and she lets rip. Sam is speechless as Donna finally tells him how much he hurt her: **The Winner Takes It All**.

In the chapel, Rosie and Bill admit their feelings for each other: **Take A Chance On Me**. Bill's amorous advances are interrupted by the arrival of the wedding guests. Donna brings in Sophie. The wedding is about to proceed, but Donna has a surprise announcement. Sophie's father is here! It is Donna's turn to be surprised when Sophie admits that she already knows.

More surprises: It turns out that Sam came back after the break-up to make amends, but believed Donna had rejected him. Harry is gay and thought he would never be a father. Sophie declares she doesn't need to find out which one is her real dad any more – and that she has learnt something about herself. She is too young to get married and Sky is delighted when she suggests they get off the island and discover the world instead.

It appears there will be no wedding, until Sam steps in and proposes to Donna. She finally agrees: **I Do, I Do, I Do, I Do, I Do**.

As the moon descends on the little Greek island, both mother and daughter are looking forward to their new lives with their new loves: **I Have A Dream**.

BELIEVE IN ANGELS

Catherine: Right from the first meeting I had a copy of a schedule. I had most of my life mapped out by Judy, but although she obviously had strong ideas, she gave me a very open brief: 'You create the story, you create the characters, you use whichever songs will suit you best. If you decide to go with twenty-five utterly unknown ABBA songs, that's fine.' I got copies of every single lyric that Björn had ever written and very quickly established that the reason why the hits were the hits was because they *were* the best songs and lent themselves completely to being used to tell a story.

I remember telling Catherine, 'The story is more important than the songs. You can choose any of these one hundred songs, not just the hits – but there are a few I will say 'No' to, that I refuse to have in *any* show!' Björn Ulvaeus

Judy: I think, or I hope, that if Catherine had gone away and come up with something featuring 'Hey, Hey Helen' and 'King Kong Song', I'd have given it equal consideration… Nevertheless, the hit songs do stand out, even though the whole point was not about simply throwing all the hits in.

Catherine: I did have the chance to listen to the whole back catalogue of ABBA CDs, but I felt the only way I could make this work was to pretend that these were my songs and not ABBA's. I didn't want to be influenced by hearing the ABBA voices singing them, so I just sat and read the lyrics. I found a voice in those lyrics, the voice that Björn had used as his storytelling voice, the voice of a woman. With a few exceptions, Björn was writing lyrics that he was not going to sing himself – he had written the songs for Agnetha and Anni-Frid – so he was going through a similar process to me, creating characters. Once I'd realised that, I knew I had to find characters who could speak like the songs.

In some musicals you find people talking in a fairly straightforward way before breaking into all kinds of verbal trickery when they start singing. That's great if you've got clever lyrics, but Björn's lyrics are very straightforward. They express what you could easily say yourself. They don't wrap the emotions up in such a way that you might think, 'That's a lovely way of putting it but I wouldn't have thought of that.' Whereas 'Breaking up is never easy, but I have to go, it's the best I can do' – I could say that, anybody could say that in real life. That proved extremely useful, because I knew that my dialogue and his lyrics were not going to bump up against each other. It would be terribly difficult to do the same thing with Leonard Cohen's songs, for example.

As well as developing the characters, I needed to find the right location. At that time I'd never really been abroad. I prefer to have been somewhere to write about it; this was the first time I had had to work with no idea of the location whatsoever. I started off by just writing 'An island' and in the process the location was somewhere off Australia, then the Caribbean. I think there was even one discussion about whether it should be Canvey Island, or something equally silly. Only much later in the day did it become a Greek island and I still had to write the script with only a collection of holiday brochures to consult.

The essential concept has stayed remarkably consistent from the very beginning: Donna, this feisty single mum, runs a taverna on a Greek island. Her only daughter Sophie is about to get married and Donna's old friends Tanya and Rosie, who she'd sung with during the 1970s in a group called Donna and the Dynamos, have arrived for the celebrations. Sophie wants her father to give her away, but she doesn't know who her father is, and so she has invited three ex-loves of Donna's – her three potential dads – to come out for the wedding…

Judy Craymer's dream and Catherine Johnson's imagination made flesh: Gunilla Backman (centre) as Donna with her two Dynamos, Charlott Strandberg and Sussie Eriksson, in Benny and Björn's hometown production of *MAMMA MIA!* at the Cirkus Teater, Stockholm.

Catherine Johnson's earliest memory of any creative writing is being asked at primary school to listen to a story on the radio and then rewrite it in her own words. 'It went down very well. The teacher liked it and read it out to the class. I thought, "Yes, I can do this." I liked the act of writing but I also liked hearing somebody say, "This is good." And I think that's very true still.'

There were, of course, many changes to the actual storyline along the way, and a number of songs I had included I had to let go. In the very first treatment Donna had a boyfriend, the crooked sheriff Stanley, who wanted to knock down her taverna *and* make way for a big casino – cue 'Money, Money, Money'. But he was thwarted by the three dads, so Donna got to keep her taverna and the love of her life. I thought that was fantastic. There was a great scene where they were all out in the boat together, the three men and Stanley, singing 'Rock Me', as they rocked the boat furiously from side to side. To this day I don't know why we had to lose Stanley.

'Fernando' was also in the outline for quite some time, as a flamboyant dance number, with Donna entertaining the clientele at the taverna. But that didn't move the story along at all and was jettisoned quite quickly; now Donna simply hums a brief snatch from the song. The storytelling had to be paramount, and 'Fernando' is a story about two old soldiers discussing the Mexican Revolution. It simply did not fit, however hard I might try.

One song which provoked a huge amount of interest was 'Just Like That', a track that ABBA had recorded but never released and which therefore had acquired a mythical quality as the Holy Grail of ABBA songs. We thought it would be cool to include it in the show, and another way of getting people to come along: twenty of your favourite ABBA songs plus the one that nobody's ever heard before. That stayed in the show right up to rehearsals as a love duet between Sophie and her fiancé Sky, but again we decided it was simply holding the story up – and out it went.

The genius of *MAMMA MIA!* was that the story left out two of the greatest hits of all: 'Fernando' and 'Waterloo'. You'd imagine a show featuring ABBA hits would first of all be set at Waterloo and the leading man would be called Fernando... Tim Rice

Judy: I had very strong feelings when I met Catherine that she was going to be the right writer for the project, but she had no track record in musicals so I had to make a bit of a pitch on her behalf to Björn and Benny. I remember working all over the Easter weekend of 1997 helping put Catherine's first presentation together, retyping it, phoning her, adding bits, and then sending it off to Björn at his country house in Henley. He had one of those American-style postboxes at the end of his garden and didn't check it for days. But once he did, things began to flow quite fast.

Catherine: I met Judy at Reading station so we could get the train out to Henley. I was incredibly nervous. I'd met Björn briefly in London, but now I had put something on paper I was working myself up into an 'Oh my God, this is going to be so nerve-racking' state as we sat there having our coffee and Danish pastries. I don't know how Judy felt inside, but she was making me feel that she was very confident, that Björn had read the treatment and loved it and that I wouldn't have been meeting him if he hadn't.

Björn: A short time before I met Catherine for the first time I had been to see *Grease* with my two youngest daughters. I realised that here was a hugely successful family musical, a musical that was uplifting, humorous and, above all, with a lot of hit songs. That evening I thought, 'Maybe this is how we could turn Judy's old idea into reality.' It was quite a revelation and I seem to remember that I called Judy immediately. 'Yes, we must give this a real chance.'

Catherine: Björn was slightly not what I expected because he had a beard – and in my mind it was *Benny* who had a beard. He was utterly charming and, gosh, he had a sense of humour. When we arrived at his house he asked me a question about something that was happening in the news at the time. I mumbled something like 'Yes you're right, that's a terrible situation…' I so desperately wanted to impress and didn't think my opinion was enough to do that. I still didn't know that I had the job, and thought they might think, 'Well, we do like the treatment but we're not keen on her, Catherine's just not our sort of person.'

Judy: Before we got down to Henley, I'd said to Catherine, 'If they ask you if you want lunch, say no. Just go in there, do the stuff, and let's go.' We got down to Björn's. I was quite anxious and Catherine was so nervous she couldn't pitch the treatment to Björn, couldn't even speak! I could see she was transfixed, thinking, 'My God, I've met Björn!', so in the end I pitched it for her. Then Lena, Björn's wife came in and said something in Swedish to Björn which was 'Would you like lunch now?' so Björn turned to us and asked, 'Would you like lunch?' and we both said, 'Uh uh'. Lena went out and came back, obviously a bit put out by this, saying something else in Swedish to Björn who then said, 'No, you have to have lunch.' So we decided it might be a good idea to stay for lunch after all.

Benny: Judy had finally come up with this idea with Catherine Johnson and Björn was quite interested in doing something. I was not. I'm very proud of the ABBA work, of the records and what we achieved, and I was thinking, 'If this were to happen, a musical in the West End with ABBA music and ABBA lyrics, if it's not good, will that take away the sincerity we had when we recorded this, trying to treat it like merchandise or something?'

Björn: At this early stage, I wasn't going to show anything to Benny. He was a little reticent about the project and I did understand that. He was worried that the show would detract rather than add something to ABBA and the songs. I have to say that during the whole process, had I felt this was not good for ABBA, I was ready to say, 'Let's stop there.' But I had liked Catherine immensely and thought if anyone could manage to do it, she could.

Catherine: My next target was producing a full script. For the theatre I had always enjoyed the process of saying, 'These are my characters, this is where it's set, this is what it's about', letting them run, and surprising myself with what happened. But with this musical whatever happened with the characters they always had to end up in an ABBA song. Initially I found that quite frustrating. The best bits were when I got to the songs because then I could just sit down and copy out all the lyrics. And I'd think, 'Hang on, if another character comes in and sings a couple of lines, by the time I've put all the spacing in that's going to be another half a page!'

Judy: While Catherine was working on the script, I was starting to bring the creative team together. One of the first people to come on board was Mark Thompson, who had recently designed the sets and costumes for Yasmina Reza's play *Art*.

Mark Thompson, production designer: After Judy had offered me the job to design her show, I met up with her, Catherine and Björn one evening after they had been to see *Art*. I thought Björn was sweet and very modest and always seemed very charming. I remember I felt a bit drunk that night because I'd been out with some friends for a drink and I was thinking, 'You've got to hold yourself together a bit'! Björn kept on saying, 'Why do you want to do this musical? You do art. I do popular music.' And when I mentioned to other people that I was going to work on this musical with ABBA music, they thought I was mad, that I was virtually committing professional suicide. I told them, 'Think what you like, just because it's populist. It will be a hit.'

Judy: I didn't follow the rulebook of How To Make A Musical, which would have told me not to bring a designer or choreographer on board before the director was in place. But I had been bowled over by the chance Mark Thompson might be interested because I had always seen him as such a magical designer. Howard Harrison, the lighting designer, was a very old friend. And Anthony Van Laast, the choreographer, was another great friend, so I really did end up putting most of the creative team together without the director.

Mark Thompson, *MAMMA MIA!*'s production designer (left) and Howard Harrison, the lighting designer (right), were brought into the team by Judy Craymer soon after Catherine's treatment had been approved. Mark knew Judy's business partner Richard East because he had designed the revival of *Joseph And The Amazing Technicolor Dreamcoat* at a time when Richard East was Jason Donovan's manager. Howard Harrison had met Judy in the 1980s when they were both involved in Tim Rice's musical *Blondel*. 'Judy,' he says, 'has always been Judy, such fun and energy and glamour, all the things Judy is. She was exactly the same then.'

On first viewing I think we all thought, 'Oh this is an easy-peasy piece, but in fact it's a really cleverly structured piece of work. I know it's not changing the world in terms of the history of theatre, but it's got everything that a Shakespeare comedy has, which is how I was briefed to design it. Mark Thompson

Anthony Van Laast, choreographer: Judy and I went out to lunch, where she explained the whole story to me and I thought, 'Actually, that's a bloody good story.' She also told me that at that stage she didn't have a director, but would I be interested in choreographing? I said, 'Well, of course I'm interested in choreographing, but also it's a caveat that normally the director likes to choose the choreographer.' Time went on, and there was no director in place, and one weekend my wife Annette and I went for a walk on Hampstead Heath. I turned

round to Annette, who's a theatrical agent, and said, 'Who do you think should direct this show?' and she said, 'Phyllida Lloyd' – Phyllida was one of her clients.

Judy: I knew a young director called Danny Slater who had been Phyllida's assistant on various operas and used to talk about her with huge respect. When her name came up I thought, 'Wow, Phyllida Lloyd.' In my mind I thought of her as a hugely intellectual director. And that was good because I knew that whoever was going to direct this musical had to have real weight, and be somebody who understood storytelling. My battle had always been explaining that this wasn't an ABBA tribute show, that it wasn't a biographical piece. I think if I'd known more about Phyllida, as I do now, I probably would never have been as fearless about approaching her, although to a certain extent I was always having to be fearless to push the whole musical forwards.

Phyllida Lloyd: When I had been at the Bristol Old Vic at the end of the 1980s, I was asked if I was interested in doing an opera for Opera North. I thought, 'What!?' It was like someone asking me, 'Would you be interested in doing a cricket net?' I had thought opera was a closed club and couldn't imagine why anyone would invite me into it, but I went and directed this opera in Leeds, and felt, despite my trepidation, bizarrely in my element. I was working on a much bigger scale, collaborating with conductors, choreographers and chorus masters, learning the architecture of operas, how to move large groups of people around a stage. Everything I would need for a show like *MAMMA MIA!*

On the other hand I'd always been quite suspicious of musical theatre. Musicals are a big deal for a director as a potentially life-changing experience,

Albert Finney in the London production of *Art*, by French playwright Yasmina Reza, with sets and costumes by Mark Thompson. The play picked up a clutch of Molière, Olivier and Tony awards, and Mark Thompson's set design received much critical acclaim for its stylish and witty minimalism.

Phyllida Lloyd (above and opposite) saw *Jesus Christ Superstar* when she was 14. 'I was blown away. I knew the lyrics to every song and used to sing 'I Don't Know How To Love Him' in harmony with my best friend at school. Apart from that I didn't get into the sung-through musicals of the 1970s. I'm not sure I thought musicals were really the right medium for a serious subject – or at least the serious subject had to be treated ironically.'

but in theory it's an opportunity that comes with 'Poisoned Chalice' written all over it. Most musicals flop. I know people who've had nervous breakdowns doing them, some who have become rich, others who have become totally miserable, others who have ended up wanting to murder the producer... However, at some point before this I'd said to my agent Annette, 'From now on we're not doing anything except high art or big bucks.' And when I say high art I didn't mean pretentious and rarefied, just something that I would feel passionately about. I wanted to edit out all the middle stuff that was not changing the world or paying the rent. So I went to meet Judy with a completely open mind.

Judy: Phyllida liked the idea of working with Catherine, because she knew of her plays at Bristol and the Bush. I don't think she was particularly familiar with ABBA but I think she had, that day, rushed off and bought herself *ABBA Gold*. And I liked her a lot. I managed to stagger through the meeting without getting egg on my face. I'd said Mark Thompson was designing the show – not quite realising that he and Phyllida were great friends and had been at Birmingham University together – with Howard Harrison lighting it and Anthony Van Laast doing the choreography. What a nerve to say to a director, 'This is going to be your team.' It's outrageous. And then we discovered we were the same age. Phyllida had just turned 40 and my fortieth birthday was only a couple of weeks away. I asked her, 'When will you let me know?' and she said, 'Before you're forty' – and, in fact, she did let me know within a week. Knowing how difficult it is to pin Phyllida down because of all her commitments, it was a miracle she got back to me so quickly.

Catherine: Having Phyllida on board was fantastic because now I knew who I'd be working with, I was going to get director's notes to help me with my writing, and it gave me a feeling that this was a process that was steamrollering on. The more people who were involved the less likely it was that it would all grind to a halt. So that was good.

The miracle was that Catherine had found even the semblance of something on which most of these songs could hang. The bare bones of the piece were very strong: the two generations, the humour. The crux from then on, for me, was to intensify it. Phyllida Lloyd

Judy: I needed to introduce Phyllida to Benny and Björn, so the three of us – Phyllida, Catherine and myself – went over to Stockholm one weekend. Görel Hanser, their business manager, picked us up and we drove to Björn's house, a little way out of the city. It was November, there were log fires, all rather lovely, and then Benny and his wife Mona came over with some other guests for this

Benny and the offices of Mono Music on the island of Skeppsholmen in Stockholm, where he still goes to work every day when he is in the city. Judy Craymer says, 'It's very exciting to be out with Björn and Benny in Stockholm. It's like being out with the king and the king – and they're totally oblivious to it.'

great long candlelit dinner. I was quite tense because I knew that Benny was not yet as supportive of the project as Björn and that if there was any slight wrong move it could all go up in smoke.

Catherine: It was my first trip to Sweden, and virtually my first flight ever. We were very up for it: champagne cocktails all round on the plane. The dinner was an absolutely gorgeous meal cooked by Lena, and we drank and drank, champagne and wine. As the years have gone by I've got worse, but even then I was a real lightweight and I got drunk too quickly. I hadn't met Benny before and I think Judy had warned me, 'Benny is not as warm to this idea as Björn is. He doesn't consider himself to be ABBA any more, so just bear that in mind, Catherine.' But after a couple of glasses I was practically nudging Benny and going, 'Oh, but Benny you *are* ABBA, you *are*, you know you are really!', which fortunately for me didn't lead to me being sacked on the spot. He seemed to find it quite amusing.

Phyllida: We were in this rather wonderful house, looking out to sea, having pre-dinner drinks and canapés served by Björn's children in little Heidi aprons. But it wasn't at all pretentious, it was just a very nice family house – and something about their down-to-earthness was very striking. The next morning we had to be at their offices at nine o'clock. We were offered whisky when we arrived and Catherine and I both nearly chundered into the wastepaper baskets.

Judy: When we arrived for the meeting at Benny and Björn's office – this heavenly space overlooking the Baltic – we'd only had a few hours' kip and didn't quite know what we were meant to be doing, but Phyllida pulled the whole thing together and said, 'We'll make a reading of it', and, of course, it was Phyllida, Catherine and me who had to read it, the boys weren't going to read it.

Catherine: It felt really bloody early to me. We sat around a big table, got the script out and read it out loud, which I found excruciating. I hadn't known this was going to happen. I thought everybody would have read it, and I would just sit there and scribble down notes. I didn't realise that I was going to be a participant. And once it was over the relief went to my head and I started trying to get Benny to go upstairs and have a look for some memorabilia – 'Please let me have a look at the ABBA costumes'; the relief had made me go a bit silly.

Judy: I remember Catherine asking whether they had any ABBA trinkets there and thinking, 'Uh oh, here we go.' In fact there wasn't much ABBA stuff around. There was a smattering of *Chess* and *Kristina* memorabilia, some gold records and posters. Life had moved on for them. They weren't living in the past, which was why doing this musical was difficult because they weren't as obsessed about ABBA as I was. And it turned out that up in the attic there were a few boxes of

ABBA items that had been packed away. Catherine begged them to find a T-shirt for her daughter and they found this tiny T-shirt, which Catherine then proceeded to wear on the flight home.

Benny: It had been a good meeting. I'm not a professional script reader, I can't tell if something is good or bad, but when you meet people who are full of enthusiasm something rubs off on you. *Kristina* was still running in Stockholm at the time and I didn't know if I would be able to be involved in anything else. But I said to Björn, 'You do Judy's musical. You take care of that and I'll be here.' There were still great gaps in the script and I must say I was still hesitant – still this reluctance of 'Are we messing with ABBA?' – but I said to Björn, 'If you like this, I think we should do it, let's go ahead.' And if this was going to be done it felt like it was in good hands.

Judy: I had a sword of Damocles hanging over my head. Because at any time Björn and Benny could have said, 'We don't need this headache in our lives.' I was overseeing everything and Björn, bless him, was overseeing the fact that he had to keep Benny happy, because Benny had told him, 'Fine, if you believe in it, run with it.'

MAMMA MIA!'s three creative dynamos: Judy Craymer, Catherine Johnson and Phyllida Lloyd. Judy compares the three of them to the three Dynamos in the show. 'Catherine's the slightly chaotic single mum, I'm high-maintenance and Phyllida's the pragmatic one.'

Richard East joined forces with Judy when she left her career in TV and film production to work on *MAMMA MIA!*. An Australian himself, he suggested in an early note that one of the three dads could be Australian: 'maybe Bill could be a bit of a Mel Gibson...'

I now had a creative team in place who Benny and Björn were comfortable with. The next job was to get the finances firmed up. A couple of years earlier I had had to make the difficult decision to leave my job as a TV producer, after coming to the conclusion that if I was going to make a go of this musical, I would have to do it full time. The very day I made that decision I had arranged to have tea with Richard East, who was Jason Donovan's manager, and who I had met when he lived in London. Richard was now based back in Australia and was just over for a visit. Over tea I told him I had given up my day job to try and make this musical happen and he said, 'Well, it sounds *fantastic*,' and I said, 'Really, do you fancy helping?', because nobody had really given me that much encouragement. We set up a company together called Craymer East, which later became part of Littlestar. What was great – and a huge relief – was that although Richard was based in Australia, I had found somebody I could call late at night who understood what I was trying to do, who was in the music business and who was well versed in the intricacies of music publishing.

I also involved Andrew Treagus as my general manager quite early on. Andrew was something of a godfather to all stage managers, one of the best general managers in the West End. I approached him and asked him to give me some advice; luckily he believed in me and would be there on the end of the phone if I needed to know how to make a deal work or how to structure a budget. Little did he know that he was going to be working full-time for so many years.

Theatre is not something that you can put a business plan together for. The whole point is that if the show doesn't work, nothing works. Judy Craymer

Andrew Treagus, executive producer: I met Judy at a time when *MAMMA MIA!* was looking like it might take off. She knew I had a background in managing musical theatre, so she asked, 'Would it be possible for you to manage this show if it goes ahead?' And after that Judy and I started having early morning meetings in a café in Old Compton Street: she told me what she wanted to do and I started putting a few things together for her.

Judy: I was very budget conscious. I had watched too many companies in the 1980s spending money on fabulous furnishings and promptly going belly up. We kept things on a tight rein. I had an assistant, Claire, who had worked with me on the film *Neville's Island*, and I offered to pay her some cash in hand. My old employers at Primetime Television offered me a space in their offices for a peppercorn rent – and in fact, we were still there when the show opened. After producing for television and film I understood the need for financial control. That mantra stayed with us throughout the production of *MAMMA MIA!*: 'This *will* work and it *will* be on budget.' In fact, I think that was part of the collaborative spirit because all of us were in it together. There wasn't anyone swanning about with superior ideas saying, 'Well, if you want me darling, I'm going to need the waterfalls and the glitter and the rain.' It was 'OK, this isn't working, let's make it work.'

However, following the meeting with Benny and Björn in Stockholm in that autumn of 1997, I knew I was going to need some more money. It was time to up the stakes with Polygram, ABBA's record company, who I'd been talking to about backing the show. I'd first gone to them earlier that year and opened up a conversation. I don't know if Benny had said to Polygram, 'If Judy Craymer comes knocking on your door, take the meeting, or at least, don't slam the door' but they had shown interest. Now I had to bring those discussions to a head.

John Kennedy, then head of Polygram UK: At the time I was finding my feet running Polygram UK. We were doing OK, had a great roster of artists and were busy signing new acts, but nothing like this musical. Roger Aimes, my boss, had been toying with Judy's proposal for a period of time but hadn't quite made up his mind. He sent it over to me and said, 'We need to make a decision on this.' For me it was very straightforward. I read a very good outline of what the show was going to be. I thought musicals were a good thing to invest in, particularly when we owned the publishing rights to the music as well. Funnily enough it even worked for me that ABBA were still slightly uncool because I thought it would appeal to an older audience who had the money, the time and the habit of going to the theatre.

The reason the project had been marked 'Quite hard to handle' was because we didn't know where the money would come from. Nothing was really happening, and Judy essentially demanded a meeting. She got a pretty senior turnout, including Roger Aimes, who was President of Polygram Worldwide, David Munns, the Head of Marketing Worldwide and David Hockman, who was Head of Publishing Worldwide. She corralled us together and said, 'I've had enough. You lot had better make up your mind. What's so difficult about this?' And basically I didn't think there was that much that was difficult about it. I did raise the thought that if I was going to invest this money, I wanted to invest in the copyright of the project, whereupon Judy made a few comments along the lines of 'Over my dead body. You don't think I've worked on this all these years to give away a share of it to you!'

From top: Andrew Treagus, executive producer, with Benny; Emma Clayton, Judy's then international assistant, with Benny, Judy and Richard East; showbiz journalist Baz Bamigboye and Judy with John Kennedy of Polygram, later part of Universal. John Kennedy says of putting up the money for *MAMMA MIA!*: 'It was one of the best investments I've ever made and one of the best investments Polygram's ever made, no question about it.'

Judy: Whatever I'd taken before that meeting I wish I could bottle it. My attitude was very much 'You're ABBA's record company, surely you can see this will work', not realising how cheeky that was. I didn't actually jump on the desk and sing to them, which is what one magazine article suggested. But I did pitch the story terribly passionately and when I think now about who was in that room I go slightly red with embarrassment. But I think that they liked that passion.

John Kennedy: In meetings people often like to find reasons to postpone any decision just a bit more. When Judy said, 'And there's going to be a workshop', we thought, 'Fantastic, a workshop, we don't have to make the decision today.

Even though she's shouted at us, we can go and see a workshop.' The truth of the matter is I don't know how many of us knew what a workshop was. I certainly had no idea what one was. We didn't think to ask where the money for this workshop would come from but we soon got a call or a letter saying, 'Somebody needs to pay for the workshop – and that somebody is you.'

Judy: The workshop was pencilled in for March the following year. I sent the draft script over to David Grindrod, who is now our casting director, and who I had been told was very busy, couldn't take on anything new. I begged him to read it and I remember him phoning me back saying, 'You know what, I think it's really fun.' We needed to find about ten performers to handle the different roles. I knew from the start that I wanted Siobhán McCarthy to play Donna, especially as Björn and Benny had already worked with her on *Chess* – and in the event she stayed as Donna right through from the workshop to the premiere and beyond, as did Jenny Galloway as Rosie and Nick Colicos as Bill, one of the three dads.

Phyllida: The workshop was an opportunity for Catherine to see how her material stood up. The performers had been chosen partly because of their experience in this kind of work, and we would put the scenes in different orders, improvise to develop the characters, explore the relationship between the songs and the scenes, and so on. And we did make a lot of progress. At the time of the workshop one of the Dynamos, Tanya, had a husband who turned up on the island with her, and one day Catherine or someone said, 'Look, shall we just not have him turn up? He really doesn't help.'

　　During a workshop there is a tension between two elements. Are we actually trying to develop this work itself, to explore and expand it, or are we in fact getting together some little bite-size presentation to excite investors? In America it tends to be the latter, with workshops performed in full costume and make-up. I was absolutely determined that the MAMMA MIA! workshop should be, as far as possible, to develop the work, which was really nerve-racking because we knew that by the time we got to the Wednesday of the second week sound systems and backing singers would be arriving, and clearly there was pressure on Judy to produce something for the potential backers. But we tried to use the workshop for the best reasons and not worry about costumes. If the actors had to change from one character to another they could just turn a baseball cap the other way around. The way the workshop was put together was quite MAMMA MIA!, very homespun, no pretension, all about the people, the music and the words.

Siobhán McCarthy, the original Donna: I don't think I've ever laughed so much through a workshop; we had great fun doing it. When it finished, a lot of people were very unsure whether this show would ever see the light of day, but I thought, 'Well, if it does take off and they ask me to do it, I'll definitely say yes, because I've got some great numbers to sing.'

The original working title of the musical, *Summer Night City*, lasted until the workshop in spring 1998, by which time the team had agreed on *MAMMA MIA!*

The workshop was a great turning point creatively. Everything changed. Catherine's script went up in the air and landed on its feet. It was exciting. Judy Craymer

Catherine: I had never done a workshop in my life. I'd always written a script, worked with the director on the rewrite and then gone into rehearsals, so this was just a totally new process for me, and I have to say I didn't enjoy it at all. Here we were in this large room with eight to ten actors, Phyllida and the creative team. We did a read-through and straightaway I realised that psychologically it was all wrong. It was downhill from then for me: while everybody else was busy workshopping, I wasn't really paying much attention, because I knew there was something very wrong with the script. I had an idea what it was and I just wanted to go home and work it out.

In the workshop version Sophie didn't want to get married, it was her mother who was pushing her towards the wedding, while Sophie was thinking, 'I'm going to do this, but I don't think I really want to' and singing 'I Wonder' – 'It's frightening, it scares me.' And I thought, 'Jesus Christ, when is this play set? Is it set now or in the Victorian age? Why on earth is this girl doing what her mother tells her?' My age group, who grew up in the 1970s, was the generation who had been saying, 'You don't need a man to have a fulfilling life.' So why was I writing a mother from the dark ages saying, 'Oh darling, it's a dream for you to have a white wedding'? I thought, 'This is so bloody obvious. I have a daughter and if she came to me and said I want to get married at Sophie's age, I would be saying, "But you're so young."' And yet here I was trying to write about a character who was my age saying the exact opposite.

The workshop for MAMMA MIA! took place from 24 March to 3 April 1998 in the old London Weekend Television rehearsal rooms. Choreographer Anthony Van Laast's son shot a video of the show still very much in embryonic form, as Phyllida and the actors worked to develop and refine the key relationships between the characters. Here, Judy (top left) and Phyllida (top middle) address the gathering. Bottom left is Siobhán McCarthy as Donna, the part she went on to play when the show opened the following year. Jenny Galloway as Rosie (left, bottom middle) and Nick Colicos as Bill also played their workshop roles in that first London production.

Having realised that, it was excruciating to watch these awful, unbelievable characters being paraded in front of me, with actors trying to make them work, and me wanting to say, 'You're never going to make them work because they don't work. They'll never work until I've gone away and rewritten it all.'

Phyllida: I think that realisation was something that came to Catherine in a blinding flash, probably whilst we were showing her something else completely. While I was, as it were, spinning plates for her, or shuffling the deck in different ways, she sat back and saw that the very fundament of this was the wrong way round.

Catherine: I didn't feel I could discuss this with anyone because money had been spent to put on the workshop and there was going to be a performance at the end of it. I didn't feel I could suddenly turn round and say, 'You know what? It's not worth us doing this because it doesn't work.' The solution – when I finally found it a few weeks later – was simple. Younger girls now have this Bridget Jones mindset, thinking, 'I've got to get married before I'm 25 otherwise my life is all over.' So it should be Sophie who was pushing to get married, and her mother who was full of doubts, wondering if her daughter was throwing her life away.

Once I'd cracked that, we were on the way to having a decent script. I think I'd had this slightly old-fashioned notion of what a musical was supposed to be like and so had been creating characters who behaved in a rather old-fashioned way. Once I'd got over that and written it as though I was writing a play then it all became a lot easier. The clouds blew away as I started to rewrite, because I knew I'd solved what for me was the fundamental problem. But despite what I'd been going through as a writer, the workshop had been very successful. The final performance was greeted with a lot of hilarity and had a very positive impact. I think that was the point when people decided that this concept was going to work.

Phyllida: The show still needed a lot of work, but there was huge potential. And I think that the cast felt the same. They were much more experienced in musical theatre than either Catherine or me, and had begun the workshop really quite half-heartedly. I don't think they had much hope for it. By the time we put it all together at the end of the two weeks they were really excited about the prospect of being in it, which was terribly important to create a buzz in the theatre world.

Judy: I was still always treading on eggshells. During the final rehearsal, the day before the specially invited audience was coming in, one of the technical team turned to Benny and said, 'How can you let these people crucify your songs?' This guy thought he was being funny, but my immediate reaction was, 'Oh no… the end of the world!' But the great thing about Björn and Benny was that they were prepared to treat things with humour. I can still see Björn rocking with laughter while we were workshopping 'Honey, Honey', saying, 'I never wrote this as a funny song.'

The most important reason for the workshop had been to get the script right. It wasn't to raise money, although the Polygram guys did come. If it had been a disaster, they would have been saying, 'Sorry, Judy, not so sure', but they thought it was fab… David Munns, who's an extremely experienced record executive, couldn't stay for the whole performance. As he left in the intermission, he turned to Howard Jones, our lawyer, and said, 'I'm going now, but don't worry, it's going to be a hit', and off he went.

John Kennedy: I hadn't known what to expect of a workshop, but I knew this was the point of no return in terms of deciding about our investment. I was going to be asked for a yes or no. I'm pretty sure I left the workshop without being pressurised, but within the next day or so I was being asked for a decision. And I said, 'Right, let's proceed to paperwork.'

There was something about that workshop that was special. There was a lot to be done but there was a little heartbeat, and you knew that with a bit of nurturing and sculpting you could make it work. Anthony Van Laast

Judy: One huge decision was made at a meeting of the creative team on the last day of the workshop. I had always told Björn we would tread very slowly, very carefully and probably open the show outside London so that he and Benny didn't feel they were in the limelight. If the show didn't work it could disappear under the radar. Mark Thompson turned round at the meeting and said, 'The show has to come straight into the West End because I don't think we can put in the kind of work we need to open in Manchester or Bristol.' So whereas before we had been working on the idea that we would be opening out of London, now the hunt was on to find a theatre in the West End.

Catherine: The August after the workshop we all got together again at the Waterside Inn at Bray. Creatively the show was really moving on. Although the bulk of my work had been done, there were still interesting developments springing up. At the beginning of Act Two, I had Sophie singing 'I Wonder', this reflective 'Should I stay or should I go?' song. This was a throwback to the previous draft where she wasn't sure whether or not she wanted to get married. Now that I had flipped the script on its head, I wondered if the song had any place there. Phyllida said, 'We're going out of Act One on this huge question mark: "Which one of you is my father?" So let's bring them back in with a song that has impact, that's very dramatic.' She turned to Björn and asked him in a very Phyllida-ish, pondering way, 'Could you possibly have, somewhere in your back catalogue, something that reflects Sophie's nightmare?' And he said, 'Yes, 'Under Attack'.' Judy said, 'Oh yes, 'Under Attack', – and they both knew what

The creative team at the Waterside Inn, Bray, in August 1998. From left: Mark Thompson, Phyllida, Judy, Catherine and Björn. Anthony Van Laast had also driven up for the day, but left before dinner. Catherine remembers, 'It was the first time I'd seen everyone since the workshop, although I had been in contact with Judy constantly. At this point I was quite relaxed and relieved. Everybody was very complimentary about the script and I felt I'd proved myself to them, even if I still felt very much the junior member of the team. I asked the waiter to take our photo – I wanted a photo of me with Björn in case the show didn't happen, to prove I was once there with Björn out of ABBA.'

What the casting director sees: headshots of the original production's principals. Clockwise from top left: Siobhán McCarthy (Donna), Hilton McRae (Sam), Paul Clarkson (Harry), Nicolas Colicos (Bill), Andrew Langtree (Sky), Lisa Stokke (Sophie), Jenny Galloway (Rosie) and Louise Plowright (Tanya).

they were talking about. Phyllida and I had no idea because we'd never heard this song. But when we read the lyrics I thought 'these lyrics really fit', and hearing the music it was, 'oh yes'.

Judy: The script had really shaped up. Things were moving forward creatively. Now we needed to confirm who was going to be on stage – even though there was no theatre in place yet.

David Grindrod, casting consultant: We held the auditions at a place called Soho Laundry. It was all a bit 'suck it and see' because the idea for the show was completely new. From the workshop we had a good idea of the balance we wanted for the three Dynamos, since we already had Siobhán McCarthy as Donna and Jenny Galloway as Rosie, and we also had an idea of the dads, but everything else was up for grabs.

Neither Phyllida or Catherine had ever done a West End musical before. There were wonderful days in the audition process where Phyllida would give me the strangest of looks. There was a moment when I said to her, 'Well, this person will swing' and she went 'Swing?', so I said, 'Yes, it will be easy for them to swing, it's absolutely fine.' There was a pause and then she went, 'What, sexually?' I said, 'No, this person will swing in and out of a role so we can put them in there, we can put them in here, they can do that.' 'Oh!'

Martin Koch, musical supervisor: Quite honestly, we didn't know what we were auditioning. It's very different now because it's very clear what we require, but at that point we were groping our way forwards. We knew, which has always been the case, that Bill could be a bit light vocally, because he doesn't really have anything to sing, whereas Harry and Sam, especially Sam, have to be able to sing. For Donna to be able to cope with her numbers, especially in the second act, the singing is crucial. We were looking for characters too. Phyllida had made it quite clear that she didn't want a Broadway or even West End type of ensemble, which can have a certain look about it – all pristine dancers and singers.

David Grindrod: What Phyllida wanted was non-dance, non-musical. She told me, 'I don't want to do a musical.' I said, 'But you *are* doing a musical!', and she retorted, 'But I don't want it to look like a musical.' So we tried to cast the characters to be as real as possible, for the audience to think that they knew the people on that stage, that you knew someone like Rosie, you knew a Bill – he didn't have to be a travel writer, but you knew somebody who was like him.

Phyllida: Of course we were all battling for our territory. I wanted people who I thought could act their way out of a paper bag. Anthony Van Laast and Nichola Treherne, Anthony's assistant, were the dance police. We wanted people who were great actors, and who could sing and dance. And we wanted all shapes and sizes. We wanted people who could sing pop – which I quickly realised is not like musical theatre, where you can weave your way around back-beating and torch-singing your way along. It's about having to sing on a beat, very very precisely and in tune. If they couldn't hold a pop tune, then they were out. We were asking a lot of established actors to come in, who hadn't done musicals before. I was willing them to be able to sing. Björn was on the whole quite forgiving and used to get quite seduced by actors trying to sing his material, whereas Martin Koch would be like a guillotine slamming down: 'Don't even think about it, don't even try it'.

Anthony Van Laast: Phyllida turned round to me one day in auditions and said quite seriously, 'Why do we need dancers?' I had to explain to her that there would be quite a lot of movement and that a lot of actors probably can't move. Part of my skill is weaving the people who *can* move in at the front. I also thought there would be numbers in the show involving quite a lot of dancing and so I had to really fight my corner with Phyllida.

I had done a show for Cameron Mackintosh called *Just So* at the Tricycle Theatre in Kilburn, in which he'd decided that he only wanted people to sing and act and at no point during the auditions was it mentioned about these people being able to move right up until we'd got into previews. Cameron then said he wanted a big production number for the opening number, and I said, 'Cam, I can't do that because we didn't hire dancers. I just can't do that. So I learnt a huge lesson that I had to make sure I had enough people in my armoury so that, if Judy or Phyllida suddenly turned round to me and said, 'We really do want a dance number', I had the personnel to create one.

Michael Simkins, actor: Actors are very gossipy. The word had gone around that there was this ludicrous, doomed-to-failure enterprise. Somebody was going to write an original show and shoo on twenty of ABBA's songs. It was going to be a turkey. And more disgraceful than that, Phyllida Lloyd, who we all thought was supposed to have scruples, to be a serious director, rumour had it that she'd taken the king's shilling and agreed to direct this dross.

But then I was asked to go up to be seen for the part of Sam. I knew all the ABBA songs; they had been part of my growing up. I'd been on a Norfolk Broads holiday with my first girlfriend Patty and 'Knowing Me, Knowing You' had been Our Song. So I really wanted to do the job. I went up for it at the Soho Laundry. In I went and they said, 'OK, would you like to give us 'Knowing Me, Knowing You'?', so I said, 'Yeah, I'll give it my best shot.' I blundered my way through the first verse, got to the chorus, looked at them all sitting there, and sang 'Knowing me, knowing you, ah ha'. And they stopped me and said, 'No, no, Michael, sorry, stop, we don't do the "ah ha"s!' It was like I'd sworn in church! 'Oh, I'm terribly sorry.' So I tried to do it without the 'ah ha's, but I dried up in the middle of the song and didn't know where I was. I did get a recall, but I sensed I'd blown it, which is always a terrible feeling. I didn't really hear much about *MAMMA MIA!* for the next year, except for the fact that it was this stonking hit.

As casting consultant of *MAMMA MIA!*, David Grindrod's job was to help piece together the jigsaw puzzle of parts, from principals and ensemble members to understudies, covers and swings (ensemble members who can slot into any role at short notice). 'David,' says Phyllida Lloyd, 'is absolutely tireless. He prepared people really well for us, and would be doing a lot of work behind the scenes to get people up to the speed we wanted them to be.' When the creative team came to see potential actors, they had one key codeword: 2MT, for 'Too Musical Theatre' they wanted a cast who would give the impression they were straight off the street. Judy Craymer remembers one actor who came in and sang a song to the panel. 'Björn said, "Is that your own song?" and the actor replied, "Yes, but if I'd known you were going to be here, I'd have sung one of yours!"'

Judy with Mark Thompson. Mark's enthusiasm for the Prince Edward Theatre was critical in convincing the creative team that the show would work there. Mark says, 'Everyone was very anti the Prince Edward, but I told them, "You're all wrong. I can definitely make the Prince Edward into an intimate theatre."'

David Grindrod: Luckily we had already found our Donna and our Rosie but we couldn't find a Tanya to complete the Dynamos. The part was cast very late in the day. I thought Louise Plowright might be right, but she was doing a play at the West Yorkshire Playhouse and I couldn't get her down for the auditions, so I told the others, 'It's all going to be done in an instant but I think I've found the woman for this part.'

Louise Plowright, the original Tanya: I was recalled for a second audition and they sent me the song 'Does Your Mother Know'. Because I don't read music, I asked my landlady in Leeds, who was a jazz saxophonist, who told me, 'Oh, you're going to have to sing this in a lower key, ask for it to be played in A minor', or whatever. 'That'll probably be right for your voice.' I don't normally dress how I dressed for that audition – I'd gone along in character because they had said Tanya was a bit like Patsy Stone from *Absolutely Fabulous*, so I wore high heels and a belted-in coat. Martin Koch, the musical supervisor, was there, and he said, 'What key would be comfortable for you to sing it in?' I said, 'Well, I've been told A minor' and it was ridiculously low, I was practically singing like a bass. Martin said, 'Well, I don't somehow think that's quite the right key', but we did make everybody laugh and there was a sense of ease after they realised that I had absolutely no clue about how to read music. I was then taken off downstairs by Nichola Treherne and put through my dance paces. I went away sweating, thinking, 'I'd quite like to do this now' despite the A-minor incident, and I got it anyway.

Andrew Treagus: One of the most difficult things was getting anybody who owned a theatre interested in us. I had heard that one theatre owner – or the person they had sent along to the workshop – said in the taxi ride back into the West End, 'Do you know who these people ABBA are?!' I had the impression that they weren't alone in thinking, 'Who wants to know about them, they were twenty-five years ago. A musical based on the songs of ABBA? No, that won't work.' But the one thing about Judy was that she believed in it so fervently. Time was running late and we were running out of options for where to go: we had looked at the Prince of Wales and the Piccadilly as a possibility and then Cameron Mackintosh quite suddenly offered us the Prince Edward.

Judy: During the autumn Cameron called me and said, 'Tell me about MAMMA MIA!, darling.' A production of *Ragtime* was due to go into the Prince Edward and I'd heard that it was not going in. Cameron offered me the Prince Edward, which was bigger than we had anticipated although it was a beautiful theatre. But I was desperate for the Prince of Wales, and he wouldn't let me have it – he was waiting for something else to go in there. 'You can't have it darling, you can't have it, take the Prince Edward.' 'Um, OK then.'

Björn: When Cameron called and suggested the Prince Edward, at first I felt, 'No, not the Prince Edward, again', because *Chess* had played there. 'No, it's too

big, no, for heaven's sake.' But we went there because that was the only logical thing to do: we didn't have a theatre. Mark Thompson absolutely loved it. He said, 'I can make it work here, I can make it look smaller than it is. Please, please', and I think he enthused all of us.

Phyllida: Most of us were feeling that the Prince Edward was far too big, and MAMMA MIA! was a little domestic show, with a lot of two-handed scenes. Mark said, 'Don't worry, leave that to me, I'll sort it', and he was the one who really had the confidence to say, 'Just take it.' He is a master at creating a balanced space, a space that looks more intimate than it might be, so much of the credit for that courageous move must go to him.

Previous productions at the Prince Edward Theatre on Old Compton Street in London's Soho – which was home to *MAMMA MIA!* for five years – included the world premieres of both *Evita* and *Chess*.
Overleaf: One of Mark Thompson's original costume designs for Tanya.

I told everyone, 'The Prince Edward's great. It's in Old Compton Street. It's in the heart of Gayworld, ABBA's a big gay thing. You cannot get a better spot for it!' Mark Thompson

MAMMA MIA! was not to look like a musical. That was Phyllida's big design brief: 'It mustn't look like a musical.' **Mark Thompson**

Phyllida: Mark is the least needy designer of anyone I've ever worked with. He will always collaborate, but he's equally happy working away on his own. He had to make certain decisions about the principles of the show before we really knew what the musical numbers were going to require. And he recognised early on that the show was an intimate, domestic musical and didn't need masses of scenery. It is part of his ethic – and one which I completely share – that set design is more about the people than how much scenery you can swap in and out, or how many flying helicopters and speedboats you can use. His taste, and mine, was for something much more economical, simple and aesthetically quite pure. He also identified that what Catherine had written was quite Shakespearean. Here was a magic island, which everyone comes to in search of something, although they don't quite know what it is they're looking for. And within 24 hours everyone has been transformed: Sophie stops needing to find her father and doesn't need to be married any more. Donna and Sam – and Rosie and Bill – discover their love and Harry is reconciled to himself. Mark identified that this was going to be a set on which you could have performed *The Tempest*.

Judy: Even at the creative meeting the summer before rehearsals, Mark was already saying, 'I see two white walls. Expensive white walls.' He'd already conceived the whole simplicity of the taverna, which I love – but it is obviously much more complex than it looks.

Mark Thompson: Phyllida's way of working involves keeping all the possibilities up in the air all of the time, so there was some doubt about the order of scenes. We had to create something that was very fluid and non-specific, so that if everything changed it was easy to do it. You start looking for clues in the script, which only defines the setting as 'a Mediterranean island, sparkling in the iridescent blue of the Aegean'. We know there's a taverna, a harbour, winding alleyways. The island is off the mainland but is that off the mainland of a bigger island or off the mainland of Greece? We always imagined it as an island like Mykonos, blue and white, big granite steps, whitewashed walls. There were scenes on jetties and a pathway off, but it also had to be an island that would light up. We wanted to go a bit funky disco!

In the old-school, especially American, musical tradition everything is visual. If it says, 'We're in a bedroom', you have to have the whole environment. There's something often rather two-dimensional about musical scenery; it's more pantomimic as we would understand it. I think in Britain we tend to create more suggestive scenery than that.

Björn: I went over to Mark's studio and found the walls papered with shots from Greece. He was looking for that blue colour that is the essence of the Aegean Sea. He came up with a powerful vision and a very, very intelligent solution.

Catherine: As a writer you have no idea what the designer is going to do with the material you have provided. Mark unveiled this seemingly very simple but very beautiful set and it just took my breath away. I felt incredibly touched by it. He had taken the very little I'd given him and done such a marvellous job. He had taken these sheets of paper with words on and created something wonderful. It was like being presented with a gift.

Andrew Treagus: When we discussed how the two major walls were going to move, I told Mark, 'I cannot sit watching the show on the first night and worry that those walls are not going to move when somebody presses a button. My life has been full of shows which have gone wrong through bad technology.' Thank goodness he agreed with me, and persuaded Phyllida to have members of backstage staff in costume pushing the walls round.

Judy: Phyllida adapted to this brilliantly. We just had to make sure we had pretty stage managers who looked great in a sunhat.

Mark Thompson: Phyllida was always saying she wanted all the walls to be incredibly light so that one little girl could go across and move a wall. There was a slightly heavy meeting towards the end of rehearsals, when they were still running around with a couple of bits of hardboard on wheels. We said there was no way that could happen for the real show and Phyllida was virtually saying, 'All right, cut the set, we'll stick with the hardboard.' It was a bit of a tense moment.

Phyllida: Mark possesses immense confidence. And the best sense of humour you could imagine, very cheeky. He is a forthright, fearless and quite impatient Aries: he likes to work fast, to see things happening quickly and to make a decision. I may have taken it for granted how important it was to me that he was part of the team… We had such shorthand, and he could tell me where to get off and what not to worry about.

Catherine: I remember sitting in the theatre during rehearsals and listening to Mark and Phyllida rowing and realising that they weren't falling out at all – they are bonded, unbreakable.

Andrew Treagus: Strangely people rather fell in love with the idea of backstage staff pushing the set round, especially Phyllida, so I think it needed a little bit of a shove to say, 'Now we are in fact going to automate the set' when we went to America.

Mark Thompson: While the set was being fitted up, I started on the costumes, because I always prefer to have the world in place first. We had a very plain white and bright blue set, so I had imagined the costumes could be really quite colourful to bring edge to it. The first time we had the company on for 'Summer Night City', when it was still the opening number, everyone was in slightly cheesy costumes

and it was just horrible. I turned to Lucy Gaiger, my costume supervisor, and said, 'I want you to get a whole load of black and blue dye. We are going to dye the entire set of costumes overnight.' We didn't tell anyone we were going to do it. At the start of the story we don't know who these people are, we need to enter a world of Greek-ish natives, and then we gradually bleed colour through so that by the end of the first act, for 'Voulez-Vous', when they really are friends, we're using purples and blues and touches of acid green. And for the wedding, at the end of these 24 hours of drama, the sun is setting before the moon. I said we should do the wedding very much in sunset colours, all pinks and orange, and that should be yummy and scrumptious and much more glamorous than a wedding would be in reality. Phyllida always laughs at the fact that I put all these people in big hats and gloves. It's pure camp. There was also a suggestion that the priest who officiates at the wedding should be wearing some kind of clerical robes. I always said no, because it's an outdoor wedding, and as we know from the script that Donna is an Irish Catholic girl, there's no way it's going to be a Greek Orthodox ceremony. It should be a priest who just happens to be there, wearing a nice soft suit, otherwise you'd have someone with a ludicrous cassock wafting around.

Judy: On one of the first days of rehearsal, Mark was talking through the costume designs with the cast and he said, in a slightly sardonic way, 'You can make comments, but don't expect changes…'

Phyllida: In some ways I feel that Mark has received very little credit for what he created, except from people who know what they're talking about. There's a danger that people think, 'It's only a couple of walls with a bit of rust running down them.' In fact it's expensive minimalism. It looks like nothing, but he had to build in space for the under-floor lighting, and the spaces Anthony and I needed for acting and dance movement, and still make these walls work poetically. The set is a fantastic piece of work by someone who really, really understands about storytelling and the architecture of the space and how to make an audience feel part of an intimate experience in a very big theatre.

THE TIME IS RIGHT

Judy: On the first full day of rehearsals, we had a 'meet and greet', or as it later became known, a 'muffin meeting': lashings of croissants, muffins and coffee, which is the traditional way to start rehearsals, especially with an original company. I actually find it rather terrifying having to stand up in front of a group of actors, but I did go down and say a few words of welcome.

Phyllida: I had been sent to an all-girls school where we were trained to make bloody good speeches to open church fêtes: I think the teachers anticipated that we would go on to marry cabinet ministers or army generals. There was one huge silver cup which was presented each speech day for 'Good manners in difficult circumstances'. This was the highest accolade that you could receive, for not crying when you learnt that the *Titanic* was about to sink. And that stood me in very good stead on the opening day of rehearsals.

It was like the first day at school, where you arrive and don't know anybody. Crowds of people, lots of talking and laughing, and then a certain amount of speechifying: 'Welcome to *MAMMA MIA!* This is going to be the trip of a lifetime.' Catherine Johnson

Phyllida: I had just finished directing my first international opera at the Paris-Bastille Opera and arrived from the opening night there direct to the first sing-through of *MAMMA MIA!*. I remember a dawning realisation as I walked into the room that this was a big deal. There was something about the fact that Benny and Björn were there, the presence of the press people – an overall sense of excitement that was unusual and slightly humbling in terms of the responsibility I was taking on. Although for me *MAMMA MIA!* was sandwiched between directing *Macbeth* in Paris and *The Carmelites* at the ENO, they were all part of one picture. There was no sense of 'Oh, now we're just doing a musical' as far as I was concerned. *MAMMA MIA!* was just as challenging as the two operas, and all of us were determined that it was going to be as good as anything we'd ever done, and that we would apply absolutely the same standards of rigour and fanatical attention to detail and dramaturgy and aesthetic beauty as we would to any other piece.

The rehearsals began at the end of January 1999, so there were only just over two months before the opening night, which was going to be in April: five weeks in the rehearsal room and then maybe three weeks in the theatre. We had some of Mark Thompson's stage set in the rehearsal room, but there were many

At the *MAMMA MIA!* rehearsals. Above: Behind Benny, Björn and Phyllida, Judy is in conversation with John Kennedy and David Hockman, both of Polygram, the principal investors in the show. Left: Björn talks with Catherine in front of Mark Thompson's original stage set model.

One for posterity: the original cast and creative team's end of term photo.

aspects of the show – choreography, staging, costumes – that were still unresolved. There were numbers that are now no longer there, and songs which were in different places. And there were whole chunks of the show where we had no idea what was going to happen on stage. But we didn't mind.

Catherine: Rehearsals and production meetings were incredibly liberating. For the first time the focus wasn't on me as the person sitting there scribbling notes down while the whole meeting told *me* what to do. Now everybody was telling everybody else what to do. For the first time I felt I didn't have to bear the brunt of the work.

The rehearsals were tough, but satisfying. I enjoy coming up with solutions, and I liked the fact that I could go away, solve a problem and go back in the next morning with a couple of pages of dialogue for people to react to. As a writer you are so used to working by yourself that there is real novelty in being with people as part of a team. And Phyllida's way of directing is incredibly inclusive. She was working with a lot of actors in the ensemble who had no lines to say and yet they were all given characters. It wasn't a case of her telling them, 'Come on stage and prance around a bit', it was 'You are part of this island. Who are you? Tell me who you are.'

Phyllida: I plunged into rehearsals as if I were doing a play, a play with music. We did extensive improvisations, exercises and games and started to build up the life of the island. We worked on weddings, hen nights and stag nights and tried to create a strong ensemble spirit, giving those members of the company who didn't have speaking roles a voice in what we were doing.

Jenny Galloway, the original Rosie: It was a very difficult, interesting rehearsal period. Just when you thought you were getting somewhere it was two steps back. It was all very tenuous, so you just put more of yourself into the role to make it happen. And that's when, as with all shows, it changes and moulds and shapes itself. It's a great mining process. Phyllida is so good at that, digging and digging and digging.

Louise Plowright: There was a lot of workshopping. Some people think it's all rubbish, but I love improvisation; it reminded me of being at drama school. Jenny Galloway, who was playing Rosie, used to do this brilliant observation of Phyllida talking to the ensemble while they were moving the set around: 'OK, everybody, I want you to push on those walls and let's see the characters, let's see the lives of these people.' All they were doing was pushing on a wall, but Phyllida would make them feel that they were making a much more important contribution.

Phyllida: In parallel with all the improvisational work the cast were going through some extremely rigorous warm-up workouts. *MAMMA MIA!* is physically very demanding, so Nichola Treherne, Anthony Van Laast's assistant, went in there to produce some finely tuned athletes; it didn't matter whether you were an actor who was slightly out of condition or someone straight out of college who was really match-fit for dancing.

Anthony Van Laast: The real nitty-gritty of the choreography happens once rehearsals start. You can only get a feel for what the show is once you see the way the director's taking things, once you've actually got the bodies in front of you, and in this case I needed to pick up on the sense of humour of the show. The role of the choreographer, I believe, is not to be in combat with your director but to assess how they want the production to flow and go along with them. It's a very delicate relationship, especially as time is short. Nichola and I would work on the dance pieces late at night, and next morning we would have thirty-five people standing in front of us, waiting to try out what we'd created.

The whole of the rehearsal period was tough. I originally created 'I Do, I Do, I Do, I Do, I Do' as a great big Busby Berkeley pastiche. I was so wrong, and it never left the rehearsal room, thank God, but I had spent weeks on it. Mark Thompson wanted Donna to go in with a pink dress and emerge in her white wedding dress on stage, and I had created a Busby Berkeley-style flower so that the audience wouldn't see Donna changing into her costume. When we did the run-through one day, I turned round to Nichola and whispered, 'That's terrible.' So I went home and rethought it. I think creativity is about setting yourself a problem, solving the problem and if you've solved the problem wrongly, having the balls to say, 'I screwed up, it's wrong' and go back to the drawing board again. Actually sometimes when you've really got it wrong it's much easier to get it right. But the key is admitting you've got it wrong.

Benny at the keyboard during rehearsals. Just behind him (in glasses) is Martin Lowe, the musical director of the original production, who took Martin Koch's arrangements, put both the band and the actors through their musical paces, and conducted the show in performance. Jenny Galloway says of Martin Lowe, 'He keeps you on the rails, but he is totally a theatre person, who understands what you're trying to do, although he will make you absolutely sing the right notes. He's a fantastic person to have down in the pit.'

Phyllida: You can see the impact of choreography straight away. To a large extent it either works or it doesn't, whereas you need time for performances to develop, for character to emerge. You have to have patience, especially with something as elusive as *MAMMA MIA!*. One minute Harry and Donna are singing 'Our Last Summer', reminiscing about their love affair in Paris, and the next moment Donna is performing 'Slipping Through My Fingers', an emotionally wrenching song about her relationship with her daughter. The journey between the two is in some ways quite an artificial thing. You are trying to breathe life into that passage of time. How you articulate that gap and how you allow the actors to have a say in that process is not simply about what words are said, but also how much space you allow. You could easily jump to one conclusion, tell the actors, 'This is what's got to happen, and that's what we're going to do every day now for the next six weeks' and miss out on something rather magical.

Working on a number like 'Dancing Queen' in rehearsal was fantastic fun. We gave Jenny Galloway and Louise Plowright a suitcase of props each – Jenny's had a snorkel, a pair of trainers, commando shorts and slippers, while Louise's was full of Clarins bottles and her hairdryer. We said, 'Right, now improvise this song using that stuff.' And they rose to the challenge magnificently. A lot of what would become highly wrought pieces of choreography came from improvising the scenes rather than Anthony or me imposing ideas from outside.

Catherine: The process was very inclusive. There was no feeling of 'OK, Catherine writes the scripts, that's her job, Anthony does the choreography, that's his job. You can't discuss the choreography and he can't discuss the script.' We were all there and all chipping in. I loved the fact that there was no demarcation, and that Phyllida invited ideas.

Phyllida: Everybody was working absolutely flat out through the rehearsal period. The show was evolving and developing all the time. Even the lyrics were changing. When Donna was feeling confused and depressed about her past catching up with her, Rosie and Tanya started singing, 'Chiquitita tell me what's wrong, I've never seen such sorrow in your eyes…' and then Björn just came out with 'And the wedding is tomorrow!', which was perfect. Knowing that he and Benny were prepared not only to accept but also to suggest that kind of subtle change was hugely encouraging. By the end of the process each song had benefited from some tiny little tinkering to provide a context that made sense for the song to exist within the storyline.

There was a moment later on while we were working on 'Super Trouper', when Anthony and I looked at each other and said, 'How is this going to go down?', because it's quite playful – there was definitely a sense of 'send up'. Benny and Björn came in to watch the number and we both thought, 'Well, this is it. We'll all be fired, or…' Björn stated tittering and then laughing. He and Benny were really enjoying it – that was a good moment.

Catherine: Although it was very rewarding sharing ideas, there were occasions where it was hard for me to watch actors playing with a scene and saying, 'Wouldn't it be interesting if we did this?' And it's not rehearsal-room etiquette for me to stand up and shout, 'Could you stop that pair of tossers now, because that will completely screw everything up.' That's a quiet conversation I would have with Phyllida afterwards. If Phyllida said, 'Yes, that's great, let's go with that', that would mean me heading back to my hotel room for a two-and-a-half-hour rewrite. But I learnt that she was allowing the actors room to explore the scene so that they would come back to where she needed them to be. And they'd have made the journey themselves, rather than her telling them what to do.

Siobhán McCarthy: Phyllida was always nineteen steps ahead of us – but she let us work out for ourselves how to develop the characters and scenes. So even though there was a huge amount of pressure to get this show right, she let it grow organically in its own space and time. Because the show had to be very naturalistic, in this rather unreal pop world, it had to be a believable journey.

Catherine: We also found that the show was over-long and we had to be hugely merciless to certain characters. So Sophie's friends, poor old Ali and Lisa – or rather the poor old actresses who had been employed to play Ali and Lisa – found their scenes being cut throughout rehearsal. I really felt for them because I felt I hadn't served them properly as a writer. But I understood precisely what Phyllida was saying, which was 'This has got to feel like a helter-skelter rollercoaster ride.' From the moment Sophie says the line 'I've got 24 hours to find out!', there should be no letting up of Sophie's and Donna's dilemmas. That's what the audience cares about.

Lisa Stokke, the original Sophie: The rehearsals were very emotional. Siobhán and I kept breaking down crying during the 'Slipping Through My Fingers' scene. We were emotional wrecks. I was far away from my family, and she was imagining her own daughter growing up. We all worked terribly hard, as you must. During rehearsals I think I gave it too much: I would go to rehearsal, come home and crawl into bed. But it paid off.

Siobhán McCarthy: Catherine put 'One Of Us', 'Slipping Through My Fingers' and 'The Winner Takes It All' almost back to back in the show – three very emotional numbers – and I said to Phyllida, 'If you do that, I'll be a snivelling wreck and the audience will be very bored; I can't sing three sad ballads one after the other.' But she knew better and she was right! I always had to hold off singing 'Slipping Through My Fingers' full out because I knew it would tip me over the edge, and you can't cry and sing at the same time. It was an incredibly poignant moment and I couldn't help thinking of my own daughter, Juliet, and the day when this might happen to me in real life. Soppy I know, but each time Lisa and I came to do it I knew if I didn't let the tears out before the opening night it would be a disaster waiting to happen, so we had a big blub during one of the rehearsals, which cleared the air – although it didn't stop the odd trickle coming down the cheek most nights.

Choreographer Anthony Van Laast with (top) his associate choreographer Nichola Treherne, and (bottom) Phyllida, Björn and musical supervisor Martin Koch. Vastly experienced across a range of dance disciplines, Anthony had recently finished work in Australia on *The Boy From Oz*, a kind of compilation show using the music of Peter Allen. He had been relieved when Judy told him that *MAMMA MIA!* was definitively not going to be another compilation musical.

Louise Plowright: The music rehearsals were tough! I suspect we had all thought at the outset, 'ABBA songs – that's a doddle, that'll be really easy.' You think you know all the tunes, but then you discover that the harmonies are unbelievably complex, with the high sopranos, low sopranos, altos, mezzos, basses and tenors all having their own little sections. I was lucky, I only had to sing my own personal harmonies as Tanya.

Benny and Björn paid a lot of attention to the detail. I remember Björn coming over to me at one point and saying, 'Louise, it's not "Chi-kah-tee-tar" it's "Chi-kee-tee-ta".' They listened critically and they wanted it to be right. I passed on that piece of advice to a few other Tanyas in my time, and always told them, 'Listen, I'm not being funny, this is something that Björn told me himself because I made the same mistake.'

Phyllida: With a musical you have to allow a lot of time for other people to do things. We had two rooms going almost all the time, sometimes three. There would be somebody having musical coaching, Nichola would be trying to set a dance number, and I would be upstairs working on 'The Name Of The Game'. There were moments when I would get slightly sulky, because Nichola would need the whole company for at least four hours and I'd be twiddling my thumbs or watching them or talking to Catherine. You did have to do a lot of sharing of the people.

Andrew Treagus: During rehearsals, everybody wants more time, especially once you have moved to the theatre, but the director is God and if the director says, 'No, I want to do this', it gets done, unless somebody can argue back and say, 'No, no that's not right.' As general manager, it's all about trying to keep the balance and make sure everybody is satisfied with their lot. If the sound team is saying, 'We must have two hours', you have to be thinking in the back of your mind whether actually one hour will do.

Phyllida: During the rehearsal process, I was learning a lot about the principal cast members, and how they responded to my direction. Siobhán McCarthy as Donna was quite untrained. She certainly felt that she had very little experience of speaking text on stage. She had done *Chess*, *Evita* and *Blood Brothers* but she'd not been in a play, so for her to do words or be asked to improvise was all completely new. During the workshop the year before I remember saying to her, 'Look, you're a natural.' She just listened to what was going on around her and responded to it, so I was able to tell her, 'You *are* an actress because you're listening.' She brought incredible charm, spontaneity and warmth to the role – and of course her voice. Whenever I listen to the original cast recording I always notice how her voice has this folky feel, the very thing that Benny and Björn wanted: a raw, folky sound, unsullied by musical theatre tricks. There was something fundamental about Siobhán being at the centre of that first production, her untutored style, her lack of artifice; there was something very *MAMMA MIA!* about that. She was just a person, a mum and someone who didn't know her own talent, who didn't really understand what her gifts were. She had absolutely no idea of her own charisma.

Above: Siobhán McCarthy brought, in Phyllida Lloyd's words, 'charm and spontaneity and warmth' to her interpretation of the songs.
Left: The *sitzprobe* (literally 'sitting rehearsal' in German), when the cast and the band meet for the first time and bring together what they have each been rehearsing separately up to this point – an exhilarating experience that still gives many of the participants goose bumps when they remember it, and is one of Benny's favourite moments.

Louise Plowright: Siobhán was a very light-hearted Irish girl. 'Look Louise,' she'd say, 'I'm going to take you down to the most fantastic shop, *great* shoes, great shoes.' She had a lovely big house in Wales; Jenny and I went and spent the weekend with her. Siobhán never stopped! She was leaping around, cooking, mixing things up and serving up these meals, while Jenny and I were half asleep in the corner, absolutely knackered. She seemed to have boundless energy.

Phyllida: Jenny Galloway is a very clever woman, witty, incredibly inventive. She was very experienced in the theatre, really spoke her mind, and was quite formidable. If anybody was going to be able to land those jokes and the physical comedy of the role as Rosie, it was Jenny. She's a clown, and you need a clown in that role. There was something about the contrast between her and Siobhán, and there was great chemistry between all three Dynamos.

Louise Plowright: Jenny is quite daunting, quite frightening. I'm the sort of person who always comes in to a room saying, 'Hello, everybody!', whereas Jenny will say, 'Oh, hi' quite seriously, which puts you in your place a little. But then you soon realise that she is such a softy. She's got the biggest heart. If you were ever upset about anything, she'd be there in a trice with her arm round you going, 'Look, sweetheart, you're going to be all right.'

Phyllida: Louise was gentle, warm, strong, with a lot of theatre and television experience. She was in her element on stage. Even though they were so different, they loved each other, those three women, and that was absolutely crucial. They worked brilliantly together. I think that Louise and Jenny looked after Siobhán, because Siobhán obviously had a vast task, belting out all those numbers every night, especially for someone who really lived the experience rather than just giving a performance. Siobhán was really laying herself out there every show.

Jenny Galloway: We three Dynamos very quickly became a unit. We had to really, whether we wanted to or not. With a new show, once the hype has died down, you've still got to find a way of getting up on stage eight times a week – and it would be a supreme feat to do that for a year if you couldn't stand your 'fellow friends'. There's only so much acting you can do…

Phyllida: I think it was quite hard for the actors who were playing the three dads. They didn't have the nuggets of gold at the centre of the show; they knew that they weren't the leads. Although everyone was busy mastering their own thing, and God knows the dads were having to learn to dance, I'm sure it was obvious to them that this was a girls' show and that they were in supporting roles. And that was not necessarily a place they would always have expected to have been.

Lisa Stokke as Sophie was this wide-eyed Bambi from Scandinavia via Liverpool and I think she and Andrew Langtree, who played Sky, thought that they'd died and gone to heaven. They couldn't believe how lucky they were. The senior generation, the forty-somethings, did quite a lot of parenting I think.

It's unusual to have a show in which the cast naturally polarised into two generations. And when you saw the forty-somethings having to get on down and learn the dance routine for 'Voulez-Vous' and how absolutely knackered they were at the end of the session, it was quite levelling.

Judy: I was very protective of Phyllida and Anthony and the rehearsal process – and because Björn was there I didn't allow the press in. Everyone thought I was crazy, because sometimes shows do invite journalists to watch rehearsals, but I didn't want anyone in there because they would not have understood the show from the rehearsals. Not that it was ground-breaking, but if someone had gone in and seen somebody wearing a tracksuit or jeans and singing an ABBA song, they wouldn't have understood the overall concept.

Phyllida: For Judy the economic stakes were absolutely massive, but she allowed us craftspeople to simply get on with our work. The production of the show was incredibly thorough, there was none of the West End commercial corner-cutting I

Lisa Stokke, who was cast as Sophie, had graduated from the Liverpool Institute of Performing Arts the summer before the show opened – and so was both playing her first professional role and making her West End debut. 'Lisa had a very kind of Juliet, young ingénue look to her,' remembers Judy Craymer.

had anticipated. During this working process, of course, there were creative areas that Judy was concerned about but the crux of the run-up to opening was that she had hired us because we were directors, choreographers, designers. We were there to direct the show and rehearse it, and so there wasn't that feeling, which I know certain musical production teams experience, of 'Oh God, the producers are in the theatre, here they come back from lunch. Shhh everyone, don't say a word!' It meant that the whole company felt like a family very quickly. Judy was the producer and she would shoulder the burdens of a producer. There was a sense underneath everything that outside the cloistered rehearsal room we were in there was a whole cavalcade going on that we were being protected from. Marketing, press, the theatre, the world press.

Catherine: I always felt very involved. Judy's enthusiasm for *MAMMA MIA!* is so huge and she wants everybody else to share her enthusiasm, so she carried me through this big build-up. There was always a feeling of countdown to this tremendously exciting thing that was about to happen.

Judy: We had finally raised the money for the show, so during this period I was concentrating on the opening, the marketing and contingency plans. You never know in a rehearsal process whether somebody will fall ill, or if there'll be an unexpected hold-up. On *MAMMA MIA!* we had a very specific gun being held to our head because Phyllida had to leave us on 7 April to go and direct *The Carmelites* at the ENO, and we wanted to open on 6 April… We'd been given two possible dates to open – the 6th and the 9th – and then we realised that the 6th was the 25th anniversary of ABBA winning the Eurovision Song Contest with 'Waterloo', so it seemed that it was meant to be. I am quite superstitious anyway, so we agreed to go with that date even though it fell just after Easter, which is not thought of as a great time to open a show because it's the school holidays and people are away.

After the rehearsal rooms, we began technical rehearsals in the Prince Edward Theatre. You walk into the auditorium and it looks like NASA because everyone's got their production desk, their computers, huge control consoles. Nobody has any idea of what's going on at all, but it is very exciting.

Andrew Treagus: We had now been involved for some time in selling the show, how the box office would work, and the relationship with the people handling the PR and the publicity. Judy and I decided to go with quite a young company called McCabes. I had said to Judy, 'I think you should go and meet Michael McCabe, because I think he's a young man who's really looking to make a name for himself.'

Judy: When I had my first job in the West End, working on *Cats*, I discovered how important the marketing of a musical was. I was aware of *Cats* becoming a phenomenon that was driven by the logo, the cat's eye, which became an icon. Phyllida had always said that the artwork should say, 'Yikes! *MAMMA MIA!*', which was a very difficult concept for them to illustrate. There was one idea about bicycles crashing, so we had an image of a girl on a bicycle. I kept showing it to people, and

'We loved the bride,' says Nancy Coyne, the US advertising director for *MAMMA MIA!*. 'She captures the joy of the show.'

they'd say, 'Um… suggests a French movie.' And then one day the art director came over for a meeting with Björn and me at the Covent Garden Hotel with a photo torn out from a fashion magazine spread on bridal wear, saying, 'What do you think of this?' – and we said, 'Now *that's* the kind of thing we want.' From that the oil painting of the bride evolved, which was much more joyful and exuberant than the photo we'd seen – she became a generic Sophie even though our Sophie might have blonde hair. And the white background for the image was so exciting: I'd always wanted something pale because *Phantom*, *Les Mis* and *Cats* were all black or dark.

John Kennedy: The Brit Awards took place in mid-February 1999, less than two months before the first night of *MAMMA MIA!*, and Pete Waterman had the idea – encouraged by Lucian Grainge at Polydor – to put together an ABBA medley for the show. Now the Brits has a television audience of ten million, and this was two months before the show was due to open, at a time when we were trying to take advance ticket sales. The medley was performed by Billie, B*witched, Steps and Cleopatra, and instantly they took ABBA's songs to a completely new generation. So whereas previously my analysis of the audience for *MAMMA MIA!* would have been 40-year-olds as couples or as groups on a night out, all of a sudden ABBA was being performed by 20-year-olds and being made known to teenagers and young kids, to such an extent that almost immediately afterwards people told me they'd be playing an ABBA record and their kids would ask them what was that group doing covering a Westlife song… This brought ABBA out more and more into people's minds, which was brilliant for the launch of the show and particularly for ticket sales.

An early rehearsal: with elements of Mark Thompson's set already in place, the three Dynamos work on their hen night 'Super Trouper' routine.

I started doing press half a year or so before the show opened, because we knew everyone in London assumed this was going to be The ABBA Story. And it was so difficult to get across the message, 'No it is not, this is something completely different.' Björn Ulvaeus

Anthony Van Laast: The night after the first preview, even though it had gone well – better than we had expected – the cast all came in with really long faces. They'd invited relatives and friends along who'd thought it was just terrible, and who couldn't understand how people were laughing at ABBA's music: was the show meant to be funny, was it not meant to be funny? Did we understand what we were doing? So Phyllida took the principals aside and I took the ensemble for a meeting. I told them, 'Do you know what, this is fantastic, it's all going to be great', yet somewhere in my heart I also felt the same insecurity. I buoyed them all up as you have to, but it's an exhausting process. During the rehearsal period, there were drafts of the script floating around the West End and odd pages had been taken completely out of context. The general vibe was that *MAMMA MIA!* was going to be risible. You knew all this was going on and whatever anyone says – and I'm as much to blame as anybody else – I think people love a huge failure more than they love a success. I'm sure everyone outside hoped the show would go down the drain. It's a wonderful feeling to prove the doubters wrong.

Andrew Treagus: I'm not great on the gossip around the West End – never have been. It's not something I particularly enjoy. There will always be rumours, and they nearly always come from theatre staff. They chatter to each other because they've seen a little bit of something or whatever. So I take it all with a pinch of salt.

Howard Harrison, lighting designer: There was a lot of negativity about the show, certainly in the West End. People were being rather bitchy about it and that inevitably has an effect on you. I think at that stage we thought that if we could run for six months in London that would be rather good.

Phyllida: After our first preview I think some of the team felt, 'This is going to be a huge hit'. I don't remember feeling that. I remember being delighted that people were jumping up and down at the end of the show, but thinking, 'Yes, but this still doesn't quite work' and being very, very focused on the problems.

Benny: When I'd seen the show in rehearsal without an audience, I couldn't say whether it was good or bad. The sound was good, the songs sounded good, but that was not the issue. Is this funny or is it not? Without an audience you don't know. That's why the previews are there. And when Sam was singing 'Knowing me, knowing you' and the audience went 'Ah ha', I thought, 'Yeah, right, they like this'. When you sit in a middle of an audience that likes something, you can feel that. So I felt that this show was going to be a good thing.

Catherine: I had a dream the night before the preview. I dreamt that the show opened, the cast came on and started singing, the audience got out of their seats and rushed down to the front, and Phyllida turned to me and said, 'They don't want the play, they only want the songs. Let's just do the songs, we won't bother with the play' and I left the theatre thinking, 'Yes, she's right.'

I told Phyllida about this dream and she thought it was very amusing. But there was a part of my mind wondering, 'How are the audience going to pay attention in the bits that aren't as much fun?', so thank goodness the audience on that night loved it! My brother and sister had come with their partners, and even Uncle Mark loved it and that meant a lot because Uncle Mark *hated* ABBA. He was practically the first one out of his seat at the end dancing along, which was thrilling.

Judy: Nothing on the creative side was a significant problem until we finally put the whole package together and realised the beginning was not working, which is what previews are there for. The commercial side of the show was in extremely good shape – we had an advance of two million pounds. However, we knew that there was something not quite right in the opening scene. But we also had a great team of people who knew that. I think some people would have simply said, 'Fine, if nobody in the audience has noticed…'

Above, from left: Rosie (Jenny Galloway), Donna (Siobhán McCarthy) and Tanya (Louise Plowright) relive their days as Donna and the Dynamos with an impromptu version of 'Dancing Queen', a moment in the show that for Catherine Johnson is about 'reminding Donna of her carefree teenage years, singing into a hairbrush in her bedroom'.
Left: Rosie and Bill (Nicolas Colicos) discover an unexpected attraction to each other in 'Take A Chance On Me'.

Catherine: It became clear that the beginning of the show was a problem. I'd thought that musicals had to begin with a big number, so my plan had been to open with 'I Have A Dream' and then go straight into a big dance number based around 'Summer Night City', all about the hustle and bustle of wedding activity, to set the scene and to introduce all the characters. But I could never make sense of it in my head; I could never see the scene properly. It always felt messy and unclear even though Anthony worked really, really hard on choreographing the dance moves. By the time we'd got to the previews in the Prince Edward it was a matter of 'Let's put an audience in front of it now' because by this time the whole number had been rehearsed out, and nobody was laughing at it any more. There had also been a piece in the *Evening Standard* along the lines of 'Is this the cheesiest idea in the world?' Someone had shown it to Judy, we'd been talking about it and we were feeling a bit depressed, thinking, 'This doesn't bode well. The show hasn't even opened and people are having a go at it.'

It was extraordinary because we'd go into the previews every night and have an audience who were loving the show, and then we would go to the Soho House club and sit around very, very gloomily and say, 'What are we going to do about the opening?' I'd think, 'Please don't make me go and rewrite the opening', and then I'd have to go back to the bloody hotel and rewrite it, a bit drunk probably, and go back in the next day to present a revamp for Phyllida to rehearse in the afternoon, along with whatever other notes she'd been given. It would go into the next available preview, and then everybody would go back to Soho House and say, 'What are we going do about the opening?' It felt like it would never be fixed.

Louise Plowright: To amuse us the cast's chef Drew would create these spoof lyrics, like changing 'Chiquitita' to 'Chicken Tikka and a nan bread' 'or 'Voulez-Vous' to 'Vol au vents, makey flakey pastry', but the first one was 'Pushing on a white wall and dragging on a chair, someone take pity' because we'd done so many versions of 'Summer Night City'.

Phyllida: Somehow the first twenty minutes of the show didn't work, and it wasn't until Donna sang 'Money, Money, Money' that the audience really knew where they were and felt comfortable; in fact it possibly wasn't even until she sang 'Mamma Mia'. The opening song, 'Summer Night City', was this big rock number with everyone jumping around, but there was something about the lyrics which I felt – and I'd had this conversation with Benny and Björn – was really unhelpful when we were trying to create life on a tiny island. 'Summer Night City' – you so *weren't* in a city. I was really exercised by the whole business of the beginning, as was Catherine. We were really tearing our hair out, so Benny and Björn said, 'Look, we'll write you something, what do you want?' and I said, 'Yes, that would be great, all our problems would be solved, but we can't do that, otherwise we might as well start from scratch and write a new show.' Then one weekend, we decided to try replacing the whole opening number with a kind of overture to avoid the problem with the lyric, to create through choreography an island in preparation for a wedding, in the middle of which you would get to know all the different characters. We had loads of props made especially for it and all these wedding presents that suddenly materialised.

Mark Thompson: There was a mime with people bringing presents and preparing the wedding breakfast. It was bonkers, completely confusing about what was happening. We had Donna arriving off a boat at one point with a load of shopping. I'd rushed off with my assistant Lucy to Liberty's and bought a stack of clothes for that night's preview; it was just crazy, because suddenly Donna wasn't just on the island, she was coming in from a shopping trip. Phyllida and I fell out – well, I refused to talk to her for a day – because she kept on adding more and more props and I remember Jane Slattery, the head of props, and Jonathan Allen,

Opposite: An example of how shows evolve during rehearsals and previews. Production designer Mark Thompson's team prepared one complete set of black outfits for the Dynamos' 'Super Trouper' routine, seen here, and one set of white outfits. But during previews, Mark decided the black costumes were not right – 'everybody said ABBA is more synonymous with white. Things are changing all day every day.'

Tanya (Louise Plowright) gives Pepper (Neal Wright), the taverna's barman, the run-around. It's obvious that something happened between them during the night of the hen and stag celebrations. While Pepper is eager to pursue the romance, Tanya is far from sure. 'Down, boy,' says Tanya. 'I'm old enough to be your mother.' As Pepper walks back to the bar he replies, 'Well, you can call me Oedipus...'

my set assistant, breaking our fingers wrapping these bloody presents at the back of the auditorium, thinking, 'These are not going to last. Same old thing, the number's not working, chuck in props.' We had hundreds of props.

Anthony Van Laast: My idea had been that while the islanders were having the wedding rehearsal all the main protagonists would arrive. It wasn't good but I kept on going, making it more and more elaborate choreographically with chairs flying around and people stepping over chairs, like *Seven Brides* meets *Cabaret*, tons of stuff going on. And then Phyllida would come and watch it and say, 'A bit too much dancing', so I'd cut some dancing. It still wasn't good. We were in previews without having solved the problem, and Phyllida was adamant it had to be got right.

Phyllida: Andrew Treagus, the general manager, said to me, 'OK, Phyllida, I just want to say I'm very impressed by the way you're all going right to the heart of this. You're leaving no stone unturned in your quest to make this into something excellent and extraordinary, but there comes a time on these big shows when we have to stop fiddling around and lock down the show so that the company know where they are and they can start playing the show.' I thought, 'Oh, the Headmaster has spoken. How am I going to get round this one?'

Andrew Treagus: I call it 'freezing' the show. And I always try to get the creative team and the director to freeze the show for at least two performances before the opening night so the company are playing the same show for at least those two performances before they're going to open to the critics and the public.

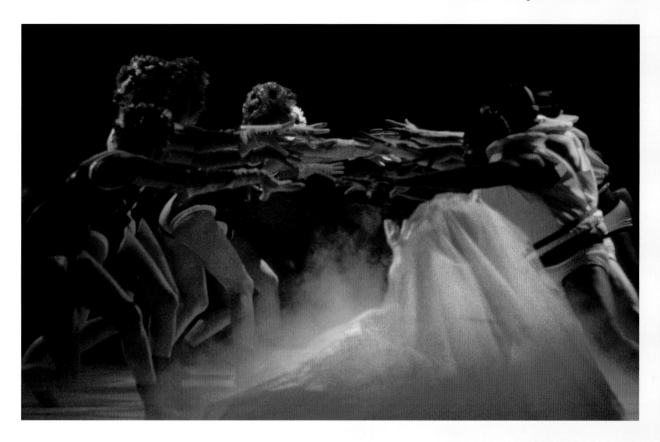

Phyllida: Andrew had said, 'Tomorrow you should make the last changes you're going to make', because we were only a few days before the opening, and I had gone away feeling slightly heavy-hearted, thinking, hoping, 'Something will come, something will come in the night...' The next day, I came in and there was a letter for me at the stage door. I had the letter in my hand and went up to a rather grotty room, which was the music director's room. Martin Koch was in there with Anthony van Laast and I was reading the letter. It had come from a relative of one of the cast members, and the gist of it was, 'Dear Miss Lloyd, I've been to see the show. I wouldn't be writing this letter if I didn't know who you were and hadn't seen your work in Opera North. I'm interested in the process you're going through and I can see you're in trouble. If you're already annoyed by my writing this, please tear up the letter now.' Of course I was rapidly turning the page. I couldn't wait to get to the next bit. 'You're trying to be something that you'll never be. You're trying to be a big, blowsy Broadway show and in fact this is an intimate, domestic story. You should be starting with the plot. Forget all the fandango, open with why we should be interested in this story. And so you should reverse such and such a scene.' What it boiled down to was that there were three scenes, A, B and C. If you reversed B and C, you didn't need A. It wasn't quite as simple as that, but that was the principle. I immediately knew that this person was right. I handed the letter to Anthony, who read it in total silence. He handed it to Martin who also read it. We looked at each other and Anthony said, 'Well, you know what you've got to do, then.'

Anthony Van Laast: Phyllida came in and said, 'I've got this letter here, and this person's got an idea about what we should do with the opening of the show. I don't really know, but it looks good.' She gave it to Martin and me to read and I

Anthony Van Laast devised the nightmare dance sequence for 'Under Attack', the number that opens Act II. Björn suggested including the song, and when Catherine Johnson read the lyrics, she found they were perfect for describing Sophie's tortured frame of mind before the audience sees her again: 'Under attack, I'm being taken. About to crack, defences breaking. Won't somebody please have a heart; come and rescue me now, 'ooo I'm falling apart.'

Opposite: Siobhán McCarthy had already created the roles of the Mistress in the original production of *Evita* and Svetlana in the stage version of *Chess*, but Donna was the first lead role she had created in the West End. In the early 1990s she had in fact recorded a couple of demos of ABBA numbers, including 'The Winner Takes It All', for Judy Craymer, while Judy was developing her ideas for *MAMMA MIA!*. Siobhán is married to Andrew Bruce, who was – with Bobby Aitken – responsible for the sound design of the show.

saw the suggestion that if we moved the third scene to the first scene and then the second scene stayed as the second scene then we wouldn't need 'Summer Night City'. I thought, 'Wow, this is brilliant.' It made so much sense. I told Phyllida, 'This is great, this is it. It's so easy, it's so easy. This is fifteen minutes' work, literally fifteen minutes' work. There's hardly even anything for Catherine to do.'

Phyllida: Catherine was out shopping and I radioed her in: 'Get your arse back here, I need to talk to you about this.' Judy was off ordering pineapple chunks for the first night party and was nowhere to be found. Benny and Björn were somewhere else. We went downstairs and found the entire company sitting in the stalls, looking slightly, 'Oh no, another note session, what are we doing this afternoon?' I said, 'Ladies and gentlemen, thank you so much for all the work you did at the weekend, especially those people who came in on Sunday. You've done such great work on that opening medley overture thing. It's cut! The show now begins with 'Honey, Honey', so we'll go from 'Honey, Honey' straight into the courtyard scene.' I could see the technical crew looking at me thinking, 'Are you insane? This isn't just a play. "Cut the opening scene?" This means the rerouting of a thousand radio mike journeys; everything will have to be completely reconfigured to make this happen.'

The company were already rather punch drunk, so they went back onto the stage like lambs to the slaughter to try the new order, but there were a few people watching who were slightly outside that first moment who immediately said, 'It's going to work.' We didn't have time to discuss it properly or ask permission, not that Judy would have wanted us to ask permission.

Catherine: I was in Marks & Spencer, shopping for knickers, when Phyllida rang. I'd just got into the store when my phone went. It was Phyllida and I remember thinking, 'I'm not going to get my knickers now', because she'd said, 'Can you come back to the theatre immediately?' When I arrived, Phyllida, in the same very good way she worked with actors, instead of saying to me, 'Right, we're doing this now', said, 'If this wasn't a musical, if you were writing this as play for the Bush Theatre, how would you start it?' And I said, 'Well, I'd cut to the chase, go straight into the diary scene…' and then Phyllida proceeded to tell me about the letter and that was it. We cut the chairs: all that remains of those chairs now is at the beginning of 'Take A Chance On Me' where we have a couple of bars of 'Summer Night City' and a bit of chair business. We went straight into the diary scene and I realised then that you don't have to start a musical with a big song and dance number. You can start a musical wherever you want to start a musical, because this is *MAMMA MIA!* and it is what it is. It isn't trying to be anything else. As soon as that was resolved, my work was done and I was able to go and get some new knickers.

Getting that opening right sums up so much for me about the *MAMMA MIA!* process. It's become a personal motto: 'The solution will come but it might not come until the last moment, as long as you can keep an open mind.' Phyllida Lloyd

Andrew Langtree as Sky with Lisa Stokke as Sophie. Both had been part of the first ever intake of students at the Liverpool Institute of Performing Arts, and shared a flat together in London, so they already knew each other very well; Andrew had already made his West End debut in the lead role of Nick in *Fame*. During rehearsals for *MAMMA MIA!* their duet of 'Just Like That', one of the very rare unreleased ABBA numbers, had to be jettisoned because it was holding up the flow of the story.

Lisa Stokke: Once 'Summer Night City' had been cut, it made quite a daunting opening for me, sitting there by myself on stage on opening night. I made the spotlight guys my allies for the whole run. I'd wave to them before the start of the show, because it was a lonely place to be and they felt like my only friends out there. On the day of the opening I was sitting on the set before the curtain came up, listening to the murmur of the audience and thought, 'OK, we'd better get this show on the road and do our best.' I think on that night I just had to trust in what I was doing, to switch to autopilot. If I'd dared to think about what that night meant I would have gone over the top on everything. If I had really got into the emotional side of it I would have lost the plot. So I just had to hold it together. I don't think I have ever concentrated so hard in all my life.

Benny: I did not really involve myself in the whats and wheres and hows of *MAMMA MIA!* but I think everybody had thought 'Summer Night City' was not really necessary. So it disappeared. And I think they did absolutely the right thing. It's this little trap: an American musical starts with a 'bang' – a big number and here we go! But *Kristina* doesn't start that way. It opens with a small number at the beginning. I think that's great, and it's the same with *MAMMA MIA!*. It just starts and there you are. Why not?

Björn: While 'Summer Night City' was opening the show, you could feel with the audience that they were slow to get into the story. Once they did they loved it, but this big production number was holding everything up. Cutting it was a drastic change, but when Phyllida told me it's what she was trying to do I didn't have to think too much about it. I think we could even have kept 'Summer Night City' in the show and it would still have been a success but maybe that little nip and tuck made it more attractive and more unusual.

Judy: It was 1 April, April Fool's Day, and we were opening on 6 April. I went down to the theatre at half past four or so and said to Martin Koch, 'So, Kochie, what's happening?' He said, 'Well, Phyllida had this letter from somebody who'd seen the show which had some suggestions and so she's taken them on board. She got Catherine in and Catherine's done some rewrites, so basically we've cut 'Summer Night City' and we're going straight to 'Honey, Honey'. I thought, 'This is an April Fool's joke. Oh yeah, very funny.' But it wasn't, and that was the greatest afternoon spent by the creative team in the theatre.

David Grindrod: From the first preview, and the cast will tell you this, the audience reaction was extraordinary. I was stunned. You could see the kids on stage thinking, 'Wow, this is something else.' The audience went wild and the phones started to ring. There were calls from Judy saying, 'Have you got any office space in the theatre because we need to set up extra phone rooms? The phones are going mad.'

Catherine: It was the audience who made *MAMMA MIA!* come to life. The sound of laughter is so seductive. I once said to Terry Johnson, the director who'd recommended me to Judy, that I'd seen somebody crying at my very first play, which he'd directed. And Terry said, 'You wait until they start laughing, that's when you get hooked.'

Andrew Treagus: What was very clear, from the very first preview, the very first time we actually let people in to see the show, and the theatre was full, was that the audience absolutely loved it. At that stage, we still had 'Summer Night City' at the start of the show. It was not right, it was clearly not right, but at the end the audience went crazy. I happened to be at the back of the stalls, by the sound desk. Björn was standing next to me and I famously said to him, 'You shouldn't expect this to happen every night, Björn…'

From left: synthesizer programmer Nick Gilpin, musical supervisor Martin Koch and sound designer Bobby Aitken.

Judy: The first-night party always falls to the producer. We would have weekly production meetings during rehearsals where Rodger Neate, the production manager, would always ask, as the last item on the agenda, 'And do we know yet where the party is?' and I would say, 'No, it's a secret.' Of course we were preparing for it to be at Mezzo's in Wardour Street. I had a budget of £40,000, which is pretty small when you've got six hundred people. It was very hands-on preparing for that party. Cameron Mackintosh was always the king of West End parties and I like to think that when we did our anniversary party in 2004 I had taken the crown on that – I always thought a good party was a fab thing to do. We also had Björn and Benny attending the first-night party so there was a lot of extra security and tension in the air. There was all the briefing of the security staff and the waiters going on, as well as making sure that the show itself was OK. The creative staff now always say, if I'm not around at rehearsals or at note sessions, 'Oh, Judy's at a pineapple chunk summit meeting.'

We had a very bad dress rehearsal which is a very good sign in theatre mythology. People were a little down. I had to be the headmistress and make sure everyone was feeling positive: it *will* be fine. I think that's when you find out what you're made of. Judy Craymer

Phyllida: My first-night pep talk would have been, 'Just do the show you've been performing. If you do any of the shows you've done in the last two weeks it will be absolutely fine', trying to calm them down, to get them to listen to each other. My approach was 'Look, don't panic' whereas Anthony and Nichola wanted lots of energy and real precision.

A lot of directors go and have dinner during the first night because they just can't bear to watch the show. My thing is that I have to watch, to witness it. This is completely solipsistic and insane because actually who cares whether I'm there or not, but I've always somehow felt that if I withdraw my energy from the building and go to the pub, something will go wrong, as if I'm Atlas and the

Sophie (Lisa Stokke) with her two
friends Lisa (left) and Ali, played by
Melissa Gibson and Eliza Lumley.
Lisa Stokke was already friends with
Eliza Lumley and implored Björn and
Martin Koch to consider her for the
part of Ali at auditions.

world might collapse if I'm not holding it up. So I was sitting, watching, and
probably scrabbling in my handbag for my notepad, thinking, 'Oh, for God's
sake, we've got to sort that out', which gives me something to focus on during
the performance, although I try and do it very discreetly because I don't want
to look like a critic. But it was a big hullabaloo. I remember people jumping up
when Benny and Björn came into the theatre. We saw them as part of the team,
so suddenly I was aware that they were obviously gods to certain people – which
of course they were slightly to us, but we'd become more blasé about it.

Benny: There was a suggestion that Björn and I should go up on stage and I said,
'I'm not going up on that stage if Catherine is not coming up with us.' There was
a little debate about this because they said, 'Well, they don't want to see Catherine,
they want to see you because you're a famous character, they know you.' I said,
'It doesn't have anything to do with that. If I'm a part of this show, Catherine is
definitely a part of it because she actually wrote the whole bloody thing. All we
did was write the songs twenty-five years ago. It's not fair, I'm not going up on
that stage if she's not coming' and it was not an empty threat.

Catherine: I didn't feel confident that we would get good reviews because I
thought the show was probably not something that was going to appeal to the
critics. However, in my mind, I felt that people might come and enjoy it for a
couple of months, so I'd been out and bought a nice dress. Then the night before
the opening I was at the hotel getting ready. My family was coming up for the

opening, and I think my kids were already up in London by then. Judy rang me really quite late, possibly even two in the morning and said, 'Benny is refusing to go on stage unless you go on stage. We're desperate for Benny and Björn to go up on stage because obviously we'll get the publicity, and that's where the photographs will be taken. We really want them on the stage and Benny wants you to be up on stage with them.' I said, 'I can't, I don't want to,' so Judy said, 'OK, it's totally up to you.' I said, 'I'll talk to them, and tell them myself.'

The following morning Benny rang me. He is probably the most manipulative man I've ever met, because he just said, 'Sorry.' I was quite nervous, because I didn't know Benny as well as Björn, and said, 'But Benny, I really can't go on stage, that's not what I do, I really don't want to go on stage.' He said, 'Yes, you do, you know you do' and I could hear myself saying, 'OK then, Benny.' So what was going to be for me a rather nice, fun, relaxing night turned into the torment of knowing that the closer the show got to the end the sooner I was going to have to go up on stage and that really was horrid. My stomach was churning, I was *so* nervous, and I had these horrible pinchy shoes on which I had to take off because I couldn't walk in them. In the end I went up on stage barefoot. It was awesome. I did feel very, very nervous and felt like I was going to throw up, and my biggest fear was that everybody was going to wonder 'Who the hell is that with Benny and Björn?', which I am sure they did. I've had to do it since, and when you're standing in the wings, that's when you become aware, much more so than when you're actually in the audience, of the noise they are making and the heat and excitement they are giving off.

The three dads. From left: Nicolas Colicos as Bill, Hilton McRae as Sam and Paul Clarkson as 'Harry the headbanger'. As Donna says in the show, 'Ye Gods, why have they all turned up now? It's like some horrible trick of Fate.' 'It is very Greek,' observes Rosie.
Overleaf: The original Stockholm cast, led by Gunilla Backman as Donna, sing 'Money, Money, Money'.

Björn, Catherine and Benny take a curtain call at the end of the first night of *MAMMA MIA!*. Catherine had been nervous about the prospect of joining them on stage – her greatest fear was that everybody would think 'Who the hell is that?' – but Benny persuaded her that she should. It has become a tradition for them to appear on stage at openings whenever all three are attending.

Phyllida: Benny and Björn were outwardly very ebullient. Benny was quite elder statesman-like, rather composed and wry. They were really enjoying it actually. They loved British theatre and they liked the whole collaborative thing. They were great collaborators. I think they liked the fact there was no führer at the top of the whole thing, beyond whom they couldn't get, or access to whom they couldn't achieve.

Judy: I think we all had our parents in during the previews and they were our barometers. Before the first night my parents came to a Saturday matinée preview. They were coming to the opening as well, but my father was very keen to check up on everything. He wasn't that well and he'd wanted to come to an evening show, but I didn't want the worry of him travelling on the tube late at night, so they watched a Saturday matinée and I came out of the show to see them in the foyer of the Prince Edward Theatre. My mother literally had tears in her eyes. They were just bowled over, they said they had never seen anything like it. It was amazing to hear that because I'd worked on lots of shows and they had never been so moved…

On the opening night, there had to be a Swedish press conference with Benny and Björn immediately after the show but just before the party, which felt to me as though someone was throwing boulders in my way just to make life more complex. After the show I got changed for the party and met up with Siobhán and Louise Plowright and Jenny Galloway, and we all went off while Björn and Benny stayed behind and did their press conference. We didn't expect the size of crowd that turned up outside the theatre, because our press people had said, 'It's the day after Easter Monday, it's a quiet day.' We had put out barriers in the streets, but it was jam-packed with people expecting to see Björn and Benny. When they did come out it was through the front of the Prince Edward Theatre. As they got into their cars, the fans leapt onto the cars and ran alongside them down the street, so there were police running down Old Compton Street like presidential outriders.

At the party I never moved from one spot at Mezzo's. The party was on two floors and I never even managed to get downstairs. As the host, you're always having to deal with tricky situations, because although everyone can bring one guest, nobody can bring more, and somebody will always come along and say, 'Can I bring in these twelve members of my family who have flown in from New Zealand?' I think it may be a very female thing to be worried about the arrangements, wanting everything to be OK, practically polishing the glasses and uncorking the wine, rather than saying, 'Get someone else to sort that out, let's go and schmooze with the right people.' It all passed in something of a haze. And I was looking forward to getting to two in the morning and having a chance finally to sit down, have a quiet drink and talk about the evening. It had been very special. This was our first opening and we didn't know if there would be any more.

Ladies and gentlemen: People of a nervous disposition should be aware that silver platform boots and white Spandex are featured in this performance.

The *MAMMA MIA!* pre-show announcement

Siobhán McCarthy as Donna: left, with Sophie (Lisa Stokke), preparing for her wedding day; below left, with Harry (Paul Clarkson), reminiscing about their romance in Paris in 'Our Last Summer'; and below, with Pepper (Neal Wright). For Catherine Johnson, the song that Donna sings to Sophie, 'Slipping Through My Fingers', is 'a fantastic song for a parent to sing to a child', and one that she – and audiences worldwide – find particularly moving. 'When we went into previews it used to make me cry every single night, missing the kids, being away from home, thinking about them. The worst night was when our guinea pig died. I was sitting next to the assistant director and she squeezed my hand thinking I was crying about my daughter, but I was actually crying about poor old Spike.'
Overleaf: The score for 'Mamma Mia'.

If I go to see the show I still find myself singing the songs. You can't get that ABBA music out of your head. It is amazing. I never get tired of it at all.

Martin Koch

Martin Koch, musical supervisor: Very early on I had a conversation with Björn and said I thought the only way to do the show properly was to absolutely *be* ABBA and have a proper transcription of each song. And the only way to do that was to be able to break it down from the original multi-track recordings. I fully expected him to say, 'No way,' but amazingly he said, 'OK, we'll do that.'

Björn: This was a very nice experiment. We asked our friend Anders Neglin, who is a composer, producer and bandleader, to help. Anders sat down in Stockholm for a fortnight or so with all the multi-track tapes – sometimes eight tracks, sometimes sixteen, twenty-four, thirty-two – writing down what was played on each track. It was very interesting because a few things came up that we hadn't remembered. And we were able to get the genuine ABBA sound through that process. I knew from experience that when other arrangers had taken on ABBA songs, it never sounded like the real thing because there are subtle details inside the song that are important but you never hear.

Martin Koch: As Benny and Björn had never created any notation for their songs, Anders Neglin took on the task of notating the instruments on each number exactly the way they had been played twenty-odd years earlier, as well as all the vocal arrangements. So we had ABBA on paper, as well as the original multi-tracks, transferred onto another format so that we could listen to each individual track on each song. And what we discovered was that they had used every trick in the book, everything that was technically possible at the time – speeding tapes up, playing things backwards. Michael Tretow, their engineer, was obviously a huge part of that, a very clever man.

Nick Gilpin, synthesizer programmer: It was fascinating being able to dissect the recordings and look at how the songs were constructed. Benny has a lot of classical influences in his music. Rachmaninov was one composer who sprang to mind whenever we listened to 'Dancing Queen', but there's also a lovely Bach fugue figure at the end of 'Lay All Your Love On Me'. And a harpsichord in 'Money, Money, Money'. You can't really hear it in the mix but it's there. And we also discovered ABBA's singing drummer. If you isolate the drum sound you can hear him singing along to the music…

Benny: We had told Martin, 'This is the sound we want to recreate.' Of course, there's no way you can recreate exactly what the song sounds like on the record, partly because they are being performed in different keys, with different artists performing the songs, and in the show you might have a guy singing a song originally written for a woman. But they did a great job. All the harmonies were exactly where they should be. There's a lot of choir work on the ABBA records and it was all in there.

Phyllida: There was a huge amount of work going on to disentangle the original songs, a mountain of spaghetti to be unravelled.

Martin Koch: Björn and I met to discuss the number of musicians we could use. We had to have a rhythm section, that was a given – a drummer and bass player. Then we needed additional percussion and two guitars. At one point we thought we might include a saxophone in the band but in the end we decided against that. And it seemed obvious to have a Benny-style keyboard that sits at the heart of the band. That is mainly piano, and is played by the music director. The rest of it we decided to spread out over three keyboards, which is where Nick did all the programming.

Nick Gilpin: I remember waking up one night thinking, 'If there are four keyboard players and there are twenty-three songs, I haven't really got enough time to do this.' I got up and started work there and then, and didn't really stop for the next six weeks.

Martin Koch: I would be in the rehearsal room and suddenly things would be changed in the way the show was being put together. I'd go back into my little room to alter all the arrangements. For the first time internet technology made life much easier. We had copyists based in south London: I could e-mail the changes over to them, they would get it all neatly set up and e-mail it back for me to print out. So within a few hours we could have the changes in place.

Benny: We worked hard to achieve the sound that we wanted for each song. But we were also prepared to allow some changes. We felt that 'The Winner Takes It All' should have more of a ballad feel. The original recording has a particular tempo. We were talking about this and I said, 'That's fine, you can take it out. It is a ballad, anyway.' That was probably the biggest change from any of the recordings.

Martin Koch: Most of the work had to be done on trust because we could only demonstrate it once the band was in place. It wasn't possible to do that until what is called the *sitzprobe*, the day when the full band and cast get to perform together for the first time. That was a very scary day because it was also the first time Benny and Björn were going to hear it and we had no idea what they were going to think. Fortunately they loved it.

Benny: For me the *sitzprobe* is the moment, apart from the opening night, which is the most joyful. I think it's the same for the band and for the company because that's when they meet for the first time and say, 'OK, let's see what this is going to be like.' It is always very uplifting. The cast have been singing along to a piano for weeks and weeks and the band has been rehearsing separately. Putting it all together is fun for everyone.

Martin Koch: We built vocal sound booths below the stage. I suspect very few people in the audience are even aware that they exist, but the ensemble spend more time in those booths behind the scenes than they

do on stage. Having proper sound booths that are acoustically treated and where the singers can use headphones means we can create what is effectively a studio set-up, which is absolutely crucial for the degree of vocal sophistication these songs require.

Phyllida: Initially I had quite a lot of difficulty dealing with the business of vocal choirs suddenly erupting in the middle of musical numbers – although it was wonderful that the company were singing live even when they weren't on stage. The whole of the second half, apart from 'Does Your Mother Know' and 'Under Attack', is a series of ballads, and yet the singers were working their bollocks off in the vocal booths creating the musical landscapes. I remember that Benny and I went through a big 'Let's take all the big stuff out from under 'The Winner Takes It All' and allow it just to be Donna' phase. Martin Koch and everyone else realised that was absolutely insane and that you needed that great epic sound to get the sense of lift-off. Luckily, we all listened to each other and the best idea prevailed. You couldn't take away all that intricate texture from the songs and expect them still to work.

Martin Koch: There was constant change up to and including the preview period. We had originally taken the 'ah ha's out of 'Knowing Me, Knowing You', and in the previews the audience sang them, which was hysterical, so we thought we'd better put them back in. We had initially removed a lot of backing vocals, many of which went back in, because the songs simply sounded incomplete. Half of the sound of ABBA was the vocals. And finally just before opening night, when 'Summer Night City' was dropped, I created an overture to get the audience in the mood and to let them know 'You're going to hear all these lovely songs.'

Nick Gilpin: It speaks volumes about the music itself that from the very first note being played at rehearsals there were smiles all round. Around the world every single band we have worked with has shown the same enthusiasm for the music. There are too many shows where the musicians are thinking to themselves, 'I'll play the notes, go to the pub and that's it.' But on *MAMMA MIA!*, they all love playing the ABBA songs.

CROSS THE STREAM

Opposite: the London cast of 2001 perform the Greek dance movements of 'Money, Money, Money', a number that Catherine Johnson always knew was going to be part of the show. 'The words say it all: "I work all night, I work all day to pay the bills I have to pay." Straight away the audience knows who Donna is – a single parent skivvying away, not a gold-digger; somebody whose feet are on the ground but who has occasional fantasies that life might be better if she didn't have to work so hard. I was always moaning about how much I had to work, and when Donna says, "I need a break, I need a holiday," it's all me in there. During the number there is a contrast between the islanders, who are not well-off, and the guests, who offer a glimpse of the rich man's world, with Tanya's gold jewellery and Chanel watches.'

Catherine: The morning after the first night I went back to Bristol and back to work on another project. Everything had been boiling up towards the opening, which was very exciting, but once it was over my thinking was, '*MAMMA MIA!* is all over for me now. It's been terrific but now I need to think about how I'm going to pay the mortgage for the next year or so. The next big occasion will be closing night.' Just as well I didn't get my frock ready – I don't think I should fit into it now.

Judy: After the opening night party, I'd gone back to the Covent Garden Hotel where a lot of people, including me, were staying. We'd arranged for a late bar, and we stayed up until five or six in the morning. Even after that I hadn't been able to sleep properly, wanting to know what the papers said. As soon as I woke up I was on to our press agent, Peter Thompson, and found out that the review from Michael Coveney in the *Daily Mail* was good, that Charlie Spencer had given it a fabulous review in the *Daily Telegraph*. Of all the critics only Nicholas de Jongh from the *Evening Standard* had hated it, so I felt very relieved. And then the day after the opening the box office sold a quarter of a million pounds' worth of tickets.

If, before we opened, anyone had said that this show would be running for so many years in so many cities, nobody would have believed it. Sometimes shows work and sometimes they don't. There's no way to tell. Benny Andersson

Judy: From very early on we had been having a great reaction from the audiences. We began to find that people wouldn't go home even after the final curtain call. Siobhán McCarthy told me that when she and the rest of the cast got back to their dressing rooms to change, they could hear them chanting over the tannoy. They would be halfway out of the stage door and the audience would still be in the auditorium asking for more. So we created an announcement in the style of the show: 'Ladies and Gentlemen, the Dynamos have left the building.' And it worked. We'd hear a cheer from the audience, or a kind of sigh, and off they tottered into the night.

Phyllida: When the show first opened in London and a lot of theatre-mad *Time Out* and *Guardian* readers were coming to see it, you could feel the audience thinking, while Rosie, for example, was trying to calm Donna down, 'Now, she's in an ABBA musical, she can *only* sing an ABBA song. What song's going to fit this moment?' And when Rosie broke into 'Chiquitita, tell me what's wrong' it would bring the house down. I loved those moments. The cast knew that the

Let the word go forth: supporting the snowball effect of audience recommendations, the marketing message of *MAMMA MIA!* has been picked out in lights above Oxford Street, lifted the spirits of jaded commuters at Piccadilly Circus tube station and toured the USA by truck.

audience knew that the whole piece was in some way a fiction, a device. The relationship between the words and the songs had to be delicately finessed. At certain times, you want to close the gap completely and make the audience believe that the song that is being performed was absolutely written for that moment. But on the whole I think it works best where the choice of song raises a smile, because you're thinking, 'Oh, how ridiculous, they're using that song' or 'Ah, that's clever.' And then there's a whole other world in which people don't know the original ABBA lyrics and just approach *MAMMA MIA!* as a new musical.

Benny: People often ask me, 'How does it feel watching *MAMMA MIA!*, knowing that you are responsible for this, that you wrote this?' I always answer, 'It's not really me.' If I see the show I don't feel, 'I wrote this song or that piece of music.' It's watching the artists perform, seeing the way they deliver the material, that gives me an emotional response. I can be quite detached from the fact that I was jointly responsible for all this music existing.

Judy: A week after we opened we had a dinner for the whole creative team. It was really just a jolly, a celebration of what we had achieved. But we were also slightly distraught that we were no longer living in each other's pockets as we had been for the previous few months. Everyone had become very close during the rehearsals and the build-up to the opening. So we sat there wondering, 'What are we going to do every day, now that we're not going to be sitting round poring over our notes with a few glasses of wine?'

But it wasn't long before I started getting calls from the States. I remember meeting one experienced producer who asked me if I had my associate directors and associate choreographers in place to roll the show out internationally. I looked at him aghast, thinking, 'No... Associate whats?' And then, funnily enough, we ended up putting the show out across the world quicker than anyone else had ever done.

It was probably in May or June, a couple of months after the first night, that we were contacted by David Mirvish and Brian Sewell of Mirvish Productions in Toronto, asking what our plans were and wanting to meet. I talked to Andrew Treagus and we decided to contact Nina Lannan from New York to advise us as a general manager: Nina had worked on *Chess*, and had been recommended by Robert Fox. Off we went to Toronto with John Kennedy. Out of that emerged the plan to do twenty-six weeks in Toronto, and then take the show to the States on tour. We talked to Björn and Benny, raised the money and off we went. That was the beginning of the journey.

Phyllida: When we started talking about the possibility of a future life for the show, and even though Judy was being wooed by Broadway, the suggestion was that it might be a good idea not to be seduced by any offer to go direct to Broadway, but to send us all to Canada and to see how *MAMMA MIA!* might work in a kind of interim world, a world that was in North America but had a little toe in Europe. It was a brilliant tactical move.

Benny: If you have success in the West End it's almost axiomatic that you should have a try on Broadway. However, because of the experience Björn and I had had with *Chess*, taking it onto Broadway cold, we were convinced that we should not do that again, but that we should try the show out somewhere else first. Toronto proved to be a very nice choice. For some odd reason the people in Toronto knew about *Chess*, which was flattering. I think there had been an official charity event with *Chess* there years before and people had remembered that. Nobody else remembered *Chess*, but they did in Toronto.

Nancy Coyne, US advertising director: I had worked with Benny and Björn on *Chess*, and I knew what they had gone through emotionally with that show. Broadway can be very very rough on newcomers, and everything had conspired against them. So not surprisingly they were a little gun-shy of Broadway, and I guess part of me was rooting for them.

Andrew Treagus: At that stage we were very circumspect about Broadway because we didn't feel that America knew ABBA at all. In fact, I think there's still a certain truth in that. I knew that some other shows had made their way to Broadway by going into other parts of America on tour. The extraordinary thing that opening in Toronto provided was not only to give us the opportunity of staying there for a much longer time and therefore putting out a brand new company for the tour, but it solidified everybody's faith in going to Broadway, almost immediately.

Any doubts about the appeal of *MAMMA MIA!* and the songs of ABBA to a North American audience were removed once the Toronto production opened, giving the production team the opportunity to send the show out on the road around America. Here Gabrielle Jones (Rosie), Dee Hoty (Donna) and Mary Ellen Mahoney (Tanya) perform the Dynamos' 'Dancing Queen' routine on US Tour One in 2001.

There were always questions about the strength and depth of ABBA's audience in North America. In fact, people knew the music even if they couldn't name the songs. ABBA have been so pervasive in Western culture.

Adrian Bryan-Brown

John Kennedy: The first stop was Toronto, so I went out there with Judy and Andrew Treagus. I thought I could help with the deal *and* keep an eye on my investment. Toronto is relatively close to New York so people could come up from there to see the show and we'd all get an idea of how a New York audience might react. By this time I was feeling pretty confident about the show, as I was about to get my money back from the investment in the UK. We met the Mirvishes, who are the aristocrats of the Canadian theatre world. They had a subscription system, whereby they had a mailing list and would send mailouts to everyone on the list telling them that over the next twelve months they'd be putting on six productions in Toronto, and their supporters would buy into all six. They clearly thought *MAMMA MIA!* would form an attractive part of their next package. Judy, Andrew and I went out to dinner that night; I was trying to get an idea of how this could work because it seemed to me that it could be quite expensive for the Mirvishes to put the show on. Judy looked at me as if I was

Overleaf: Louise Plowright and Siobhán McCarthy, as Tanya and Donna, sing 'Super Trouper' in the original London show. There are twenty-four different elements to Donna's Super Trouper costume: main fabric; sleeve and leg frills (specialist-pleated); thin lycra to edge sleeve and leg frills; silver piping; diamante strip; eyelets; heavyweight zip; belt beads (from Australia); belt, backing and lining; perspex buckle (custom-made); shoulder pads; lining; interlining to support fronts; sheer flesh soufflé for front panel; silver cord elastic for facing; star-shaped diamante stones (large); star-shaped diamante stones (small); triangular iridescent stones; round iridescent stones; lozenge-shaped glass stones; star-shaped earrings; silver boots; bra; diamante hair grips.

Above: The dads from the original North American cast, left to right: David Mucci (Bill), Gary P Lynch (Sam) and Lee MacDougall (Harry). Opposite: Louise Pitre was already a big name on the Toronto theatre scene when she took on the role of Donna.

mad and said, 'No, no, no, they don't put it on, we put it on.' The plan was, we would sit in Toronto for six weeks, get some income which would help us earn some money back and then take the show on a tour of the US. My heart sank. I was just about to recoup my money in the UK, and I suddenly realised that the money I was getting back from there would go straight into Canada. I was now playing at two roulette wheels.

Phyllida: Before going over to Toronto I was very wary of the idea we might have created A Product, which we could now simply manufacture. I don't know whether I had thought this through consciously, but my instinct was very strongly that we should try to reorientate the show for a Canadian audience. It seemed so clear to me that the audiences were gaining most of their pleasure from the fact that they were seeing themselves on stage, and therefore *MAMMA MIA!* in Toronto had to be a Canadian musical. If we went to Toronto and recreated it with an Irish Donna and her two English Dynamos, we were going to kill it. And if that meant changing the jokes or making adjustments to the text to make it sit more easily in the mouths of Canadian actors then we should do that.

We worked really hard on the Toronto production. I don't think we were conscious, or I wasn't, of how close we were to New York and how we were being watched in minute detail by the whole Broadway community. Phyllida Lloyd

Catherine: We've always made a point of trying to introduce slang, dialect, little place references, anything that will enable an audience to feel this is our *MAMMA MIA!* In Toronto you're not watching the London *MAMMA MIA!* and in Japan you're not watching the Dutch *MAMMA MIA!*. They are all very site-specific.

The characters remain the same characters; they just come from different places. So the actors will have worked out where Donna hails from, and where she met the Dynamos. They might say, 'Well, the Dynamos are from Detroit and they could have been Diana Ross and the Supremes if they hadn't been white.' There are plenty of immovables in the text: when the story started, twenty-one years earlier, Donna and her two friends were working in a club on the mainland, she met Sam, she had this passionate affair. But the cast have to work out how they got there. Sam knows he's an architect, but who was he, how old is he, what's he been doing, why is he an architect on the Greek mainland? So I think it's great fun for them – that sounds slightly patronising, I think it's really bloody useful for an actor to know exactly who they are, and what they had for breakfast, before they come on and we see them.

David Grindrod: I took a phone call from Judy, who said, 'We want to put *MAMMA MIA!* on in Canada. Would you consider being our casting consultant? You can have five minutes to think about it and ring me back' – well, I couldn't say no. So I flew over to Toronto with Martin Koch and Nichola Treherne.

We were the missionaries dispatched to convert the Canadians to the cult of *MAMMA MIA!*, and to start putting a company together. We were given a free rein, and I think that's what has given the show its life. Phyllida didn't want another 5' 10" blonde playing Tanya or another four-foot-something actress playing Rosie. What I was looking for – and this does sound a little corny – was whether the actors had what we call 'the *MAMMA MIA!* Spirit'. I can't define it, but I know what it is as soon as an actor comes into the audition room. 'You can be in my party, I understand you. You're a bit wacky, you're a bit mad, you're not conventionally pretty or handsome.' We also try not to take the process too seriously, we have a bit of a laugh. In Toronto I was concerned that people should not see us as these British ogres trying to take over their turf. I wanted it to be light-hearted, so that even if someone didn't get a role, they would go away with a good feeling about the show.

We didn't want to hire in 'stars'. Phyllida and Judy wanted people who were good in their roles. We felt that if we put in stars it would throw a dynamic of the show, unbalance it somehow. I think the show itself has become the star.

David Grindrod

Phyllida: We tried to behave as if the show had never been done before. We didn't talk about how we'd done it in London or say, 'This is what we do, this is what we think is funny.' Of course we wanted to build on the massive amount of work we'd done, particularly Anthony's choreography, because we knew those elements worked. But in the auditions we were painstaking in our attempts not to measure the actors against the existing template. A friend of mine, an opera director called Francesca Zambello, rang me up one day and told me, 'I've met this woman called Louise Pitre. I can't use her for the productions I'm working on. She's not right for me, but she's absolutely right for Donna.' When Louise walked into the audition and sang 'The Winner Takes It All', it was amazing, like hearing her make up the song as she went along. And she had the most astonishing voice.

Louise Pitre, the first North American Donna: Because Francesca Zambello had mentioned my name to Phyllida, almost from the start there was a special little connection. I was asked back twice, and both times I sang 'The Winner Takes It All'. The second time I went back there were all these women my age in the waiting room, and I thought, 'Oh my God.' But Phyllida came out and called me in by myself. She said, 'Sit down. We want you to be our Donna.' I had never been told I had got a part there and then in an audition room. I could not believe it. I actually got up off my chair, hopped and skipped around the room. And I screamed. And then I sat back down and pretended I was smoking a cigarette. And they said, 'The reason we called you today was we wanted to meet your potential Dynamos.' We spent an hour and a half doing this scene with all these women, but I knew I had the job!

Phyllida: There was a great moment at the *sitzprobe*, this exciting point when the cast, after rehearsing with a piano accompanist, finally get to perform with the band. Benny had flown over for the occasion. There had always been this insistence about having to sing 'The Winner Takes It All' on the beat, because the vocal backing choir was coming in on the beat. But when Benny heard Louise sing I remember him being very moved and saying, 'Tell her she can sing it how she likes, forget about having to hit the beat', because he heard this kind of Piaf quality in her voice.

Louise Pitre: My most beautiful moment was when Benny came over for the first time, for the *sitzprobe*. And he told me that the way I had sung 'The Winner Takes It All' was the way he had always imagined it. Because he had written it as a *chanson*. I am French-Canadian, and to me that melody always sounded like a Piaf song.

    At the end of this *sitzprobe* Benny was sitting at the back and of course the band were incredibly nervous. During the finale Benny went up to stand next to one of the keyboard players and started playing one hand of the part, so for the ending the keyboard player told him, 'OK mate, you can take the whole thing.' Benny sat down and went straight into this piece of mad keyboard rock insanity. The whole cast just stopped singing and starting screaming. It was a fantastic moment of festivity.

Phyllida: Once again, as we had been with Jenny Galloway, we were blessed by finding a brilliant clown for the Toronto production: Mary Ellen Mahoney, who played Tanya. Mary Ellen was like something from a real vaudeville act, like Lucille Ball. So we gave her and the other Dynamos the same suitcase I had given

Above: Tina Maddigan as Sophie and Adam Brazier as Sky from the original North American cast. Below: The Royal Alexandra Theatre, Toronto, often described as 'an Edwardian jewel-box'. The brief to the architect, John McIntosh Lyle, from the leader of the theatre's founders was concise: 'Build me the finest theatre on the continent'.

The Toronto cast in 'Under Attack'. Louise Pitre remembers the opening night at the Royal Alexandra Theatre as 'magical, deliriously wonderful. By the time we were singing 'Waterloo', it was difficult not to jump out of your skin'.

Jenny, Siobhán and Louise in London, and instead of telling them what those three had come up with, I let them take the props and improvise from scratch. And, of course, they came up with all kinds of good things that then got integrated into the show, not only in Toronto, but were inserted back into the London production.

We were in the Royal Alexandra Theatre, a beautiful theatre, which was much more intimate than London. So there were aspects of the show in terms of its intimacy and domestic detail that we were really able to develop and exploit. And we had an audience that culturally seemed to really get it. They knew the songs, although I don't think they knew them as well as we did in the UK, and the Canadian sense of humour might have been a little more akin to ours than it is in the States. It was a good thing that Judy had not succumbed to the overtures from New York. We'd been allowed to develop the show somewhere slightly less exposed.

There were a couple of Americans on the stage management side in Toronto. Wondering if we were involved in a potential culture clash with some of the team being American and others being Canadian, I asked one of the Americans, 'So what does Canada mean to you?' There was a pause and he said, 'I don't really ever think about it' and I remember thinking, 'OK, right...' We also had an American woman playing keyboards in the band. She told me that when she was a child at school, the map of North America had the border clearly marked and all the States filled in in great detail. North of the line it was just white, there were no towns or cities marked, so when she was 19 and flew to Toronto for a university interview she said she nearly died at the realisation that there were buildings and skyscrapers there.

Toronto was an amazing rehearsal period. It was absolutely joyous and brilliant and brought tears to my eyes many, many times. It really felt like we were on the crest of a wave. Anthony Van Laast

Catherine: The box office had been very strong during the London previews, but after the opening it went bananas and recouped very quickly, which was the first indication of how well it was doing. I had always promised the children I'd take them to America whenever I earned some decent money and we went over on a trip to New York the August after the opening. So I must have very quickly decided that I was now able to go to America and not have to put the money aside for a rainy day. That was the start of me stopping thinking of *MAMMA MIA!* as a job that I'd now finished, and the first glimmer of a realisation that this was going to be a job for life.

Later in the year I went over to Toronto and continued the process I had worked on in London, although obviously with much more confidence now that the show was up and running. I think we did feel that the script was quite British and that it would help if we made it sound comfortable in a North American tone. I would work through the lines with the actresses and actors so that we could adjust anything that sounded incredibly English. The cast weren't as blatant as declaring, 'I could never say that line, darling.' They would simply suggest, 'We don't say "I mustn't do that", it's "I can't do that".' And they gave us little idioms as well; I love language and slang. 'Pepper my snapper' came out of Toronto, that was suggested to me by Mary Ellen Mahoney (the actress playing Tanya)

Keith Kemps as Bill and Corrine Koslo as Rosie from the 2003 Toronto cast take a chance on each other. 'It's a fun number,' says Catherine Johnson. 'Rosie's character came totally out of 'Take A Chance On Me'; it's all about chatting somebody up. I like the bits where I divvied up the lines so that Rosie sings "We can go dancing" and Bill is like, "Well we can go walking".'

and it got such a laugh, it's now in every single production. We didn't know what a snapper was. We knew it was a fish, but we didn't know what it was a euphemism for in North America. Boy, did that one go down well.

Anthony Van Laast: We were able to make a number of improvements during the Toronto rehearsals. I had choreographed 'Money, Money, Money' during the first week of rehearsals in London, before Phyllida had arrived from Paris, and it had stayed in for the first year of the London production, but as soon as we went to Canada I cut it as quickly as possible because although it had been apparent it was absolutely the wrong number, we hadn't had time to change it for London. That's an interesting example of what happens if you start something without the director there to tell you when you are going badly off course. I felt if I was going to be out in Toronto I wanted to get the show right. I went through the whole show, and there was hardly anything left untouched. By the end the show was really finding its shape. And then we added 'Waterloo' as well.

Catherine: 'Waterloo' went into the show due to popular demand, and after an incredible amount of debate. It was the one song that didn't earn its place in the show by being story-driven. The megamix was a device being used a lot at the time, so we had decided we were going to have one too. But because 'Waterloo' wasn't in *MAMMA MIA!* and because we were still being slightly purist about this being 'the smash hit musical based on the songs of ABBA' rather than The ABBA Musical, we felt we should only megamix the songs that were in the show. So we did 'Mamma Mia' first and then the girls would come on dressed in their 'Super Trouper' costumes and the house would erupt. But two songs just didn't seem enough. People were still clamouring for more.

We made the decision that we were going to introduce 'Waterloo' in Toronto and that if it worked there, we would gradually put it back into London as well. We had also received another letter from an audience member, this time from a young boy who'd been to see the show and had come up with a way of adding 'Waterloo', so Judy was able to write back to him to say, 'Thank you and – guess what – we are putting it in as the finale!'

The first time 'Waterloo' was performed in the megamix, I knew that the three dads were going to come back on dressed in male ABBA outfits but I had no idea what it was going to look like. Benny and Björn didn't even know this was going to happen so it was fantastic to be sitting next to them when the three guys came on dressed in those very peculiar costumes – and they laughed and laughed. I think it's a great moment. Everybody goes out feeling that they've had their money's worth. And I found I had no problem about the song not being in the show. I just thought, 'Yes, of course, this is the moment where we break out of the constraints of the book and we go into a celebration of ABBA, so it's totally natural to have 'Mamma Mia', 'Dancing Queen' *and* 'Waterloo'.

Michael Simkins: The 'Waterloo' curtain call came into the London show during my first year as Sam. I was being fitted for this bloody 'Super Trouper' outfit, and I got so po-faced. I was standing there saying, 'I can't believe we've sold this show out. Look at me, what's happened to the integrity of the dads? I'm coming on in a lamé codpiece; it's never going to work, the shame of it.' I later heard that the people who were fitting me said, 'The look on Michael's face when we fitted him for the lamé codpiece could have curdled milk at a hundred paces.' Louise Plowright came in while I was being fitted, burst into laughter and told me, 'I've never seen anybody looking so unhappy.' So I went on to perform the finale imagining it would be the most terrible, tacky thing and, naturally, the moment I walked on, I thought, 'Of course, this is what they've been waiting for.' I had thought including 'Waterloo' would debase the show, but it doesn't at all. It actually augments it. It's wonderful.

Phyllida: The story was ultimately more important than cramming all the numbers from *ABBA Gold* into the show. As far as adding 'Waterloo' was concerned there were two schools of thought. I was with Björn in the puritan camp – we felt that it was somehow unethical to have a curtain call and bung in numbers that we couldn't fit into the show – and then there was another faction, which must have been Martin Koch, Benny and probably Judy, who thought, 'What is your problem, just lighten up!' Looking back, I totally agree with them, because when we did put the number in, it was a great pay-off to finally see the dads in the clothes that they might have imagined wearing in the 1970s. It made the circle complete.

Nina Lannan, North American general manager: When you sat in the middle of the London audience and felt its energy, and then saw the same thing in Toronto, that's when, if you had any doubts at all, they had to dissipate. The show was clearly such an audience pleaser. After a preview in Toronto we were sitting at the back of the house while the creative team were giving notes. A man in his seventies, an audience member, was leaving the theatre. As he went past us, and he knew we were working on the show, he turned and said, 'You have a fabulous show, this is one of the best.' And I thought, 'My goodness, this show has something.' You can't really quite explain why it works, but it works!

Andrew Treagus: The day after we opened in Toronto, I sat down with Brian Sewell of Mirvish Productions and we immediately said the same thing to each other: 'We can do more than twenty-six weeks here'. I spoke to Judy, got everybody together for a meeting and told them we wanted the show to stay in Toronto. People now talk about this being 'the *MAMMA MIA!* route', but there was no genius thinking behind it. We were doing what was possible and what really made it possible was the fact that *MAMMA MIA!* was loved by every audience who ever came to see it.

Kevin Samual Yee as Pepper from the 2003 Toronto cast spars with Nicole Robert as Tanya in 'Does Your Mother Know'. Catherine Johnson relished the opportunity to take the song, originally sung by Björn, and give it to a woman to sing. 'There's been a lot of emotional stuff going on, so it felt right to take a breather, have a bit of a laugh. Everyone's down on the beach getting tanked up before the wedding and Pepper's trying to come on to Tanya after the previous night's shenanigans, which Tanya is drawing a veil over. He keeps on and on, so she just turns and gives him a great little knock-back. I suppose it's every middle-aged woman's fantasy to have a load of 20-year-old boys drooling over you.'

The Toronto production seemed just as fresh and funny and peculiarly Canadian as it had seemed fresh and funny and peculiarly British when we'd seen it in London. The buzz went sky high again, and we knew we had another hit on our hands. Catherine Johnson

Judy: Andrew Treagus thought it was a great idea to stay in Toronto, to create a new Toronto company to sit down there and send the current company out on the road, as we had scheduled. I thought it was a great idea too but at the same time I was thinking, 'Will we get all this achieved in time?', because that meant we had to start reauditioning to find the company to sit down, and we'd have to build another set. But that's why Andrew is so brilliant – because he understands all the technical possibilities. When we sat down with the creative team in the auditorium of the Royal Alexandra and Andrew pitched this idea, he asked them how they felt about it because obviously they had to be working on both simultaneously. It was Phyllida who said, 'I'm not sure' and she was quite right to do that on behalf of the cast, who would have other actors taking over their roles in Toronto. But it was also very funny because Mark Thompson was kicking the back of her foot, and whispering to her, 'Phyllida, do you know what you're saying? This is an offer not to refuse.' As Phyllida suspected, the cast were a little uncertain, but they changed their mind once the tour started, and Louise Pitre, who was our Donna in Toronto, became our Donna on Broadway.

Phyllida: Just before the Toronto opening in May 2000, we changed the London cast. We had tightened up the shape of the show in Canada, but this was going to be a radical change because we would be altering the cast who had made the show with us in the first place. I think I was the one who said, 'Ask Louise Plowright if she can sing 'The Winner Takes It All',' because I felt that somewhere inside Louise was a Donna – something to do with Louise's warmth and rock chick-ness.

Louise Plowright: Phyllida rang me and asked me if I would be interested in taking over the role of Donna. I had never even considered myself to be a Donna and yet I felt more right for that part than I've ever felt for anything. It seemed completely right up my street, much more me than Tanya had been. And there are so few roles for women of that age. I was so excited because not only was I going to be learning to be someone new, I was going to be in a romantic situation. I had never played romantic, so I was going to have a romantic leading man, I was going to have two brand-new best friends and, even better, I was going to have my own daughter.

Michael Simkins: When the cast change happened, I was called back for another audition. This time I went out onto the stage at the Prince Edward and there was Björn sitting in the stalls. I sang 'Knowing Me, Knowing You', not too badly, and I saw them all get into a huddle, with Phyllida leaning over. I don't know what they said – and I've never asked – so this is my interpretation. I imagine Björn was saying, 'Look, he's obviously a good actor and he comes with a very good CV but he's very square and he's singing it like a Donald Pears. I think he's just not funky enough for what we want', and I can see Phyllida going, 'Mike does a lot of stuff, he's renowned for getting on with things.' Then one of them asked me, 'I don't suppose you know 'SOS'?' 'Of course I do, I know all the songs. I've never sung it but if you want me to have a go, I will.' A couple of days later I had been offered the part of Sam. So I went to see the show that night and sat in

The second London casting saw Louise Plowright, the original Tanya, take on the role of Donna. Having already decided to leave at the end of the first year, Louise had a phone call from Phyllida Lloyd asking her if she had ever considered herself to be a Donna… Louise was delighted to accept. She says, 'It was such a fantastic role, and there are so few roles for women of that age.' Here she is seen in her new role in the finale (right and below), with Michael Simkins as Sam in 'I Do, I Do, I Do, I Do, I Do' (bottom left), and in 'Mamma Mia' (bottom right).

Adrian Bryan-Brown, the show's US press representative, with Nina Lannan, the North American general manager. Both are long-established members of the Broadway theatre community. Adrian Bryan-Brown says of the show, 'On one level you can just have a good time with the ABBA songs, on the other there's the drama of finding out where you are in this world. Now that sounds fantastically pretentious, doesn't it!'

some side seats behind a gauze. It was all very discreet, like a Venetian ball. And I had the best time. I found myself getting quite emotional about the reaction at the end. I sensed that the audience had just had the most fantastic time and there is something very emotional about seeing an audience having their thirty-five quid repaid in spades because it often doesn't happen – in the theatre you have to kiss a lot of frogs before you meet a prince.

Frida first came to see *MAMMA MIA!* during the second year in London, which was my first year in it. Word got round that she was really enjoying the show, and then at the end of the interval the message came through that 'Frida wants to come on at the end'. At that point 'Dancing Queen' was still the end of the show, we hadn't added 'Waterloo' into the medley. Philip Effemey, the company manager, said, 'When you come on to join up with Lou for 'Dancing Queen', Frida wants to come on from the other side.' I said, 'Philip, look, it's going to be a disaster. Frida's still a beautiful, elegant woman but nobody's going to recognise her.' Boy, was I wrong! I'd put one foot on from the wings and from the other side Frida had barely placed her ankle on stage before the whole audience went 'YEAH!' They knew exactly who she was and it was the most exhilarating moment.

Benny: I can't recall talking to Frida and Agnetha at all about *MAMMA MIA!* No big deal. What was there for them to say? Maybe Judy spoke to them, maybe Björn did, but I doubt it. The input in ABBA from the girls was immense – it could not have happened otherwise. ABBA was Anni-Frid, Benny, Björn and Agnetha, nothing else. So, what would I feel if I were a singer and the girls were the writers and they were doing this musical, with other people involved? I think they still feel that they are as big a part of this as they ever were. They've both been to see the show. Frida's seen it many times. Agnetha was at the Stockholm opening and she's seen it a couple of times. She likes the fact that it is working.

Björn: Agnetha and Frida were OK with the show. They could have said, 'Um, I don't like that', but I think I would have gone ahead anyway, using my own judgement as to whether it was good or bad for the group. But with all those people involved who were so completely one hundred per cent committed, it couldn't go wrong. They were devoted to it, all of them.

Judy: Nina Lannan plotted the tour of the States, playing big ABBA-friendly cities – San Francisco, Los Angeles, Washington, Chicago, Boston – where we were playing for quite a long time. We planned to play ten to fourteen weeks in those places even though we were only guaranteed for a few weeks. But judging by the box office in Toronto and London it was a risk we wanted to take, even if we were sometimes having to start from scratch again. People were still telling us, 'You'll have to change the title because people will think *MAMMA MIA!* is an Italian restaurant', but we battled on.

Nina Lannan: We decided to start the tour in San Francisco. We didn't really want to go direct to Boston or Washington because those cities were too close to

New York. In addition to being ABBA-friendly, San Francisco had the advantage of a beautifully run theatre with a good, built-in subscription audience. Los Angeles, which we briefly considered for the premiere, had the disadvantage of a spread-out audience that would have been much harder to reach. Carole Shorenstein Hayes was so proud to present the US premiere of *MAMMA MIA!* in San Francisco. She had no doubts about the show. She lobbied for it. When I asked her if she thought the show could run for three to four months, she said, 'Yes. This is just right for the dot commers in the San Francisco Bay area, and it definitely should play San Francisco before it plays Sacramento!'

David Grindrod: In San Francisco, we opened on a Wednesday afternoon. I was quite apprehensive because I felt that ABBA was not known in the States at all. But I sat in the middle of this matinee audience and what I observed was they were intrigued by the story. They got into the story straightaway and when the dads came on, they said, 'Ah, they've arrived'. I was thinking, 'Who's arrived? What are you talking about?' But they were absolutely hook, line and sinkered with the narrative. I can still feel the goose bumps now.

Benny: Someone else could have taken the songs, written something nice, put it up on the stage, and it could have been a total disaster, like it has been with a number of these back catalogue musicals. You can't just take a bunch of songs and stick them into some kind of order. You need your Catherine Johnson, so we were very lucky that she wanted to do it.

To answer the demand for *MAMMA MIA!* in the US, a second national tour opened in February 2002, and had played in eighty-three cities by 2006. Top: Tiffani Barbour as Ali, Sara Kramer as Sophie and Joelle Graham as Lisa in the 2004 cast of that tour. Above: Monique Lund and the 2002 US Tour Two company in 'Money, Money, Money'.

Nancy Coyne: The course *MAMMA MIA!* had taken proved to be wildly successful and turned out to be a marketing strategy as sound as anything I have ever worked on. It broke new ground. People had opened shows in Toronto before, but then they had moved on; *MAMMA MIA!* stayed there. With the second company out on the road, and a third company due to open in New York, we had the equivalent of a huge grassroots marketing campaign across the country. When 64 per cent of the people in a Broadway theatre come from out of town and you are able to open on Broadway with five US cities and Toronto already having had huge campaigns and 'sold out' signs, then you come in with a certain sort of muscle. It was really a steamroller.

Judy: In November 2000 we were in San Francisco, then we opened on Broadway the following October and in between we put on the show in Australia and re-made the Toronto company. No wonder I'm exhausted. Blimey.

Adrian Bryan-Brown, North American press representative: The press coverage had built and built ever since *MAMMA MIA!* opened in London. There was a buzz, and plenty of speculation, about the show coming over to New York. It was a time when there weren't many shows being created out of pop music, so there was a novelty aspect – some intrigue, mixed with a certain amount of sniffiness. A lot of the New York press had been up to see the show in Toronto. It was good timing, because the Canadian dollar was very low, and it was an attractive weekend option for

For the original Broadway production Louise Pitre as Donna had two new Dynamos: Judy Kaye (above) as Rosie, and Karen Mason (opposite) as Tanya – both established Broadway actresses. Judy Kaye had won a Tony award playing Carlotta Giudicelli in *Phantom Of The Opera*, and Karen Mason brought all her musical theatre experience to bear on the role of Tanya, delivering, in the words of *The New York Times*' Ben Brantley, 'vivid bite' to the part.

journalists. After Toronto, the ink just kept coming. It was encouraging to find that there was a lot of smart press. Features writers in New York were not just approaching us to interview the ABBA boys, they were asking, 'Who are these three women who got this show together?'

Judy: Broadway was quite a terrifying prospect. It really can make or break you. But there was so much goodwill, such a strong word of mouth and the reviews were all so positive that it seemed the way to go. The way we went into Broadway was very well planned because we didn't go there in an arrogant way, shouting, 'Here we are, we're a hit in London, we're storming into Broadway.' We had very gently dipped our toe in the water, we had created a buzz and all the New York press had been to see it in Toronto and in San Francisco. Michael Riedel from the *New York Post* in particular had been very supportive. There had been a tradition on Broadway that critics could open and close a show. It's less true now compared to the days of Frank Rich when everyone read his reviews in the *New York Times* – there's much more marketing involved now, although it is still a risk if the newspapers are negative. However, when the show first opened in London, Clive Barnes and Ben Brantley, two of the principal New York critics, had flown over and written favourable reviews and once that's happened, they can't take that away from you. Ben Brantley called it 'Clunkingly endearing' or 'Endearingly clunky' and we took that as a great positive.

John Kennedy: Now we come to the one we'd all been nervous of, Broadway. Björn and Benny had had a painful experience with *Chess*, and right from the very beginning Broadway was something which might not even have happened because it was too much of a risk. It's like the music business, where you can have artists who sell huge numbers of records round the world and when it comes to America they sell none – Robbie Williams is a classic example. Just because you've had a hit somewhere else you can't assume you will have a hit on Broadway.

In the meantime Polygram had been taken over by Universal, so there was now a different set of parameters. That actually suited me quite well, because during the takeover I was not really answering to anyone – I was able to keep moving this money around and I didn't have to explain. But it was also back to the stage we had been at with Judy before: it was hard to get a decision out of anyone, nobody wanted to make the commitment for the extra money we needed to open on Broadway. There was no doubt in my mind that we were going to do it; we were in this partnership together and it would be a terrible breach of trust to pull out. I was trying to get permission from the local CFO in America because the figures had gone well above my terms of reference and all I wanted to do was say yes. He told me, 'I've looked at all the figures and I'm not sure.' I said, 'OK, I've got a great idea. If you don't want to invest, can you confirm that I can invest personally.' He said, 'You wouldn't really do that, would you?' and I said, 'Absolutely, I have no doubt.' So he said, 'In that case we'll do it.' Perhaps I shouldn't have been quite so enthusiastic. I should've tried harder to persuade him to let me invest because I would have made a fortune.

It had reached the stage where we were taking all our chips and were about to play at the Broadway roulette wheel, which was the most dangerous one of all. John Kennedy

Catherine: Broadway is so different. Broadway just takes a show and gives it that old razzle-dazzle. It becomes A Show, it's beyond being *MAMMA MIA!*, the little show from England that made good. It's *MAMMA MIA!* the Broadway Show, and it is a slightly different production. But it still worked, with all that Broadway-ness about it. You could still feel that the story was coming through. It's not a show that relies on huge spectacle. It is about relationships and that is still as emphatically important on Broadway as anywhere else.

Nancy Coyne: Many shows get hung up on pleasing the highbrow critics, or targeting the Tony awards. This show always positioned itself as a popular musical. *MAMMA MIA!* never seemed to care about anything except the audience.

Phyllida: All my friends who had worked on Broadway were impressing on me that this was going to be a very different experience. There were quite a lot of caveats and warnings. We were lucky. It wasn't as bad as it can be sometimes. You hear about people doing Broadway shows where there are eighteen different producers' names above the title and not only do they think they know how to do it, all their grannies, aunts, uncles and cousins come to see the show during preview, and they all have an opinion about who should be fired, who should do this. We were really insulated from that.

Perhaps the biggest difficulty on Broadway was casting the show. The essence of *MAMMA MIA!* is that you are watching a reflection of the audience on stage, every kind of person is up there. But the people who are performing on Broadway are a particular creature, they're *not* the kind of person who's let themselves go physically. They are by definition not all shapes and sizes. In London we could say, 'This person sings really well, they're a great actor. OK, they've got two left feet', but then that's very *MAMMA MIA!*, 'Let's make that work.' But to get a job in a Broadway musical you've got to be a thoroughbred beast and therefore the sort of slight chaos of the show was in danger of becoming more polished if we weren't really careful. If I was to give out two suitcases and the props and say, 'Right, here's 'Dancing Queen'. Your objective is to entertain Donna, cheer her up, delight her with your inventions', they would look at me as if I was mad. The feeling was 'Tell us what you want and we'll do anything you want.' The idea that the responsibility was being thrown back at them was anathema.

David Grindrod: I'd never casted on Broadway before and I thought this was going to be the Great White Way, fantastic, wonderful, marvellous. But things were very different. The people coming for audition often didn't understand the games I'd ask them to play. They couldn't take them on board. It was most bizarre. They didn't take us seriously; it was the whole thing of the Brits coming over.

Judy Craymer outside the Cadillac Winter Garden Theatre, Broadway, where *MAMMA MIA!* opened in October 2001 replacing an eighteen-year run of *Cats*.

Paul Garrington, associate director: I was on Broadway as an observer, preparing to take the show into Europe and watching Phyllida in action. During any breaks the actors would disappear and be straight on the phone to their agents before coming back into work. There was also a tendency on Broadway for people to want to formularise something that is much looser and much more idiosyncratic. Some of those slightly older Broadway performers really wanted to practise a little walk to get it right, to get the laugh on the beat.

Catherine: There must have been some discussion about whether we needed a Broadway star, but we really, really wanted Louise Pitre, who had played Donna from right from the start in Toronto and was currently on tour with the show, and we wanted Tina Madigan, who played Sophie, to go in as well because we loved both of them, we felt they were perfect. It would be Louise's first starring role on Broadway. And it didn't feel like we were suddenly being confronted with a Broadway legend taking on our show. Louise was a legend, but she was *our* legend.

Andrew Treagus: Broadway is much tougher than anywhere else. It's more highly unionised, particularly the guys who work on stage in the theatres. It's not like that in the West End. Stage hands in London work for the theatre, and get paid just about a living wage. On Broadway those jobs are very well paid. The people who have them guard the jobs with their lives and hand them down through the family. It's a very different way of working and a much tougher environment. To become a general manager or a company manager on Broadway you have to pass an exam, whereas in the West End that is not the case, and so it can attract the dilettante. And on Broadway you have to consult the unions continuously. I've often said to Nina Lannan, 'Nina, if I had to do your job, I wouldn't be doing it.' I just wouldn't. With everything else that it takes to put on a show, it is very nerve-racking to have that extra pressure.

The company felt like old friends rather than big scary Broadway people. I think Judy dealt far more with those people than I did. She has to, it's what she gets paid to do. I'm all right, I can slope off into the background.

Catherine Johnson

Björn: Broadway is the most regulated market of any kind in the world with all those unions and the weak producers, the unions deciding what to do and the producers not being able to say no. But even with that and our *Chess* experience, for some reason you want to go back.

Catherine: Broadway opened right after 9/11. I'd been over to New York for rehearsals in case anybody wanted to talk about their character with me, but had left and was in Memphis on that day. All the company were still on Broadway, so I remember a very anxious day trying to dial out and find out if everyone was OK.

Above left: Donna was Louise Pitre's first Broadway appearance. Her impressions of Broadway were of 'a concentrated bubble. It is teeming with energy. For me, coming from Toronto, it was the sheer volume of activity that was fascinating.'
Dean Nolen as Harry (above) and Ken Marks as Bill (left) sing 'Thank You For The Music'. Catherine Johnson needed a song where Sophie sang with her dads, and they were brought together by the music. 'She's thanking them really for her life, saying, "I wouldn't be alive if it wasn't for one of you three."'

There was some discussion about whether or not we would go ahead. It's hard now to remember just how scary a prospect that was. There was a question mark about whether it was the right thing to do – not whether it was the safe thing to do but whether it was the appropriate thing to do.

Judy: On the Sunday two days before 9/11, the big annual event called 'Broadway On Broadway' took place, when all the shows gather to give a free concert in Times Square. *MAMMA MIA!* had not yet opened on Broadway, but we were asked to participate since the show was about to open. Every show uses a gimmick to grab attention, and our theme was upbeat and holidays and we wanted to throw beach balls out into this huge audience of 95,000 people in Times Square. But then Nina Lannan got a call from someone quite high up in the NYPD to say they had serious concerns. They didn't like the idea of the beach balls and they'd also heard that when people came to see the show they got up and started dancing. The authorities were really concerned that we were going to start a riot in Times Square. It makes you realise how the world changed, because that was the police department's biggest concern on 9 September 2001.

On 9/11, I woke up early because I was going to the dentist to have root canal fillings, which I was dreading. I turned on the television about eight o'clock and saw that a plane had gone into the towers. I instinctively called my mum in London but the phone went dead while we were talking. She very astutely called the Littlestar offices and told them, 'Judy's OK, I've spoken to her' – and then all the phones went dead. I managed to get across to the dentist on the Upper West Side and had the root canal filling while listening to the news continuing to come in on TV and with the dentist being called away several times during this intricate procedure because he was getting calls from people whose friends were missing. The rest of the day was spent trying to locate everyone and make sure they were OK. The touring show was in Boston; the Monday had been a day off and a lot of the cast had come into New York to visit home or see relatives or to check their apartments, so we needed to track them all down. They couldn't get back to Boston because the area had been declared an emergency zone. And there were some of the Toronto company who had come in to New York and they couldn't get back either. The Boston show was cancelled on 9/11, but the next night we somehow managed to get the show on, although everyone was a bit wobbly. Out of respect, Boston and all the shows worldwide held a minute's silence before the performance.

Phyllida: I had walked down to the rehearsal room on Union Square. There was a vast crowd looking straight down the street at the towers engulfed in black smoke. I went into the rehearsal room and the company was in a really bad state. There were kids who we'd brought in from Canada, a country which has barely had a shot fired in anger on its land, and the rumour was that the island of Manhattan had been closed, that nobody could get in or out and the island was under attack. People were absolutely terrified.

We told everyone to get back home. Anthony, Nichola and I left the rehearsal room and we set off to walk back from Union Square to where they were staying

up by the Lincoln Center. As we walked through totally empty streets, one guy shot out of a sidestreet with a tray of snowshaker scenes and a sign that said, '$25 – with twin towers' and Anthony looked at me as if to say, 'It's tempting, isn't it, because by the time you get to the first night there won't be any of these left.' And a few blocks later someone else popped out of another side alley with a laminated sign, clearly done that morning: 'Upset by today's disaster? Ring 1-800-something.' I thought, 'Talk about turning everything into a marketing opportunity.'

Anthony Van Laast: We walked back uptown and sat at a café outside the Lincoln Center having a glass of wine and eating a lovely meal in the sunshine. It was truly the most surreal experience: four miles away was one of the world's greatest catastrophes and there we were having something to eat uptown as if we were in another world.

Phyllida: We came back together a couple of days later. We sat in a circle and thought it would be a good idea to ask everyone to say what they felt at that moment. We talked about what should we do. One person said, 'I think we should make sandwiches for the fire brigade', which we knew they needed. Someone else suggested we should all go and give blood, and another said, 'Whatever we do, the one thing we shouldn't do is this, the thing we're doing, rehearsing a musical.' Then one of the senior members of the company replied, 'But this is what we do. Some people are trained to flip burgers, drive subway trains or be nurses but this is what we are trained to do. They may not need us now but the time will come when they do and we have to be ready.' It was very sobering. It did make one, especially me as the director, profoundly conscious of how we conducted ourselves, what our purpose was in the whole scheme of

The original Broadway boys prepare Sky (Joe Machota) for his stag night in 'Lay All Your Love On Me'. From Catherine Johnson's point of view, 'all the great love numbers seemed to occur between the oldies, so it was time to give Sophie and Sky a song. Once I had found the line, "I wasn't jealous before we met; now every man I see is a potential threat," I was up and running. This is two young people saying how much they like each other, and telling each other not to waste that emotion. And then to move it on a level we brought the rest of the stag party into the song.'

Above and opposite top: Karen Mason, Louise Pitre and Judy Kaye let rip as the Dynamos in the finale of the Broadway opening. 'Opening night on Broadway was like opening night in Toronto, but to the power of 100,' says Louise Pitre. 'This is how I took my bow: I went back on stage for my one solo bow and I got down on my knees and kissed the floor of the stage, and I hit it with my hand, so hard that I hurt my hand. I hadn't planned it. It was "I am here, I did it. And it's a gas." They could have all booed, it would not have mattered. I was so proud.'

things. We also felt very lonely, because the whole American response was so terrifyingly martial, 'Let's nuke 'em out of their foxholes.' We'd felt completely at home up to that moment and now we suddenly felt that we were the aliens. Everything seemed very fragile.

Anthony Van Laast: Phyllida and I both believe there is a place in our society for theatre. It's a mirror to our life and the joy it brings people is immeasurable. So that afternoon I started teaching a few simple ballroom steps from 'I Do, I Do, I Do, I Do, I Do'. And we got the whole thing going again. But it was a very tough time to be there. The New York experience was hard.

Judy: Phyllida quite rightly wanted to continue with rehearsals although in her heart, I'm sure like all of us, she must have felt it was the most ridiculous thing to be doing. I think the rehearsals became a comfort to the cast because everyone was drawn together and they could talk about the horror of what had happened and what was happening. Those days were more medicinal and therapeutic than anything else. We were all desperate to help in any way we could. We made a decision that we would raise money for the American Red Cross Fund and the World Trade Center Relief Fund. I contacted all the investors, theatre owners and creative teams of the five productions then running worldwide and they immediately agreed to donate their income from 5 October, the first public preview night on Broadway.

Benny: I arrived in New York on 14 September. There was no one on the plane… There was a sad feeling in New York, American flags in all the shop windows and empty streets. I think it was a good decision not to put a lid on the show, especially as it was a common decision with the cast, the crew and the band. They all voted to continue.

Björn: I did discuss with Judy whether we should postpone the opening or even cancel it. But she'd had so much input from New York saying, 'Please, please, please don't do that. Because what we need now is something like *MAMMA MIA!*, something to cheer us up.'

Judy: We went into virtually complete shutdown in terms of marketing and publicity. The New York media in any case had been completely overwhelmed by 9/11. But we were in a very fortunate position because we had a huge box office advance of about $27 million. There were shows that suffered, which is the fragility of theatre: if your audience is down for even a couple of nights you can start to lose your foothold, but as we hadn't opened our advance was solid. And the question of the first-night party was raised. My instincts told me that we should have one, but it was a sensitive issue. It was a very wise New Yorker who told me, 'You know, Judy, if you cancel the party, you put the car companies in jeopardy, the restaurants, the caterers, everyone will lose out financially; they're banking on those jobs.' So we did go ahead, but what had happened only weeks before never left anybody's thoughts, not even for a second. You were always very respectful, but you just had to get on.

Above: New York Mayor Rudy Giuliani was a backstage visitor at the Winter Garden, obeying his own exhortations in the weeks following 9/11 for visitors to 'come to New York and see theatre'.

It did turn out to be an appropriate thing to do. The sensation I got on opening night was that people were really celebrating the fact that a musical had opened. Mayor Giuliani had been begging people to come to New York, not to be scared off. It felt like we were giving a big thumbs up, and being supportive with our presence. Catherine Johnson

Above: Opening night on Broadway – Louise Pitre (seen with Benny and Björn at the opening-night party) remembers ending up at the after-party party singing Piaf songs with Benny at the piano until three or four in the morning. 'Even though we had a show next day, it didn't matter.' Opposite: Joe Machota as Sky and Tina Maddigan as Sophie on Broadway. Overleaf: Dance notations by Nichola Treherne.

Louise Pitre: The Broadway previews were the most incredible time. The audience reaction was what we were hoping for. But what I was not ready for was what happened at the stage door. People would stand waiting outside and I got hugged and kissed I don't know how many times. 'Thank you,' they said, with tears in their eyes. 'We need this.' It was extraordinary to be thanked for doing your job.

Nancy Coyne: We were fortunate that Giuliani was a very charismatic mayor. I received a call from a local radio station two days after 9/11. The mayor was coming in and they wanted to know if there was something the theatre industry wanted him to say. I wrote a very quick script, which he read out word for word. The basic message was, 'Come back to the theatre. It's the right thing to do. Show everyone that New York has not stopped.' And people responded; they felt it was patriotic to come and see a show. It was doing something that was quintessentially New York, that was supporting the city's economy, and something that was communal in nature with your fellow New Yorkers. People came out of the theatre incredibly moved by the experience. It felt so right.

John Kennedy: We opened against this background of devastation. It was quite astonishing that a pop musical could have such an impact at that time. *MAMMA MIA!* wasn't responsible for people coming back into New York, but it did give people the idea that it was OK to go.

For the first night performances of *MAMMA MIA!* I would try to arrive at the last possible moment and leave at the first possible moment, because I had a large business to run and going to the premieres meant giving up quite a lot of time. I took this to an extreme on Broadway by arriving on the afternoon of the show, going to the show, on to the party and then catching the 8 am flight back to London. Björn, Benny and I had been drinking in the hotel bar after the party, very excited and patting each other on the back. Benny sat down to play the piano again – which was absolutely fantastic – and we literally drank through until six in the morning. As we left the bar I was pretty much arm in arm with Benny. I called the concierge and asked him to bring my bag. Benny said, 'What are you doing?' and I said, 'I've got a plane in two hours' time.' Benny thought I was mad, but I said, 'I'm not sure I am, because I'm going to get on a plane, have a good long sleep and wake up at home.' You're going to wake up with a hangover and you'll still have to get home!'

At the opening night were some of the firemen who had been to hell and back. It was wonderful to see all these Irish-American firemen enjoying themselves. One of them turned to me and said, 'This is the first time since 9/11 that I've seen my wife smile.' Judy Craymer

People often say that there isn't a lot of choreography in *MAMMA MIA!* It may not be kick, kick, kick, but the amount of musical staging is huge. Most of the movement is based on naturalism, which was a very deliberate choice. Anthony Van Laast

Anthony Van Laast: The dance world is in reality a number of very different worlds. There's the contemporary dance world – which is where I gained most of my experience – in its own little bubble, and then you've got the classical ballet world, which is definitely its own little clique. And after that you've got the commercial world. In the UK, ballet looks down on contemporary dance, and they both look down on commercial dance. And then all of them look even further down on musical theatre. It's not the same in America at all. It's very different there because there is a tradition of great choreographers like Jerome Robbins, who worked in both commercial theatre and ballet. And Susan Stroman choreographs for ballet companies and yet she'll also do *The Producers*. It's quite normal in the States to work in both fields.

Because my background was not exclusively in musical theatre, when I started working with Phyllida on *MAMMA MIA!*, I was able to relate to how she wanted to do it even though her approach was totally unconventional. When I'm working as a choreographer on a musical, I believe it should be director-led. I have directed shows as well, so I know what it entails. On *MAMMA MIA!* this had to be Phyllida's idea and my interpretation of her ideas.

Phyllida: I learnt a huge amount from Anthony. He has a great sense of how to structure a piece of musical staging, which can look like very little but is really a kind of musical storytelling. It wasn't necessarily about who steps where and which dance steps are going to happen, it was about how to get from, say, Donna saying 'I do, I do' to the moment where all the chairs have been cleared, Donna's done a costume change and everybody is dancing in that slightly Peggy Spencer style of ballroom dancing.

Nichola Treherne, associate choreographer: At auditions, some of the actors would be in an absolute panic, not realising that Phyllida, Anthony and I love people who are not dancers, as long as they have rhythm and a willingness to learn, because they come across as natural. An audience should come to watch *MAMMA MIA!* and say, 'That could be me, or my sister, or my mother.' If you have a cast member who physically can't do something, there's no point in forcing them. We wanted the actors to create the roles. That is where Anthony is so good, because he will work to what a director or a writer requires, rather than creating a production number that will make people say, 'That's a wonderfully choreographed show.'

The key was to think 'natural and normal' at all times. Often Anthony and I would create some moves, and then say to each other, 'No, no, that's too dancer-ish.' We had to reflect what was in the script. It was people at a party dancing along with the music. Or the Dynamos, who had a routine back in the 1970s that they had made up themselves, so it shouldn't look slick. It was absolutely clear in the script who these characters were. The Dynamos aren't really dancers. The dads definitely aren't. Even for Pepper, if he's a fantastic dancer it can work against him, because when he's dancing in 'Does Your Mother Know', it should look like he is really trying hard to impress Tanya, like a kid on a beach who's watched a video and thought, 'I'll try and do those moves.'

Anthony Van Laast: A good example of how I went about creating a number in *MAMMA MIA!* is the opening of Act Two – 'Under Attack', which was Sophie's nightmare sequence. I'd sit on my exercise bike at home, start listening to the music and in a way my brain would become a piece of blank videotape.

For that number I was thinking about dreams and dream characters, and I thought that the number should have a contemporary Pina Bausch feel. First I came up with the idea of using the bed, and then I imagined what a dream image would be – like perhaps seeing yourself in a wedding dress. And then the nightmare would be that it actually turned out to be your husband in the wedding dress. It was about that feeling in a bad dream when you're running and running but you get stuck and can't run any more.

Nichola Treherne: In rehearsal, while the cast were learning the music, we would talk through ideas, and Phyllida would give us an idea of what she wanted something to look like. We would feel the music and start to improvise the number, including doing some improvisational work with the cast to help keep the whole thing natural. If you're putting on a pure dance show you work out every step in detail. But because we were working organically, we would structure it with key markers. There are no two productions of MAMMA MIA! that are the same, but there are structures within the show that are consistent. It is all written down, in a mixture of Benesh dance notation and longhand notes…

Anthony Van Laast: I work very closely with Nichola. In my mind I can envisage the overall structure for a number. But I'll come to her with some ideas and we'll workshop steps together and play with sequences together. Nichola is the one who will write down where everyone goes. I don't know whether they go left or right or whatever. I'll say, 'Over there a bit, over there a bit, you walk through here.' I'm sure Phyllida would often come to watch what we'd done and think, 'What the hell is that?' – I think it's quite different to what she had imagined.

Phyllida: Anthony Van Laast is the most positive person I've ever met. Very practical, very paternal, never negative. He must have a dark side, but I haven't seen it: he's irrepressible and never depressed, which was extraordinary. And he and Nichola both had that same sense of humour that the core team shared, which got us through any difficult moments.

Anthony Van Laast: The rehearsal period on a new show is intensive. We only had a few weeks. It's like a Grand Prix. The flag goes down and you're off. I'll finish rehearsals during the day and then be working in the evening with Nichola from six until nine or ten. It's very hard to get the right momentum and the right creativity going to make major changes in the show, and bloody difficult to make changes during previews; you have to lift the energy of twenty or thirty people on stage. There are two months of constant change. I very rarely end up with the same thing I started choreographing in the beginning – I'll keep changing it, modifying it, see if the characters develop. You have to be open to new possibilities and not think that the first effort you put down is going to be the correct one. Editing, that's the choreographer's job.

Nichola Treherne: MAMMA MIA! is not a dance show. The challenge was always to get actors moving and make production numbers with a lot of people who weren't dancers. And the cast achieved it. We structured it, but they did it. 'Voulez-Vous' takes a long time to teach: four morning sessions and the actors have to work so hard. You have a roomful of people, over half of whom are probably thinking, 'I will never learn this', and four or five days later they are singing and dancing it up to speed.

Michael Simkins: MAMMA MIA! is a show with two different generations, each of which has a slightly different agenda. Most of the younger generation, by dint of the fact that they have to dance and sing so much in each performance, are constantly working out at Pineapple. Whereas the only thing us oldies are working out at is steak and kidney pie between shows. But I can say in all honesty that the youngsters tend to keep the old ones young and the youngsters, I think, really enjoy the fact that there is this older group of actors hanging around who can help them with things that they are weak on. But boy, do we need help from the youngsters – particularly in the dance routines. They cover up a multitude of sins with their energy and their technical proficiency; they hide the fact that the old crocks are sometimes slightly struggling.

STILL ANOTHER MILE

Rhonda Burchmore, Australia's Performer of the Year in 1999, played Tanya in the original Australian cast of *MAMMA MIA!*. A previous highlight of her career had been creating the role of April in David Atkins' *Hot Shoe Shuffle*, the first Australian musical ever to open in London's West End.

Judy: There had always been massive interest in *MAMMA MIA!* going to Australia because ABBA had been – and continue to be – so huge there, and of course it was where most of *ABBA: The Movie* had been shot. To fit an Australian production into what was becoming quite a complex logistical jigsaw we slotted it in after Toronto and the US tour, but before Broadway. So the team went out to Australia in the spring of 2001 and opened the show in Melbourne in June, which meant I had a turnaround of about a month before I was due in New York to prepare for the Broadway opening and planning a second US touring company.

The great difference about being in Australia was that we found ourselves in a place that didn't feel threatening in any way. There was none of the intense sense of competition with other shows opening around the corner or down the block that you experience in the West End or on Broadway. We were being extremely well looked after in a heavenly place with a heavenly climate. Melbourne felt like our own personal venue: *MAMMA MIA!* was coming to town and everyone was excited. In other cities the existence of theatres and shows is taken for granted to a certain extent but in Melbourne the opening was much more of an event and the party, let me tell you, was a stunner. The world was also a different place then, just before 9/11. You jumped on a plane to travel to Australia and no one was worried about terrorism in quite the same way.

Because Catherine couldn't join us in Australia, I wrote her a diary, which I called 'Judy Goes To Melbourne Without Catherine', and in it I described everything that happened from the moment I got into the British Airways lounge at Heathrow right through to the opening night, including all the madness, exuberance and ABBA craziness of the Australian coverage. I distinctly remember flipping TV channels one day and finding one TV show – and I don't think I was hallucinating – featuring a man who had had the word 'Frida' tattooed on his penis...

Catherine: Yes, I totally missed out on Australia, I wasn't very well at the time and couldn't travel, so I have memories of receiving a series of raucous e-mails which led me to believe that everybody was having a bloody good time there, especially the Dynamos – I mean my two Dynamos, Phyllida and Judy – without me. They were having an absolute blast!

Judy seemed to drink champagne for the entire twenty-one hours we were on the plane. I think she refuels on the stuff! Whilst she did a fantastic job she made sure she enjoyed herself after all the hard work. John Kennedy

Phyllida: As the production moved into new territories, there would be a squad who went in first to set up the show, and would be obliged to say, 'This is what we do' – and then Anthony Van Laast and I would turn up saying, 'Oh! Was it like this? Well, let's try something new', and start unearthing new possibilities and seeing if we could improve the show. Which is not necessarily the usual way to behave on a musical that you're trying to replicate around the world…

By now we had become a real team. Whenever we were recceing the places where we were going to be staying, we each had our own priorities. Martin Koch would get down on his hands and knees and start feeling around for the modem points around the wall. Nichola Treherne would go straight into the bedroom testing the pillows and the mattress to see whether the bed was all right for her bad back. Anthony would want to check out the gym. And I was always getting out my compass trying to find out whether the apartment was facing south, because I will only sleep in a south-facing apartment. Of course, I came a cropper when we went to Australia and asked the estate agent whether it was a south-facing apartment. He said, 'Madam, I can show you hundreds'…

Nichola Treherne: We were now an extremely close-knit team. Together we were able to solve any problems that might crop up, and we were having fun, too. In Australia Anthony celebrated his fiftieth birthday, so we organised a surprise hot air balloon flight. He is frightened of heights, so we had blindfolded him to get him on board with the rest of us. Judy refused to go – not, as we thought, because she didn't want to get up early, but because she wanted to ensure that at least one member of the creative team of *MAMMA MIA!* would survive.

Judy: I had actually phoned Andrew Treagus in London to check we were insured! And then later that morning I had a phone call from Phyllida, in a very bad Australian accent, claiming that she was from the balloon company and they had lost the entire party somewhere over the outback.

Top: Phyllida Lloyd in rehearsal with original Australian cast members, left to right: Peter Hardy (Bill), Nicholas Eadie (Sam) and Anne Wood (Donna). Above: Anthony Van Laast with Lara Mulcahy (left) and Anne Wood. Anthony's associate choreographer Nichola Treherne remembers Australia as the territory that was most fanatical over Benny and Björn, bringing back memories of ABBAmania in the 1970s.

The Australian production of *MAMMA MIA!* was launched with panache with an after-show party at the Park Hyatt in Melbourne. Judy Craymer remembers breaking a glass by accident. 'I told Alistair Paterson, the party organiser, "I'm afraid I've broken a champagne glass in the toilet." He turned to me and said, "I'll radio for help immediately."'

Nichola Treherne: Phyllida would also arrange for us to visit the opera in Melbourne, and beforehand talk us through what the opera was about, so in return we took her to see Kylie Minogue in concert.

Phyllida: At the time I was studying Wagner. Every morning, while Nichola and Anthony were rehearsing the choreography, I was at the Victoria College of the Arts studying *The Ring* with Dr David Kram, who is the head of the opera department and a genius Wagnerian specialist.

Judy: The *MAMMA MIA!* spirit received an extra boost from the Australians' sense of humour. We ended up doing ridiculous things. I remember having a Dynamos drinks party in Phyllida's apartment. The three Dynamos had got hold of a camcorder and were doing a *Through The Keyhole* spoof, going round her rooms holding up and dissecting everything she had, from fake tan to books on Wagner.

Phyllida: We loved the culture gap between the Brits and the Aussies. The stage manager in Melbourne came up to me one day and said, 'Philly, any obs if some rellies of the prinnies come in and watch a little bit of corry this arvo?' I said, 'OK, sit down, bring a dictionary and let's just talk that one through' – and we worked out that what she wanted to know was whether I had any objections if some relatives of the principals came to watch the choreography that afternoon. But notwithstanding the language barrier the audiences completely got the show. They shared the same sense of humour as we did and fifteen hundred people would have a belly laugh at lines that might have been lost on some of the coach parties who'd come in to see other productions of the show. And they could not believe that the script had not been written by an Australian. As far as they were concerned it was unthinkable that it had come from anywhere else.

Catherine: Of all languages and dialects, Australian is my favourite – I am a complete *Neighbours* aficionado. Nothing is allowed to interfere with my daily dose. I love the broadness of Australian, the fact that wherever you come from there, everyone uses a very expressive, colourful language whether they're a bartender or the Prime Minister. In the West Country, and especially from Bristol, where I come from, we've always spoken with that little upwards inflection at the end of the sentence. It's a very Bristolian habit and, of course, the Australians do that too. Whether that was because most of the early convicts came from the West Country, I don't know, but the Australians just seem to be my sort of people.

David Grindrod: We had held auditions during the blizzards of Toronto, now we were in the heat of Australia. We started doing these mad auditions travelling to Melbourne – sitting in a sweltering dance studio with no air conditioning, just a couple of fans turning – and heading over to Sydney and then across to Perth for half a day and back: a three-hour plane ride each way with a four-hour time change thrown in, which was fun. We were still casting as we were trying to get on the plane to come back to the UK. It was a challenge to get a cast together in

The three original Australian Dynamos, from left: Rhonda Burchmore, Anne Wood and Lara Mulcahy. Lara later played the role of Rosie in the London production.

Australia because there wasn't such a large pool of musical theatre actors available, but what we loved about the Australians was that straightaway they were wacky and wild. I had brought Anne Wood in to audition, for a possible Tanya, but Phyllida turned round to me and said, 'She could be Donna. Get her in tomorrow with no make up' – Phyllida has that eye, and she was spot on.

Those Aussie women were the most outrageous Dynamos because they just *are* Dynamos. Australia does not have a huge constituency of actor-singers to draw on but we found some great people. Phyllida Lloyd

Benny: Australia is so bloody far away. I thought about going, but you can't go down there to see a show one night and then come straight back home. You need to take at least a week off. So I'm sad to say that I talked to the people down there and said, 'Yes I'd like to come, I really would', but it didn't happen for whatever reason and I just didn't go.

Judy: By the time we had the North American shows and the Australian production up and running, the stone really was gathering moss. There was intense pressure to put on productions in countries where English was not the first language. We had a huge file of foreign-language proposals. We decided we weren't going to license the show, but were going to do it ourselves with a partner. They would take responsibility for financing the production, but we could retain overall creative control; the first of these productions was going to be in Hamburg with Joop van den Ende's theatre company Stage Holding, who would also produce the Dutch version. Moving *MAMMA MIA!* into non-English language territories brought up the whole issue

The Beatrix Theatre in Utrecht – the home of the original Dutch production, which was supposed to be the first version of *MAMMA MIA!* to be played in translation. In the end, that accolade went to the German show in Hamburg, while the Dutch opening was delayed until November 2003.

of translation. Initially everyone who was interested in staging the show wanted the ABBA songs to be in English because they were so well known and they thought that the songs were the meat and potatoes of the show. But we felt that the whole point of the show was to tell the story using the lyrics as the source material. So having Catherine's text in German, for example, and the songs in English didn't seem right. Phyllida said, 'No, it must all be in one language.' I think Björn and Benny warmed to that idea because they had been quite reticent; their fear would have been that this was simply an excuse to put ABBA songs on stage.

Björn: I really hadn't wanted to do *MAMMA MIA!* in any other language. The idea was to try it out in the Netherlands, which is good ABBA territory but a relatively small market. But the Dutch show was delayed, so Germany became the first European production. I was thinking, 'Should we really try it in such a huge territory? We don't have a clue whether this will work.' But we decided to take the chance.

Phyllida: Because the direction of the new productions was now going to be handled by Paul Garrington as associate director, my contribution to the European shows, aside from going to watch runs, was in helping power through the decision to translate the lyrics. Catherine concurred; we shared the same feelings about how important it was to translate the lyrics as well as the script as soon as we went into a non-English speaking country. This was really very contentious. ABBA's songs had never been translated; a lot of people felt that they couldn't be translated into German. Björn was really apprehensive about this, as were the Dutch and the Germans. I was at a party where some German actors told me, 'You can't translate this. Everyone knows the songs in English.' So I said, 'OK, two things: first, tell me what the second line of 'Dancing Queen' is' – which they couldn't remember – 'and secondly translate "Chiquitita, tell me what's wrong" into German for me here and now.' I explained the set-up for the song, the scene where Donna comes into her room, distraught, throws herself on the bed, wraps herself in the duvet and is not going to come out. And I said, 'Now sing "Chiquitita, tell me what's wrong" in German and then sing it in English. Which is funnier?' I could see them to starting to laugh when they sang it to themselves in German. And they did admit, 'Maybe it does have potential.'

Catherine: Eventually everyone agreed that the whole show should be translated so that we would have what English-language audiences got, which is a seamless marriage of the words and the lyrics, or as seamless as we can make it. My job has been to keep an eye on the text and make sure that it makes sense and retains the spirit of the show. Because in general I don't speak the local language, I have to rely on back-translations – where the German version, for example, is translated back into English. What usually happens is that the adapter will come and see the show, we talk about it, they ask questions if they need to, they go away to do their translation, and I get the back-translation. I make notes on anything that doesn't seem to be quite right and then we talk again. The translator can then tell me, 'This has been a particularly clumsy back-translation, and this is what I actually meant' or agree to adjust a particular nuance, because although we do want every territory to feel that it owns *MAMMA MIA!* there are certain points where you can't stray too far without losing the characters or the plot. You have to capture the sense of drama and narrative. With the lyrics it's extremely difficult because not only do you have to factor in aspects of rhythm and rhyme but the last line of the dialogue must slip straight into the first line of the lyrics.

Björn: Phyllida, Catherine and I were absolutely convinced that the songs should be in German. I had seen *Chess* done with the songs in English and the dialogue translated, and, oh, what a mess! So they found this wonderful collaborator for me, Michael Kunze, a German songwriter who had even written something for the Hootenanny Singers in 1965 or 66. He's such a good lyricist and I know some German so I was able to contribute, and the lyrics actually turned out very well.

Judy: We were lucky that the translator for the songs in Germany was Michael Kunze, who's brilliant at what he does, and Björn felt very relaxed with him. And the translator of the book was this wonderful woman called Ruth Deny, who had never written for the theatre before but was a translator of major movies. She had translated films like *Trainspotting* and *Men In Black*, so she understood how to work with the humour and style of the piece. She wasn't trying to 'make a play'.

Paul Garrington: You end up having a very close relationship with your translators, so selecting them is an extremely important decision. The right person is not necessarily someone who has worked on *Phantom Of The Opera* or *Les Mis* if they don't really understand how to handle ABBA lyrics, which have a very specific style. Likewise with the book, communicating Catherine's sense of humour and the feeling of her writing is essential. We really struck gold in Germany with Michael Kunze, who was probably the best person we could have found to translate the songs, and Ruth Deny, who was in her early forties, had been a Hamburg rock chick and loved ABBA. They both really understood what was needed.

There was no pop musical theatre tradition in Germany. Their experience was in classic belt-'em-out shows. There were loads of great young dancers who could sing and act, but for the age group we have to cast from for most of the principals – women and men in their forties and fifties – finding performers who could really deliver the songs and be really convincing actors, or vice versa, was quite a hunt.

Having resolved the translation issue, we now also had to address the notion of whether these should be German characters, or whether they should be English characters who just happened to speak German. Phyllida, Catherine and I were very keen that the show should feel German, that *MAMMA MIA!* shouldn't be a UFO that had landed in the middle of Hamburg. The compromise we arrived at was to take away the specific Englishness of it and prevent the audience from even asking the question by creating a sense of the show being international. Rosie could be pronounced Rozi, and Tanya was spelt Tanja, so the story could be told without anyone thinking, 'Hang on a minute, which airport has she come from…'

Top: Simone Kleinsma as Donna with the original Utrecht company in 'Money, Money, Money'. Paul Garrington, the show's associate director (seen above, in rehearsals) describes her as 'a Dutch institution'.

Judy: There was one moment when Catherine and I were with Ruth Deny, talking about the dads. Harry had started out as an Englishman, Sam had originally been Scottish, but could be American or English, and traditionally Bill was Australian. So we were asking her whether Sam would be German, or maybe they were *all* German, and Ruth said, 'Oh no, Donna would never have slept with three German men.' Catherine and I both giggled, but to this day we don't know what she meant.

MAMMA MIA! really is a play which demands skilful acting and directing. You can't approach *MAMMA MIA!* as if it were just a musical. That would be fatal.

Paul Garrington

Opposite: Carolin Fortenbacher with the Hamburg Dynamos Kerstin Marie Mäkelburg (Tanya) and Jasna Ivir (Rosie).
Below: Carolin Fortenbacher (Donna) and Katja Berg (Sophie) in the original Hamburg production.

Judy: We held a press event a few months before the Hamburg opening and all the German journalists were still asking, 'Why are you translating this? We love it in English', which was worrying, but I wondered if there might have been a touch of snobbery involved, because the journalists all spoke such excellent English. For us the idea is that presenting the show in the indigenous language reaches out to a much wider audience. And what was so great about the Hamburg opening was that it was obvious the audience absolutely loved hearing the songs translated. They had a huge sense of humour, a very raucous audience.

Benny: I think everyone had been a bit hesitant about translating *MAMMA MIA!*, because it was based on the original lyrics. But Catherine had always said she used the songs as a piece of the writing and that the story lay within the songs – and she's obviously right. I went to see the first German preview in Hamburg, wondering, 'How is this going to work with everything in another language?' And it worked, amazingly, helped by a very good cast, by the way. The audience knew these songs in English as 'Thank You For The Music' or 'Knowing Me, Knowing You', but they still worked as 'Danke Für Die Lieder' or 'Ich Bin Ich, Du Bist Du'.

Paul Garrington: The first preview in Hamburg was the most insane event. The Germans love an event; they are fantastic at that sense of festivity and know how to really launch a show. The Operettenhaus had been running *Cats* for millions of years. After that closed the theatre was completely redesigned and for the reopening it was wrapped in a massive piece of silk with a big bow. The production company closed down part of the Reeperbahn, invited the public and put a stage outside the front.

Judy: Both Björn and Benny were due to be there, but Björn couldn't make it, so Benny came on his own. He doesn't really like doing press, but he was fantastic. We had been told that there would be a bit of an opening ceremony to unveil the theatre, a few fireworks, all fairly low key. So we set off from the hotel, with the cars in radio communication, all 'Foxtrot to teapot'. I was in a car with Benny and Phyllida, and as we approached the theatre we could hear this throbbing music as though we were coming up to Wembley Stadium in the middle of some vast concert. The car

was driving between huge crowds with this music pumping out and suddenly a microphone voice in German came booming out, saying *'Und ein großer Wilkommen für Ben-ny Andersson, Ju-dy Craymer'* and we were all saying, 'Oh my God', and I was thinking, 'Oh no, Benny will never do anything for us again.' There was dry ice everywhere, the car pulled up and suddenly we were on a red carpet, climbing up some steep wooden steps onto a platform in front of two thousand people being introduced – 'And now Ju-dy Craymer is going to say something and Ben-ny Andersson is going to say something' – aargh. This was followed by the pressing of the buttons to set off the fireworks, *'Eins. Zwei. Drei.'*, which triggered a gigantic explosion on top of the theatre and this huge cloth fell away from the Operettenhaus.

In Germany we now have two productions running – in Hamburg and Stuttgart. It's the first time in history that the same show has had two German productions running simultaneously. I wish I knew the secret.

Andrew Treagus

Below: Judy Craymer introduces *MAMMA MIA!* to Japan – she remembers Japan as being 'filled with speeches'.

Paul Garrington: Almost simultaneously with Germany, I was working on the production for Japan, where we were dealing with a completely different set of cultural references. Trying to establish an argument between Sophie and Donna, mother and daughter, was incredibly difficult because the actors would say, 'No, I would never, ever do that', so my job was to look for a slightly different way into it and say, 'OK, it's not an argument, but you really want to say this.' And to have Sky and Sophie kiss on stage in Tokyo was virtually impossible, almost illegal!

Phyllida: We had to be understanding. The producers in Japan didn't want Paul to see the translation and he kept saying, 'Well, if you won't show me the whole translation, could we just see a little bit of the translation?' 'Ah yes, yes' – meaning 'no'. Eventually, after some weeks, he was allowed to see the back-translation of 'Gimme! Gimme! Gimme! (A Man After Midnight)' and it came back as 'Give Me, Give Me, Give Me (Some Hope In My Heart)'. Paul said, 'Obviously, that's not really a translation, is it?' and the answer was 'No, because a Japanese lady would never say this.' So he felt it was probably best not to enquire any more.

Judy: I was in Japan for the previews. It was a beautiful production and at the end of the show the applause seemed to last forever. Someone told me, 'It's because it's rather impolite for the cast to leave the stage while the audience is applauding, and vice versa.'

Andrew Treagus: The Japanese audiences *are* different. They tend to contain their feelings and you can actually find yourself thinking during the show, 'Are they getting this, are they enjoying it?' And at the end they go crazy. After the final curtain call, they take at least another three. It goes on and on and the audience are going wild. It is quite incredible.

Left: The firework display announcing the opening of *MAMMA MIA!* at the Operettenhaus, Hamburg in November 2002.

Above: The cast of the Stuttgart production, which opened at the Palladium Theater in July 2004.
Left: Backstage fittings and costume work for the Stuttgart show.

Chizu Hosaka, one of the long-time principals of the Shiki theatre company, as Donna (second from right) and company in the original Tokyo production.

I went out for a few days before the opening after which it was time for everybody to come home. First-night parties in Japan tend to be rather austere. The cast and the theatre employees are not allowed to eat or drink anything until the VIPs have left – the VIPs being us – but there were speeches. I had to give a speech, Paul gave a speech thanking everybody, and when it was time for us to go, everybody was in floods of tears – including the Japanese, which was the most moving experience because they tend to be very reserved. And I have to say we were all equally moved, including even the hardest-bitten members of the team.

Paul Garrington: I had thought the Germans were well organised, but in Japan the sense of professionalism and organisation and commitment was on a different planet. They worked so hard, it was so dedicatedly brilliant, but the first public show was performed in almost total silence. I sat there, utterly terrified, thinking we'd screwed up completely before the audience went ballistic at the end.

We learnt that *MAMMA MIA!* wasn't a boring show to repeat. Whoever was cast in it added their own life. The show always developed a distinctive local personality. Nichola Treherne

Paul Garrington: I don't think a Japanese woman would have escaped to a Greek island and slept with three Japanese men. It doesn't really fit with their cultural code. So the solution was for us to have Japanese actors doing this show that was about English people, which was a little strange. I did some press interviews for the Tokyo opening, and the journalists would want to talk to me about the 'tragedy' of *MAMMA MIA!*, this tragic story about a single mother, who sings

out her tragedy. They saw her as a slightly sad and lonely woman caught in an awful predicament. Whereas in Korea they thought she was a whore! 'Oh, so you're having a leading woman who's really a prostitute?' 'What? Not quite'.

Judy: The audience in Korea is much younger, because musical theatre is relatively new. And the same applies to the cast – there weren't many people over 35.

Paul Garrington: Seoul is like Tokyo on speed. Slightly more chaotic and manic, but probably more closely linked, slightly more Western – although I hate using that word. It was the very opposite of Tokyo, because they were very inexperienced about doing something on this scale. They had put on shows with great passion and great chutzpah, but never anything of this kind of size. It was in the Seoul Arts Centre, the city's opera house, which was a major and very classy national venue. To have *MAMMA MIA!* there was a huge event for the Koreans, which they brought great heart and gusto to. The timescale was tight because we were having to teach the show as well and we were working through translations of varying degrees of accuracy. It often felt like we were in a Korean version of *Lost In Translation*.

Park Hae-Mee as Donna, top with the original Seoul cast in 'Money, Money, Money' and above in 'Mamma Mia'.

Judy: Now that the European and Far East productions were starting to roll out, our attention turned back to the States, and in particular Las Vegas. Once again, we'd had enormous interest from early on, particularly from Steve Wynn, who'd built the Mirage and Bellagio and put on the great Cirque du Soleil shows *Mystère* and *O*. But Steve had wanted a total exclusive on the show that would have prevented us from touring *MAMMA MIA!* in the US, which we of course were not prepared to commit to. So Vegas had dropped off our radar for a while. We were still playing in Toronto, we had toured the major US cities, opened on Broadway and we had set our sights on US Tour Two, as it was called, which was going to be light on its feet compared to the first tour, because that show

Opposite: Dynamos from around the world. Clockwise from top left: Jeon Soo-Kyeong, Park Hae-Mee and Lee Kyeong-Mi (Seoul); Lara Mulcahy, Anne Wood and Rhonda Burchmore (Australia); Simone Kleinsma (Utrecht); Charlott Strandberg, Gunilla Backman and Sussie Eriksson (Stockholm); Jasna Ivir (Stuttgart); Geraldine Fitzgerald, Helen Hobson and Joanna Monro (International Tour).

had been quite cumbersome to move and set up. This new, faster-moving tour required a number of technical design adjustments, but we didn't alter the quality of the show or the look. The planning for that had been in hand even before we opened on Broadway, so US Tour Two was able to open in Providence, Rhode Island in February 2002. It was somewhere around that time that we were approached by the Mandalay Bay in Vegas. Andrew Treagus thought we should agree to put on a production there, and I thought he meant in a couple of years' time, but no, it was going to be ASAP!

Nina Lannan: I started in the business in 1980, so I remember a time when theatrical shows would go and sit down in Las Vegas hotels for stays of several months: the original companies of *Annie* and *42nd Street* had both done that. Then there had been a period when that didn't happen. As soon as I saw *MAMMA MIA!* I thought it would be perfect for Vegas, but none of the proposals we received really made sense until all of a sudden we got a call in the office saying that the Mandalay Bay Hotel was looking for a show to replace *Storm*. The Mandalay Bay had hosted a long run of *Chicago*, but *Storm* hadn't done too well, so they wanted a branded international hit. Their executives flew out to San Francisco to see *MAMMA MIA!*, and they were very happy with the show and with the audience reaction. Within six months of that visit we had a show on in Vegas.

Judy: We were insistent that the show wouldn't be Vegas-ised. As we had on Broadway, we encountered a certain amount of spin. A lot of people had their penny's worth to say: 'Oh, Broadway and West End shows don't work in Vegas.' But the Mandalay Bay people were very determined it should work there, and I was determined that the show should stay full length, right down to the complete megamix curtain call. I'm sure I slammed the door a couple of times when it was suggested we make it a tiny bit shorter. We were also being told, 'Ah, but you don't understand the Vegas audiences. The main thing is to get them back out into the casinos.' It was certainly a different environment. You have to walk through the casinos to get into the theatre. And Vegas audiences weren't used to having an intermission and the full megamix finale – unlike anywhere else in the world, where we had to work hard to get the audience to leave at the end because they wanted to see more, in Vegas, as soon as the lights went down, they'd be out of there, which increased the number of voices telling me we should shorten the show. I put my foot down. 'No, no, no.' My view was that we were selling the show on the basis that this was the Broadway production in Vegas, not an express version. And in any case the megamix finale was exactly what *not* to cut: it was so Vegas.

Catherine: *MAMMA MIA!* has already been pared down as much as it possibly can be. It is quite tightly structured, so if you take anything out it has such a knock-on effect on what's to come that you would end up having to rewrite the show from scratch. Judy just insisted that it was my way or the highway, as she said.

Top: The Mandalay Bay Hotel, *MAMMA MIA!*'s Las Vegas home. Above: The bride gets a Vegas makeover. Nancy Coyne remembers 'Judy was over and I said, "What's the hottest new merchandise?" She put on a cowboy hat, and we all said, "Oh my God, that's so Vegas."'

Adrian Bryan-Brown: Las Vegas is a town where people go to see the absolute best in entertainment; they have outsize – supersized – expectations. *MAMMA MIA!*, in its rather charming way, delivers the promise of being a hit around the world, so the idea is that the punters are getting to see a global hit, but in a very convenient way: 'One of the most successful shows in the world is downstairs, tonight.'

David Grindrod: I wouldn't have missed Vegas for the world. I had worked for a couple of years at Sun City in South Africa, so I was used to casinos, the gaudiness, and the bar-room crooners trying to sound like Sinatra. And I had put on Vegas-style shows with waterfalls and swimming pools, what I call 'tits and feather' shows. When we first arrived we were staying at the Luxor. The oddness of it all flowed over me but when I got down to the foyer of the hotel I found my associate director with his head in his hands. 'What in heaven's name is wrong?' I asked him, and he said, 'I can't stay in a room with the Eyes of Nefertiti in it.' I told him, 'Whoa, hold it, whoosh, just calm down. We *are* going to do this show here. They pay our bills and we just have to get on with it, whatever your thoughts about the place are. Take a big gulp, we're all in this together and we all jump together.' If you're not used to Vegas, it is the most bizarre place in the world and the most bizarre people come to audition – one day we had a snake charmer show up. And there was one girl who came in for the Vegas auditions. Gorgeous she was, and I could tell she'd had a lip job done, so I sent a note down the table: 'Look at the lips.' And the note came back with 'Look at the Adam's apple.' From then on we knew what we were in for.

Phyllida: On the first night in Vegas I remember that there were real brides and grooms sitting in the audience, fresh out of the wedding chapels. And if a mobile phone went off, the person would answer it – 'Oh, hi, I'm just watching the show.'

Nichola Treherne: Vegas was fabulous, because I'm a gambler at heart. Of all the shows this was the most physical, because we had more dancers than anywhere else by pure chance. We could teach the moves and they would learn it straightaway. The next day it was perfect, 'Wow.' We were rehearsing in what we could only imagine was a porn studio, which had a selection of boudoirs out at the back.

Paul Garrington: Robert McQueen had been Phyllida's associate director not only for Las Vegas, but also for the second Toronto company and US Tour Two. I was now responsible for bringing the show to Europe, in Holland and Spain, and putting together a European tour. And we found that in each country we had to adjust with the local theatrical culture. The comedy that people respond to in Madrid is more physical, on the edge of becoming slapstick. And then of course there's a specific theatrical style in Spain, the tradition of dark comedies and Lorca. The Spanish actors have big, bold personalities, which you can't and shouldn't interfere with too much. A Spanish Donna is a completely different animal to a Dutch one. The Dutch Donna – and I'm making a terrible generalisation here – is this adorable, down-to-earth, slightly chaotic woman who got into a bit of a muddle and slept

with three men. Whereas the Spanish Donna is passionate, sexy and a little bit scary! It's amazing how one character can sustain those kinds of differences.

Nichola Treherne: In Madrid the cast found it difficult to maintain the choreography. Each day it was almost like starting again. They would not go home and practise the moves. They'd go out and party. It took them a little while to get going; they don't wake up till five in the afternoon.

Judy: In the early days of thinking about where the show might go, Scandinavia had definitely not been on the list. In any case I would never have talked to anyone about going to Scandinavia, and especially Sweden, without talking to Benny and Björn. There were a lot of additional issues for them to bear in mind. But I have learnt with *MAMMA MIA!* never to say never, whether it's making a cast album, or going to Broadway. It must have been some time after the show had proved to work in Germany and then Holland that they thought, 'Why not?'

Björn: After the Dutch and German shows I didn't really have any excuse not to go to Stockholm, but I was reluctant to revisit those old lyrics and translate them back into my mother tongue – that seemed a little spooky. So I chose to have Niklas Strömstedt, a good friend and very accomplished lyricist, as a collaborator. We did the same thing as I had with Michael in Germany: Niklas did the bulk of the work and then we bounced it back and forth. It was odd noticing all the things that I would have done differently. But in the end, the Swedish lyrics seem completely natural to me.

Judy: The Swedish translation was always going to be an interesting challenge for Björn. He'd written those lyrics thirty years before when he probably wasn't anywhere near as fluent and erudite in the English language as he is now, but he seemed to feel comfortable working with Niklas Strömstedt.

Above: Mariona Castillo and Alejandro Vera as Sophie and Sky in 'Voulez-Vous' from the original Madrid production, which opened in the Teatro Lope de Vega in November 2004.
Below: *MAMMA MIA!*'s general manager Julian Stoneman with Helen Hobson (the International Tour's first Donna) with Judy Craymer at the first night in Edinburgh. This English-language tour opened at The Point in Dublin in September 2004, and has visited a long list of European and South African cities.
Overleaf: Anna Madgett and Mark Uhre, who played Sophie and Sky in Toronto's 2003 cast, sing 'I Have A Dream' in the show's closing scene.

MAMMA MIA! celebrated five years in London in April 2004, shortly before relocating to the Prince of Wales Theatre. From top: Frida, who Judy says was 'always so supportive'; Judy with Cameron Mackintosh; Benny and Björn with Vivien Parry (Donna).

Catherine: For all of us, our home town is what matters, isn't it? Benny and Björn didn't want to fall flat on their faces in Stockholm, any more than I'd like to in Bristol.

Benny: There had been the odd Swedish lyric of 'Honey, Honey' and a few of the other songs. We discovered that a number of our songs had been translated by Stig Anderson, but they had never been recorded. There was an opportunity when we were translating the songs to rewrite them, so they could fit into the show more than they actually do. But we avoided that. Björn said, 'No, no, we should be as close to the original lyric as possible even if it does not fit in with the show.'

Paul Garrington: Stockholm was very special. Preparations and rehearsals took place over the winter, working through days when it would just be creeping towards daylight at two in the afternoon, before going dark again. We were there for Christmas, which is delightful in Sweden, fabulous, very festive… and very cold. There was an added element of risk, a real sense of 'Are we going to pull this off in Sweden?' The pressure on Benny and Björn must have been acute, and they were both very keen to make it work for a Swedish audience. Björn was there all the time working with Niklas, changing and adjusting things. The auditions were obviously going to be quite intense and Benny and Björn were very much part of the audition process, both very keen to have only the best voices possible.

Nichola Treherne: What I noticed in Stockholm was the sound of the singers' voices. It didn't matter who they were, whether they were the principals, the ensemble or the understudies and covers, it was incredible: they all had this beautifully pure ABBA sound, nothing like the belters who'd turn up for auditions on Broadway.

Björn: It was a magical night, in typically Swedish winter weather. The production was so well received, and we knew this was going to be a deliberately restricted run. We had decided that whatever happened we would stop at the end of 2006. Even if we had 98 per cent ticket sales throughout, we would stop, because that was what we'd promised the actors. And it made the show like a limited edition.

Phyllida: The best aspect of the Stockholm show for me was the experience of watching a Swedish audience hearing the songs translated into Swedish for the first time. They were overwhelmed with excitement at that, something which presumably they'd never imagined would happen.

Judy: On the opening night there was a lovely idea for us all to go over to the first-night party in a horse-drawn sleigh, but I was totally unprepared because I was in ballet pumps and a short dress with bare legs, so in the end I drove up there. It was snowing, there were candles everywhere, in this beautiful theatre just by the Baltic. It was quite magical. It felt very much that we had come full circle.

There was never an ambition to take over the world. It just happened. Judy Craymer

Left and below: Niklas Riesback (Sky) and Nina Lundseie (Sophie) from the original Stockholm production of *MAMMA MIA!*, which opened at the Cirkus Teater in February 2005. Catherine Johnson explains how 'I Have A Dream' came to end the show, as Sky and Sophie walk towards the moon. 'Nichola Treherne came up with this brilliant suggestion. The show starts with 'I Have A Dream', we've gone through this journey with Sophie, her dream has now changed, she no longer wants to find her dad, she wants to get off the island and discover herself. It makes perfect sense.'

Right: Gunilla Backman as Donna and Charlott Strandberg as Tanya from the original Stockholm company.
Far right: Judy Craymer and Catherine Johnson at the Stockholm opening in February 2005. The four members of ABBA all attended, though they did not appear in public together.
Overleaf: Bobby Aitken's sound design for *MAMMA MIA!* at the Prince of Wales Theatre, London.

The first time I met Benny and Björn I discovered they are both very, very audio-savvy. They have enough understanding and experience of sound to make good judgements. Bobby Aitken

Bobby Aitken, sound designer: There were very opposite ideas about what the show should be in terms of the audio. Benny and Björn were looking to hear over twenty pop songs at pop-song level, but Phyllida thought she was about to direct an unamplified opera. She once said to me, really earnestly, 'I don't understand at all why we have to have loudspeakers.' And the answer was that however quietly you play pop music there's still a dynamic within the song that an unamplified voice can't produce. These songs were meant to be performed with electronics.

At the time MAMMA MIA! was opening, there was a development in loudspeaker technology called 'line array', a way of grouping loudspeakers together to give what is essentially a more focused sound with a longer throw. This was just becoming trendy and, in fact, it was Benny and Björn who asked us to look at this new technology. It sounded fantastic – and we've always used it on all MAMMA MIA! productions since.

Björn: We had used a fairly new French sound system for Kristina, with such good sound, such wonderful sound, so Benny and I agreed that we should use the same system in the West End. At that time the sound systems in most theatres had not followed developments elsewhere in the music business. They always sounded rather hard and hollow. I thought one thing that MAMMA MIA! must have is better sound than any other show. It's what audiences would expect from us.

Phyllida: This rather smoochy French guy, who was more scientist than technician, had invented these incredible speakers with a very strange shape that had never been used in musical theatre. What was extraordinary was that somehow his system made it feel as though the voices and the music on stage were right there in front of you.

Bobby Aitken: It's not always about the technology itself, it's about what you do with it. MAMMA MIA! is a very human story and the audience has a real relationship with most of the characters on stage. We tried very hard not to interfere with that feeling – in fact to enhance it. The tendency in musical theatre was to have the actors' microphones low down on their heads, and therefore often visible. Clearly the closer you get to somebody's mouth the better it will sound because you have more isolation: when I push up your fader I hear more of you and less of somebody standing next to you. But with MAMMA MIA! we fought really hard to keep the mikes as invisible as possible, even though that means we may lose the odd word. I think that's what makes the show work – it retains its naturalness, the sacrifice of the few for the good of the many. We also try to keep absolutely focused on where each person is, so you can have your eyes closed and almost point to who is speaking.

There was a lot of discussion during rehearsals about sound effects and what we could try. I have always found using effects very difficult in musical theatre. I feel there can be so much aural information competing for attention. It can often be a distraction from the audience's relationship with the characters on stage. In the end there are no sound effects in MAMMA MIA! at all! They all got cut one by one. What remains is sonically leaner.

Benny: Every time I see the show a part of me is checking, 'What's the sound guy doing today?' because the sound is like a living creature. The whole thing is dependent on the man or woman sitting behind the console. At the end of the day it becomes a personal matter because each person mixes the show differently within the overall parameters. So you need to be sure that whoever is doing that really has a feel for the show, because the actors deliver different performances every night. That's why people like to go to the theatre.

My priority was to make the world of *MAMMA MIA!* a real world, and to make it believable. I'd been to Greece a year or so before the show opened and remembered the pureness of the light. Howard Harrison

Howard Harrison, lighting designer: I believe that ideally an audience should not really be aware of lighting. Good lighting should just feel right; it shouldn't draw attention to itself, although there are parts of *MAMMA MIA!*, like the finale, where there are sixteen lights pointing in the audience's face, and they are clearly going to be aware of the lights at that point.

The show had to be bright and upbeat and vivid. In the late 1990s we were emerging from a phase of musicals where the mood and the visuals were rather dark, so it was refreshing to do a show where suddenly the feeling was bright and fresh and clean.

There was nothing much I could do until Mark Thompson had finished working on the set designs. So much of my job is dependent on what the designer comes up with – I can only respond to that. I remember going to his studio to see the set model for the first time; there were lots of little model people wearing bikinis and lying on sun loungers, which I thought looked rather jolly. The principal difficulty for me was that the set was effectively a sealed blue box, which we had to light and make iridescent as well as achieving all the other effects we wanted to achieve for the show. We were somewhat restricted in terms of the number of places we could light the show from.

And we were also rather limited when the show first opened because lighting technology was going through a huge transition at that point. It was a period of development when new equipment was coming out all the time, so we found ourselves heading down an avenue using equipment that at the time was state of the art, but it then soon became superseded by more sophisticated technology. The opening happened about a year too early from a technical point of view.

Phyllida was always very clear from the beginning, and rightly so, that *MAMMA MIA!* was a play and should be lit like a play, including the musical numbers that form part of it. But then the whole of the second half of Act One, from 'Super Trouper' to 'Voulez-Vous' – the hen night in the taverna – has a completely different atmosphere from the rest of the play. It's hotter, sexier. The rest is much more grounded in the reality of the island. And that has driven the changes and improvements we've added to the show since it opened. For example, the original version of 'Money, Money, Money' in London was a kind of fantasy sequence, which was subsequently changed. Originally everyone was part of a fantasy inside Donna's head and so the lighting was full of saturated colours, whereas the version that is now in the show is very much about Donna and the inhabitants of the taverna.

Even during the rehearsals for the Stockholm opening I was still making changes. There was something in 'Gimme! Gimme! Gimme!' that I had never been happy with and had wanted to change for ages, so finally we were able to alter it and now we've inserted it into all the productions around the world. It was a really simple thing. We had been using a whirly pattern of lights on the floor, which I always hated and thought was a bit naff, even though it worked. But we've now replaced that with some pools of light that I think are a bit sexier. The great thing about *MAMMA MIA!* is that everyone is very happy for you to go in and change things, to improve what's there, even if it's working. I can never sit back and think it's all perfect: there's always going to be something you can do to make it better. Listen, we are lucky. How many shows are there where you get the chance to do it sixteen times?

THE MOVIE: THE WONDER
OF A FAIRY TALE

Onwards and upwards – With the movie version of *MAMMA MIA!* completed and hugely successful, the dream of Judy Craymer (seen opposite with the London 2003 company) continues, as further foreign-language productions of *MAMMA MIA!* are in the pipeline and significant anniversaries of the existing productions are stacking up, always providing her with a fresh set of challenges and opportunities.

Judy: As far back as 2001, when the very first US tour was in Los Angeles, I was having discussions about the possibility of making a film version of the show. At eleven in the morning of the opening in LA, I had arranged a meeting with CAA, the Hollywood agency, and one of their clients. I'd imagined it might be a handful of people so when I came downstairs and found this posse of eager faces waiting for me it took me quite aback. But the same bravado, or foolhardiness, or whatever you want to call it that had kicked in when I was asking Polygram to commit to the show surged up again. And despite being confronted by these seasoned film people, I refused to relinquish any rights in *MAMMA MIA!*. I sat there and said, 'No, we're not going to sell the film rights. I am not going to be swayed.' I look back again and think, 'My God, I did that.' But they all kept in touch over the years. The clients who had been at that original meeting, Playtone – Tom Hanks and his partner Gary Goetzman's production company – had been after *MAMMA MIA!* for a very long time. Tom Hanks phoned me personally at the Littlestar offices to try and persuade me. Everyone in the office was beside themselves and one of the girls working for us then was going 'Come in Houston', and there was Tom – but I was not to be swayed…

John Kennedy: I remember having a conversation with Judy quite early on, when we were excited about how well *MAMMA MIA!* was doing, and I joked that one day we'd do a film. She said, 'No, no film.' I said I thought it was the next logical step and that it would be fantastic – the glamour, the Hollywood stars, the Oscars – but she was absolutely adamant that there wouldn't be a film. And then grudgingly she said, 'Well, maybe in ten years' time', but only if it remained completely under her control. Her argument was very convincing. She explained that some musicals can gross around the world as much as some films do, which I didn't know, and she was proved correct with *MAMMA MIA!*.

Judy: Despite not yielding to Tom's blandishments, when I wanted to really move the film forwards and realised that I would need a partner, Playtone were still there and willing to be that partner. That would not have happened five years earlier because they didn't yet know how the show would evolve or how we could operate. I think that Björn and Benny really warmed to the idea that they would be working with somebody who knew their way around Hollywood, because they knew *MAMMA MIA!* would be right in the spotlight when it became a film.

The prospect of making a movie was very exciting, something that I had never done in my life, and neither had Benny. A whole new experience. Björn Ulvaeus

Björn: Even reading Catherine's screenplay, there was a different language to learn. And with a movie, there is music underscoring the action, which of course is something we understand and know how to do, but all the rest was new to us.

Benny: It is difficult to read a screenplay, scene by scene, with all the technical directions. I was always clear that I would want to produce the music for the film. The songs existed already, of course, but we would have to re-record them from square one, as well as creating any linking music and additional scoring, and that meant we would need to know who was going to be in the movie, the keys they'd want to sing in and so on: a lot of work.

Phyllida: When we started having discussions about the movie, we'd have conversations where all kinds of information would emerge. Judy would suddenly say, 'I've never liked 'I Do, I Do, I Do, I Do, I Do'. I hope it's not in the film.' 'What, now you're telling us!' And we'd discover we each had our own personal un-favourite. It was a chance to be absolutely open about anything that we felt worked and didn't work in the show.

Judy: There was a marvellous moment when we were discussing the movie and deconstructing the music in particular. We were talking about the fact that in the stage show we have the vocal group singing on stage, but that in a film it's not so easy to have all these people running around singing. You need a reason for them to be there and to be singing. So we were having this discussion and Benny said, 'Maybe we take the backing vocals out,' and Björn said, 'Oh, don't be so ridiculous.' But it proved that everything was up for grabs. Nothing was taken for granted.

Catherine: We'd been talking about a screenplay for quite a while. Judy and I would have chats from time to time. We went on holiday to Madeira once ostensibly to talk about doing the screenplay, although we ended up lounging around in the sun and only talked about it for an hour on the plane back. When it came to the crunch and I needed to start work, I was listening to the overture to the show, and I thought, 'OK, so you could have everybody arriving on the island throughout the overture, and then crack on with the story'. And I just wrote it the usual way, with blood, sweat and tears.

When you're writing for the stage your aim generally is to construct a suspension of disbelief, drawing an audience into the world you are creating so that everybody is caught up in the moment. On film you can explore what people are doing when they're not on stage, when you're not seeing them.

I wanted the movie to be infused with the spirit of *MAMMA MIA!*. I wouldn't want anyone who'd seen the stage show to go to see the film and say 'Oh, that's not *MAMMA MIA!*.' But it should also be as much an individual movie experience as the stage show is a theatrical experience. The template I had in mind was very much *Grease: The Movie* – it's so glorious and I wanted to make something that would be as joyous as that.

Adapting the book of the stage version into a screenplay was a sharp learning curve for Catherine Johnson, but one she tackled with relish and enjoyed completing: 'I love writing THE END,' she says. 'It's the best bit.' In the final version 'One Of Us' had been dropped, 'When All Is Said And Done' introduced as a number for Sam, and 'Under Attack', and 'Knowing Me, Knowing You' converted into instrumental moments. 'Thank you For The Music' was also cut. Catherine says, 'It's a number that works on stage with everyone staying in the courtyard because the audience can suspend their disbelief, but we realised it wouldn't work in the movie. And I was also able to change 'Our Last Summer' into a scene where all the dads could talk to Sophie about their experiences with Donna, a chance for her to build a relationship with each of them, rather than just with Harry.'

When it was clear that the movie was going to become a reality, I felt I was back at the top of the rollercoaster, that exciting blend of exhilaration and dread: 'Here we go again!' Judy Craymer

Phyllida: *MAMMA MIA!* was always a movie: the ultimate fairy tale, set on location on a magical island. In many ways, it was bursting to get off the stage and into the cinema, but I had no idea I would be the person who would get to direct it. And indeed I think that Judy may have been urged by the sensible people to look for a proper film director… Of course *MAMMA MIA!* meant everything to me, but I decided that I wasn't going to let it ruin the next few years of my life if I found out that Steven Spielberg was directing it. So it was a big surprise when Judy rang me up one day and said, 'Catherine and I want you to read the screenplay, and if you like it, I want you to do it.'

Judy: I had never thought of anyone else directing the film. One of the conditions of any deal was that Catherine would write the screenplay and Phyllida would direct. I was determined to keep us together, even though some naysayers said I'd never get that through Universal, especially as musical films still have something of a hit-and-miss reputation in Hollywood. There were certainly quite a few hurdles to clear, but clear them we did.

Gary Goetzman: There were three original dynamos, Judy, Catherine and Phyllida. Obviously we felt that it was really important to keep that trio together for the film to capture all the great fun and energy that *MAMMA MIA!* on stage has. Even though Phyllida Lloyd had not directed a major motion picture before, and even though Catherine Johnson hadn't written a major screenplay, those were non-starters as issues, because they both know exactly what *MAMMA MIA!* is.

Judy: Meryl Streep was very much our first choice to play Donna, although many other names were suggested by other people, of course. We knew she had seen the show on Broadway a few years before, as she'd written a rather wonderful letter to the cast telling them how much she loved the show and how she'd wanted to get up on stage. And like schoolgirl fans, we had kept this letter. When we approached Meryl's agent in November 2006, everybody wished us luck, assuming we weren't going to get her. Apparently, Meryl was driving in her car when her agent rang and told her we'd offered her the part of Donna, and she screamed, 'I *am* MAMMA MIA!'. Phyllida and I flew out to New York to meet her for coffee in the Lowell Hotel on the Upper East Side, and as we were settling ourselves down, she said, 'So, you want me to play Donna?' 'Ye-e-s,' we squeaked, amazed that this was her opening question. 'You really *really* want me to play Donna?' Another 'Ye-e-s,' from us. 'Wow', she said.

Top: The announcement that *MAMMA MIA!* is to be made into a movie makes headline news in the trade publication *Daily Variety* in April 2006. Bottom: Producer Gary Goetzman, co-founder with Tom Hanks of Playtone, who was to produce the movie with Judy Craymer for Universal Pictures.

Above: The jetty scenes were shot on the Greek mainland at Damouhari, a hamlet on the eastern Pelion coast, but the other locations for the fictional island of Kalokairi were all on the *bona fide* island settings of Skiathos and Skopelos in the Sporades – each of these locations inspired the film's Greek Cypriot cinematographer Haris Zambarloukos. Phyllida Lloyd remembers how fantastic it was to be able to dive into the sea at the end of a long day's shooting.

Below: Sam, aka Pierce Brosnan, here with Judy Craymer, says of ABBA's music, 'Everyone has their favourite song. Everyone's listened to ABBA; everyone's danced to ABBA; everyone's sung ABBA; everyone's been driven nuts by their songs. But, ultimately, people just love the songs and they have a place in their hearts for them.'

Phyllida: We knew that Meryl sang. We knew she wanted to do a musical. She combined everything that was required. She's one of those unique actors who can laugh the world's laughs and cry the world's tears. That's what *MAMMA MIA!* needed, and we had it in her.

Judy: Once the news about Meryl got out the world sat up and took the movie very seriously. Meryl became completely supportive of and ambitious for the project – later on Phyllida and I joked that we should get T-shirts that said, 'We were here *before* Meryl!' For the rest of the casting, we had to do a little detective work to find out who could sing – we couldn't really ask these A-list movie stars to come in and audition the way we could for the role of Sophie, for example.

When we had first been developing the stage show in the late 90s, I was an avid watcher of *Cybill*, the Cybill Shepherd sitcom, and was obsessed by Christine Baranski as Maryanne, and from then on, in my head at least, she was Tanya, fragile, bright, always reaching for the next Martini.

Christine Baranski, Tanya: So often we say that women don't matter enough in the industry and why aren't there stories about women? Well, this is it. This is an example of a woman with a vision for ten years who said, 'There's something here in this musical.' And she was right.

Judy: And for Rosie we needed the best comedienne we could find, who else but Julie Walters? When *her* agent rang her about being in the movie, Julie's first words were, 'Make my day, tell me I'm going to be the fat one…'

Meryl Streep, Donna: You can see built into *MAMMA MIA!* something very forgiving about being human and being female and all the things that go with it – things women understand.

Colin Firth, Harry: This is not unfamiliar to me, I have to say. I have been there before. You could say that the Jane Austen world is similar. The Bridget Jones films are seen though a woman's eyes. So they tend to wheel me in whenever they need someone to be the side salad.

These women have created their own world, their own life-force. And we guys are just the chicks. Pierce Brosnan

Judy: We did try to avoid making the decision about the three dads entirely on the basis of 'Cor, who do we fancy?' I knew Pierce Brosnan could sing, and sent a copy of him singing in the movie *Evelyn* to Benny, Björn and the musical director, Martin Lowe, to prove it. We met Pierce in London for dinner after he'd seen *MAMMA MIA!* and he told us that night that he was up for it. Colin Firth, however, was definitely not a big fan of musicals, though I think he is now. And Stellan Skarsgård was a suggestion from our casting director Ellen Lewis. He didn't get the role because he is Swedish, but when Benny and Björn asked if he could sing, Stellan was able to say, 'I'll pop down the road and show you.'

Phyllida: We had three men with incredible warmth and humour, and each of them had the skill to take us on this incredible journey from a place in their lives where they're all a bit stuck, a bit lost, to their liberation and literally letting their hair down on a magical island.

Colin Firth: There's a real tenderness about the notion of these three grizzled, middle-aged men who find out there's more to their lives than they thought.

Pierce Brosnan, Sam: I don't think I have ever been so nervous about a job, but Martin Lowe, the musical director, instilled such confidence in me. He came out to California and we set up in my office and started banging out the songs. For the next few months, I listened to them day in and day out, driving the kids to school. When it came time to record, I walked into the studios and there were Phyllida and Judy, and Benny and Björn… Show time! I wasn't alone because I had Stellan and Colin right there, equally terrified. In the end, I surrendered to the whole experience, and had a great time doing it. It's actually quite exhilarating to sing and to express your emotions that way.

Judy: The songs were pre-recorded in April 2007 at Air Studios in London. Benny got the original ABBA backing musicians together – 'The music sticks in the fingers,'

Above: Christine Baranski, Meryl Streep and Julie Walters as Tanya, Donna and Rosie. Christine Baranski says, 'One of the great challenges and pleasures for me – and Meryl and Julie – was creating this sense of an old and textured friendship', while Meryl Streep comments, 'I was really doing this to embarrass my 20-something-year-old children. The dancing part will mortify them. They'll have to move to Alaska or someplace. Just the overalls alone are gonna do it for them.'
Below: Colin Firth, Stellan Skarsgård and Pierce Brosnan as the three dads Harry, Bill and Sam. Stellan Skarsgård enjoys the fact that the men are the supporting roles. 'Nobody is interested in our psychology. We are the bimbos in the film!'

Opposite top: Christine Baranski's Tanya performs 'Does Your Mother Know' on Kastani beach on Skopelos. Phyllida Lloyd recalls, 'We had to put concrete under the sand to create a really good dance floor, because the sand was just too squishy for us to get lift-off.' And Christine Baranski remembers, 'You're on this beautiful Greek beach, the sun pounding down in your eyes, and you're singing over many takes at full throttle, going for broke every time. It was exhausting. No matter, they wipe you down like a prizefighter, fan you down and then you're back in it again. But it was a gas.' Judy Craymer, says, 'I'm sure Christine enjoyed it hugely. Who wouldn't dream of doing a free concert on the beach with 25 gorgeous boys oiled to within an inch of their lives in sun-tan oil?'
Opposite far right: Donna climbs the goathouse, built in Pinewood studios and created by production designer Maria Djurkovic. Meryl Streep says, 'I was told that I was going to climb up the goathouse wall while singing 'Mamma Mia'. I thought, "How big could a goathouse be?" The goathouse turned out to be this sheer wall. I was basically doing a Spider-Man stunt. It was the first week, and I thought, "Whew! I better do my exercises every night."' Judy remembers that at their very first meeting in New York, 'Meryl said she wanted a project that would take 100%, or 110% of her energy. She definitely got her wish.'

he said, – and the backing vocals were by the Stockholm cast. To have Benny and Björn reworking the music and recording with the actors was an incredibly exciting prospect, and in the studio Benny was particularly hands-on; everything came under his command.

Meryl Streep: The songs are timeless. They just enter your body. When I came to learn them, I found I knew every single one.

Christine Baranski: There's a tendency to think ABBA songs will be easy to sing – perhaps because they're so catchy – but they are much more complicated than one would think. Benny and Björn are superb musicians, and their harmonies and rhythms are complex. They are very exacting about what they want.

Björn: We had such fun in the recording studio. There was such a relaxed feeling. We knew that they were primarily actors – of course they were – but they were all delivering exactly what we had expected them to do.

Stellan Skarsgård, Bill: Benny and Björn are so calm and very Swedish. Here were two other fellow Swedes standing there, being very encouraging; they just let me sing on.

Benny: It was tremendously joyful, especially collaborating with the actors who were so incredibly well prepared, a totally uplifting experience.

Judy: After the movie had been cast and the songs pre-recorded, we had the first read-through at Pinewood – for new casts on the stage show I usually had a little tongue-in-cheek line that 'in MAMMA MIA!, the ABBA songs are the stars', but looking at Pierce Brosnan, Meryl Streep and the others, I said I thought for once that just might not be true, though Pierce assured me it was…

Phyllida: When we got out to Greece we had to be prepared to abandon all our best-laid plans. We had fallen in love with some of these locations quite a long time before. Then, suddenly, we'd find that a perfect little beach had been eaten up by surf and we had to pick up sticks and dash into the woods and do something different. But throughout the life of the show we've always been excited by changing what we're doing according to the context. It was very much meat and drink to us to have to adapt to the terrain.

Judy: Shooting on location was a real white-knuckle ride. Although the settings were glorious – we weren't stuck out in the Sahara – the tight schedules meant it was intense for everyone. But there was a great mood and camaraderie throughout. At one point Benny arrived and we set up a party within 24 hours, tracked down the only piano on the island in case he fancied playing – and he did, with all the cast singing along. Fantastic.

Left: Dominic Cooper as Sky and Amanda Seyfried as Sophie, who landed the role after the production team had run extensive auditions in London, New York and Los Angeles. Judy Craymer remembers, 'There were a lot of talented Sophies out there, and a lot of young actresses who were extremely interested in the part, but Amanda, who we saw in LA, ticked all the boxes: she had an impish, loveable look and a fabulous voice, and even looked like Meryl. Dominic has a charming yet playful factor. He can sing, and the girls love him. He was perfect in the role of Sky.'

Top: Director Phyllida Lloyd on location in a landscape she first backpacked across at the age of 17. Bottom: Amanda Seyfried as Sophie approaches the wedding ceremony on local transport. Amanda says, 'I love the music so much. It makes your heart pump and want to dance and be in love with the world!'

Christine Baranski: It was one of the happiest sets I've ever been on. This thing that Phyllida calls the MAMMA MIA! spirit is all about sensuality and a sense of fun. The movie is like a tribute to Aphrodite, the goddess of love and beauty. There is really something fundamentally joyous and kind of erotic that people connect to on a deep level.

Julie Walters, Rosie: We were all learning stuff that none of us did. Well, we could all sort of do it, but we're not West End Wendies, we weren't appearing in musicals all the time, and that really is bonding.

Meryl Streep: Phyllida was always demanding that we locate the real stuff in what could be just fun. So she was where we located ourselves, our lodestone. She was where we started from. It's a great quality in a director, that level of sureness and certainty.

Colin Firth: She had an amazing way of informing moments that didn't seem important with texture, or using an angle that could make the moment more interesting – wonderfully economic and precise filmmaking.

Phyllida: I was determined that the camera language was going to be different for every song. Not just for the sake of it, but so that it would do something different to the audience, according to what the plot required at the moment. I wanted to get inside the scenes, because I'd always been outside them in the theatre. I parked myself right in the middle of a piece like 'Voulez-Vous' and presented Sophie's point-of-view with my camera.

Gary Goetzman: You can't help but move and stomp your feet. You forget you're actually shooting a movie. All that quiet reverence that the cast and crew normally have by the camera, all of a sudden it's out the window. *Everybody's* rockin'.

Stellan Skarsgård: When you're a middle-aged man and everyone else is a twenty-year-old professional dancer, you do feel slightly intimidated. Dancing was something I hadn't done sober in thirty years.

Phyllida: We filmed 'Voulez-Vous' using five cameras over four days. There is something very exhilarating about shouting 'playback' with 50 or 60 people on the dancefloor and you've agreed to run to the end of the number, whatever happens. That was when we saw the fruits of all the rehearsals, of everybody knowing each other, and of me being able to set up certain kinds of improvisations and say, 'OK, I'm not going to tell anyone exactly where they're going, but I'm going to give you certain boundaries, like "Don't stand right in front of the camera".' We tried to create this energy where anything was possible, this sort of Bacchanalian fever. And it was the very first time that I felt any sense of relaxation. All the women came hurtling into the bottom of the courtyard, the music started and I thought, 'I'm in movies. I'm directing a mega blockbuster Hollywood movie!'

Judy: I am very proud of Phyllida. She set herself an almost impossible task with 'Voulez-Vous', a huge, complex piece with all the lead actors, the ensemble and so much intricate choreography. After all the intense work from everybody involved, the movie was the perfect celebration for this extended *MAMMA MIA!* family that keeps growing and growing in ways I could never have dreamed of.

Catherine: After all the premieres had finished one of my happiest moments was seeing the film again on holiday in Mykonos, in an open-air cinema, at 11 o'clock at night, under a beautiful moonlit sky. It was just like *Cinema Paradiso*, with very few tourists in the audience, mainly Greek locals. It was a wonderful experience, because whereas we all look at the locations and think, 'That would be a great place to go on holiday', for them it was their backyard. They roared with laughter – there must have been a fantastic translation for the subtitles – and surrounded by all the nighttime sounds and aromas of a Greek island it was as if the scenes on screen had come alive.

Judy: : For the credits we wanted to use a megamix finale just like the stage show, but since in most movies the audience leaves as soon as the credits roll, our idea of a communal experience wasn't really a Hollywood concept. Ann Roth, the costume designer, had prepared some fabulous costumes, but we didn't get the green light until just before we shot the sequence back at Pinewood. I have to say the dads were extremely keen to get into platform boots and Lycra. As we packed up, I had a panicky call from the dressers: Colin Firth didn't want to leave without his Lycra suit! And then we needed to find a role for Björn. Benny had turned up on location in an amazing 1920s motor yacht called the 'Haida G' and we shot 'Money, Money, Money' on the yacht, with Meryl doing her *Titanic* spoof on the bow. Later Benny got his Hitchcockian cameo dressed as a Greek fisherman playing the 'Dancing Queen' riff on a piano on the jetty. And of course Björn wanted to know what he could do. So Phyllida said, 'Tell Björn to get himself to Pinewood in a Greek costume for the finale and he's in.' Björn said, 'I'll be there': he turned up and there he is as Apollo, having to lip-synch to himself on 'Waterloo'! We have this little mantra on the show that came from a review of the Broadway version: 'Let the joy wash over you', and it has, right to the very end – and beyond.

The Swedish premiere of the movie on 4th July 2008, held at Benny Andersson's Rival Hotel in Stockholm, saw all four members of ABBA reunited with the *MAMMA MIA!* team and the stars of the film. From left to right: Benny, Pierce Brosnan, Amanda Seyfried, Meryl Streep, Agnetha, Anni-Frid, Christine Baranski, Colin Firth, Catherine, Phyllida, Judy, Björn and Dominic Cooper.

CHRONOLOGY

1945
APRIL — Björn Ulvaeus is born in Gothenburg.
NOVEMBER — Anni-Frid ('Frida') Lyngstad is born in Bjørkåsen, Norway.
1946
DECEMBER — Benny Andersson is born in Stockholm.
1950
APRIL — Agnetha Fältskog is born in Jönköping.
1963
Polar Music is founded by Stig Anderson and Bengt Bernhag. The first act they sign is the Hootenanny Singers, a skiffle group featuring Björn Ulvaeus.
1964
OCTOBER — Benny Andersson joins the Hep Stars, one of Sweden's most successful groups.
1966
Benny and Björn meet and begin to write together.
1967
SEPTEMBER — Frida wins a Swedish talent competition. After appearing on national TV, she is offered a recording contract with EMI. Around the same time, Agnetha establishes herself as a pop singer, and goes on to have several hits in Sweden.
1968
Björn meets Agnetha while both are on tours of Sweden's folkparks.
1969
Benny meets Anni-Frid, also while touring the folkparks. Over the next three years, the four future members of ABBA will collaborate on and contribute to each other's records before gradually coming together as a group.
1972
JUNE — 'People Need Love' is the first release credited to all four members of the group. They are not yet known as ABBA.
1973
FEBRUARY — 'Ring Ring' is released in Swedish and English versions.
MARCH — The Ring Ring album is a Number 2 hit in Sweden, but the single fails to get into the running for Eurovision.
1974
MARCH — Waterloo is released in Sweden. Swedish- and English-language versions of the title track are also released.
APRIL — 'Waterloo' wins the Eurovision Song Contest in Brighton, and goes to Number 1 in the UK and Number 6 in the US.
NOVEMBER — ABBA embark on their first major European tour.
1975
APRIL — The album ABBA is released together with the single 'I Do, I Do, I Do, I Do, I Do'.
JUNE — 'SOS' is released and peaks at Number 6 in the UK.
SEPTEMBER — 'Mamma Mia' knocks Queen's 'Bohemian Rhapsody' off the Number 1 spot in the UK.
NOVEMBER — Greatest Hits, the group's first compilation, is released.

1976
MARCH — 'Fernando', an English-language version of a track written for Frida's 1975 solo album, is released. It will reach Number 1 in 11 countries, including the UK.
AUGUST — 'Dancing Queen' is released and becomes the only ABBA single to reach Number 1 in the USA.
OCTOBER — Arrival is released. It is to be ABBA's first Number 1 album in the UK, and goes on to top the charts in ten countries.
NOVEMBER — 'Money, Money, Money' is released.
1977
JANUARY — ABBA open their first world tour in Oslo. Their set includes the mini musical The Girl With The Golden Hair.
FEBRUARY — 'Knowing Me, Knowing You' hits the charts. At the end of February the world tour reaches Australia, where filming for ABBA: The Movie will take place.
OCTOBER — 'The Name Of The Game' hits the charts.
DECEMBER — ABBA – The Album, the group's fifth album in 5 years, is released. It will reach Number 1 in the UK chart.
1978
JANUARY — 'Take A Chance On Me' goes to Number 1 in the UK and Number 3 in the US.
MAY — A double A-side of 'Eagle' and 'Thank You For The Music' is released.
SEPTEMBER — 'Summer Night City' appears.
1979
JANUARY — 'Chiquitita' is the first single to be taken from the Voulez-Vous album. All royalties are donated to UNICEF to mark the charity's campaign for The Year of the Child.
APRIL — Voulez-Vous is released and tops the charts in 11 countries. 'Does Your Mother Know' is released as a single at around the same time.
AUGUST — The single 'Voulez-Vous' is released.
OCTOBER — Greatest Hits Vol. 2, planned to coincide with ABBA's North American and European tours, is released together with the single 'Gimme! Gimme! Gimme! (A Man After Midnight)'.
DECEMBER — 'I Have a Dream' makes Number 2 in the UK.
1980
JUNE — Gracias Por La Música, ABBA's first Spanish-language album, reaches Number 5 in Spain and Number 4 in Argentina.
JULY — 'The Winner Takes It All' rises to Number 8 in the US chart as well as hitting the top spot across Europe.
NOVEMBER — Super Trouper is ABBA's seventh album and another international hit, again reaching Number 1 in Sweden and the UK. The title track is released as a single in the same month and becomes ABBA's ninth UK Number 1.
1981
NOVEMBER — The Visitors, the eighth and final original album, reaches Number 1 in eight countries.
DECEMBER — 'One Of Us' is the first single to come from The Visitors and ABBA's last major single success worldwide.

1982

NOVEMBER — ABBA celebrate ten years as a band with a double album entitled *The Singles – The First Ten Years*. It is also in the autumn of 1982 that Judy Craymer meets Björn and Benny for the first time while working on *Chess*.

1983

FEBRUARY — 'Under Attack', the band's final single, is a hit in Belgium and the Netherlands.

1992

SEPTEMBER — *ABBA Gold* is released. It will go on to be re-released twice and sell more than 22 million copies worldwide.

1997

JANUARY — Judy meets Catherine Johnson. They start to throw out ideas for a musical play based on the songs of ABBA.

FEBRUARY — Judy and Catherine present Catherine's ideas to Björn.

APRIL–MAY — The first draft is completed and delivered.

JUNE — Björn, Judy and Catherine go to see *Art* in London and meet designer Mark Thompson, who then joins the creative team.

NOVEMBER — Phyllida Lloyd comes on board as director. Judy, Catherine and Phyllida meet with Benny and Björn in Stockholm.

1998

MARCH–APRIL — There is a ten-day workshop, attended by Polygram executives and creative team members.

1999

JANUARY — Rehearsals begin.

APRIL — *MAMMA MIA!* opens at London's Prince Edward Theatre.

AUGUST — The original cast recording is completed. Over the coming years it will go on to sell millions of copies worldwide.

2000

MAY — *MAMMA MIA!*'s first international production opens at the Royal Alexandra Theatre in Toronto.

NOVEMBER — The US National Tour opens. It will play 1,522 performances before closing in August 2004.

2001

JUNE — The show premieres in Melbourne, Australia.

OCTOBER — *MAMMA MIA!* opens at the Cadillac Winter Garden Theatre on Broadway with huge advance sales. Within a week of opening it sets a new house record.

2002

FEBRUARY — A second US National Tour opens. The same tour has since played in almost 100 cities.

NOVEMBER — The first foreign language production of *MAMMA MIA!* opens at the Operettenhaus in Hamburg, Germany.

DECEMBER — A Japanese-language show opens at the Dentsu Shiki Theatre and plays at full capacity at every performance until November 2004.

2003

FEBRUARY — *MAMMA MIA!* sets a new house record within a week of opening at the Mandalay Bay Hotel in Las Vegas.

JULY — The show admits its 10 millionth audience member worldwide.

NOVEMBER — A Dutch language production opens at the Beatrix Theatre in Utrecht, Holland.

2004

JANUARY — Korea's version of *MAMMA MIA!* opens with the highest advance in Korean theatrical history.

APRIL — The show celebrates 5 years in London on the 30th Anniversary of ABBA winning the Eurovision Song Contest.

JULY — A second German-language production opens in Stuttgart, Germany. It is the first time that a major musical has played concurrently in two German cities.

SEPTEMBER — The International tour begins in Dublin, Ireland.

NOVEMBER — The first Spanish language version opens in Madrid. This is the fourteenth production of *MAMMA MIA!* – and the fifth foreign language production – to open worldwide.

2005

FEBRUARY — *MAMMA MIA!* reaches ABBA's homeland, opening in Swedish at the Cirkus Teater in Stockholm, Sweden.

MARCH — The show celebrates 2,500 performances in London.

MAY — With 1,500 performances on Broadway, *MAMMA MIA!* surpasses the original Broadway runs of such hits as *The Sound Of Music*; *Damn Yankees* and *The King And I*. The same month, the Toronto show closes on its fifth anniversary, having become the longest-running production in the 96-year history of the Royal Alexandra Theatre.

JUNE — *MAMMA MIA!* plays its 1,000th performance in Las Vegas, becoming the most successful and longest-running full-scale Broadway musical ever to play the Las Vegas Strip.

2006

OCTOBER — *MAMMA MIA!* celebrates its fifth anniversary on Broadway and opens in Russian in Moscow.

2007

JUNE — Filming for *MAMMA MIA!* the movie began at Pinewood studios.

AUGUST — The global smash hit musical *MAMMA MIA!* celebrates 3,500 performances in London and becomes the longest running show ever at the Prince of Wales Theatre, passing the record previously held by the musical *Aspects of Love*.

OCTOBER — *MAMMA MIA!* slides past the performance record previously held by Mel Brooks' *The Producers* to become the 18th longest running show in Broadway history.

Judy Craymer, global producer of the smash hit musical *MAMMA MIA!* is presented with an MBE by His Royal Highness The Prince of Wales, at Buckingham Palace in London. *MAMMA MIA!*'s fourth German language production opens in Berlin.

NOVEMBER — A second Spanish production opens in Barcelona at the Barcelona Teatre Musical.

2008

MAY — *MAMMA MIA!*, the longest-running Broadway musical on the Las Vegas Strip celebrates 2,000 performances at the Mandalay Bay Resort.

JUNE — World premiere of *MAMMA MIA!* the movie in London, England at the Odeon cinema, Leicester Square.

JULY — Swedish premiere of *MAMMA MIA!* the movie in Stockholm, Sweden.

AUGUST — The soundtrack to the summer's blockbuster hit *MAMMA MIA!* the movie reaches Number 1 on the Pop Catalog of Billboard's Top 200 Chart in the U.S., and achieves platinum status, after only its fifth week of release.

SEPTEMBER — *MAMMA MIA!* the movie announced as officially the highest grossing movie of 2008 in the UK, Norway, Sweden, Greece, Austria, Hungary, Iceland, Holland and Cyprus.

2009

MARCH — A Norwegian language production opens at the Folketeatret in Oslo.

APRIL — 10th anniversary of the original London show of *MAMMA MIA!* at the Prince of Wales Theatre.

PRODUCTION DETAILS

LONDON

Original venue Prince Edward Theatre

Other venue Prince of Wales Theatre

Opening date 6 April 1999

Original principal cast
Donna: Siobhán McCarthy
Sophie: Lisa Stokke
Sky: Andrew Langtree
Tanya: Louise Plowright
Rosie: Jenny Galloway
Sam: Hilton McRae
Harry: Paul Clarkson
Bill: Nicolas Colicos
Eddie: Nigel Harman
Pepper: Neal Wright
Ali: Eliza Lumley
Lisa: Melissa Gibson

TORONTO

Venue Royal Alexandra Theatre

Opening date 23 May 2000

Closing date 22 May 2005

Original principal cast
Donna: Louise Pitre
Sophie: Tina Maddigan
Sky: Adam Brazier
Tanya: Mary Ellen Mahoney
Rosie: Gabrielle Jones
Sam: Gary P Lynch
Harry: Lee MacDougall
Bill: David Mucci
Eddie: Nicolas Dromard
Pepper: Sal Scozzari
Ali: Nicole Fraser
Lisa: Miku Graham

US NATIONAL TOUR 1

Opening venue Orpheum Theatre, San Francisco

Tour route San Francisco, Los Angeles, Chicago, Boston, Minneapolis, Detroit, Philadelphia, Washington DC, Denver

Opening date 17 November 2000

Closing date 29 August 2004

Original principal cast
Donna: Louise Pitre
Sophie: Tina Maddigan
Sky: Adam Brazier
Tanya: Mary Ellen Mahoney
Rosie: Gabrielle Jones
Sam: Gary P Lynch
Harry: Lee MacDougall
Bill: David Mucci
Eddie: Nicolas Dromard
Pepper: Sal Scozzari
Ali: Nicole Fraser
Lisa: Miku Graham

AUSTRALIA & ASIA TOUR

Opening venue Princess Theatre, Melbourne

Tour route Melbourne, Sydney, Brisbane, Perth, Adelaide, Auckland, Hong Kong, Singapore, Brisbane, Melbourne

Opening date 9 June 2001

Closing date 9 June 2005

Original principal cast
Donna: Anne Wood
Sophie: Natalie O'Donnell
Sky: Jolyon James
Tanya: Rhonda Burchmore
Rosie: Lara Mulcahy
Sam: Nicholas Eadie
Harry: Robert Grubb
Bill: Peter Hardy
Eddie: Alan James Davies
Pepper: Shaun Rennie
Ali: Katrina Talbot
Lisa: Alicia Gardiner

BROADWAY

Venue Cadillac Winter Garden Theatre

Opening date 18 October 2001

Original principal cast
Donna: Louise Pitre
Sophie: Tina Maddigan
Sky: Joe Machota
Tanya: Karen Mason
Rosie: Judy Kaye
Sam: David W. Keeley
Harry: Dean Nolen
Bill: Ken Marks
Eddie: Michael Benjamin Washington
Pepper: Mark Price
Ali: Sara Inbar
Lisa: Tonya Doran

US NATIONAL TOUR 2

Opening venue Performing Arts Centre, Providence

Tour towns and cities include
Akron, Albuquerque, Appleton, Atlanta, Austin, Bakersfield, Baltimore, Birmingham, Bloomington, Boise, Buffalo, Calgary, Charlotte, Chicago, Cincinnati, Cleveland, Columbus, Costa Mesa, Dallas, Dayton, Denver, Des Moines, Detroit , East Lansing, Edmonton, Eugene, Fort Lauderdale, Fort Meyers, Fort Worth, Fresno, Grand Rapids, Greensboro, Greenville, Guadalajara (Mexico), Hartford, Hershey, Houston, Indianapolis, Iowa City, Jacksonville, Kalamazoo, Kansas City, Lincoln, Little Rock, Long Beach, Louisville, Madison, Memphis, Mexico City, Miami, Milwaukee, Minneapolis, Monterrey (Mexico), Montreal, Nashville, New Orleans, Norfolk, Oklahoma City, Omaha, Orlando, Ottawa, Pasadena, Peoria, Philadelphia, Pittsburgh, Portland, Providence, Raleigh, Regina, Richmond, Rochester, Sacramento, Salt Lake City, San Antonio, San Bernadino, San Diego, San Jose, Scranton, Seattle, South Bend, Spokane, Springfield, St Louis, Syracuse, Tampa, Tempe, Thousand Oaks, Toledo, Tucson, Tulsa, University Park, Vancouver, Washington DC, West Palm Beach, Winnipeg

Opening date 28 February 2002

Original principal cast
Donna: Monique Lund
Sophie: Kristie Marsden
Sky: Chris Bolan
Tanya: Ellen Harvey
Rosie: Robin Baxter
Sam: Don Noble
Harry: James Kall
Bill: Pearce Bunting
Eddie: Tommar Wilson
Pepper: J.P. Potter
Ali: Bethany Pagliolo
Lisa: Elana Ernst

HAMBURG

Venue Operettenhaus

Opening date 3 November 2002

Original principal cast
Donna: Carolin Fortenbacher
Sophie: Katja Berg
Sky: Jörg Neubauer
Tanya: Kelstin Marie Mäkelburg
Rosie: Jasna Ivir
Sam: Frank Logemann
Harry: Cusch Jung
Bill: Ulrich Wiggers
Eddie: Wolf Wrobel
Pepper: Guido Zarncke
Ali: Bettina Oswald
Lisa: Florence Kasumba

Translators
Book: Ruth Deny
Lyrics: Michael Kunze

TOKYO

Venue Dentsu Shiki Theatre

Opening date 1 December 2002

Closing date 28 November 2004

Original principal cast
Donna: Chizu Hosaka
Sophie: Asami Higuchi
Sky: Yoichiro Akutsu
Tanya: Izumi Mori
Rosie: Yayoi Aoyama
Sam: Kiyomichi Shiba
Harry: Masaru Yamaki
Bill: Masuo Nonaka
Eddie: Yuji Kawaguchi
Pepper: Ryuhei Mochizuki
Ali: Yuki Morizane
Lisa: Kae Igarashi

Translators
Book: Hiromitsu Yukawa
Lyrics: Keita Asari

LAS VEGAS

Venue Mandalay Bay Theatre

Opening date 13 February 2003

Original principal cast
Donna: Tina Walsh
Sophie: Jill Paice
Sky: Victor Wallace
Tanya: Karole Foreman
Rosie: Jennifer Perry
Sam: Nick Cokas
Harry: Michael Piontek
Bill: Mark Leydorf
Eddie: Felipe Crook
Pepper: Brandon Alameda
Ali: Courtney Bradshaw
Lisa: Danielle Ferretti

UTRECHT

Venue Beatrix Theatre

Opening date 9 November 2003

Closing date 12 February 2006

Original principal cast
Donna: Simone Kleinsma
Sophie: Celine Purcell
Sky: Oren Schrijver
Tanja: Ellen Evers
Roos: Doris Baaten
Sam: Hajo Bruins
Harrie: Jon Van Eerd
Bart: Filip Bolluyt
Eddie: Jeroen Luiten
Pepper: Paul Boereboom
Ellie: Manon Novak
Lisa: Suzanne de Heij

Translators
Book: Daniel Cohen
Lyrics: Coot Van Doesburgh

KOREA

Original venue Seoul Arts Centre

Other venue Daegu Opera House

Opening date 25 January 2004

Original principal cast
Donna: Park Hae-Mee
Sophie: Bae Hae-Sun
Sky: Lee Gun-Myung
Tanya: Jeon Soo-Kyeong
Rosie: Lee Kyung-Mi
Sam: Sung Ki-Youn
Harry: Joo Seong-Joong
Bill: Park Ji-Il
Eddie: Jung Eui-Uk
Pepper: Jung Chul-Ho

Ali: Lim Eun-Young
Lisa: Seo Eun-Sun

Translators
Book: Chul-Lee Kim, Soo-Jeong Seong
Lyrics: Jin-Sub Han

STUTTGART

Venue Palladium Theatre

Opening date 18 July 2004

Original principal cast
Donna: Jasna Ivir
Sophie: Ina Trabesinger
Sky: Armin Kahl
Tanja: Franziska Becker
Rosie: Iris Schumaker
Sam: Andreas Lichtenberger
Harry: Tilo Keiner
Bill: Marc Hetterle
Eddie: John Ramsten
Pepper: Till Nau
Ali: Julia Berger
Lisa: Marianne Tarnowskij

Translators
Book: Ruth Deny
Lyrics: Michael Kunze

INTERNATIONAL TOUR

Opening venue The Point
Theatre, Dublin

Tour route Dublin, Edinburgh,
Johannesburg, Cape Town,
Durban, Tallinn, Lisbon, Brussels,
Paris, Cologne, Oberhausen,
Munich,Erfurt, Leipzig,
Frankfurt, Berlin, Austria,
Switzerland, Belfast, Edinburgh,
Cape Town, Pretoria, Manchester

Opening date 9 September 2004

Original principal cast
Donna: Helen Hobson
Sophie: Emily Dykes
Sky: Michael Xavier
Tanya: Geraldine Fitzgerald
Rosie: Joanna Monro
Sam: Cameron Blakely
Harry: John Langley
Bill: Ulrich Wiggers
Eddie: Mark Willshire
Pepper: Barnaby Thompson
Ali: Jayde Westaby
Lisa: Kaisa Hammerlund

MADRID

Venue Lope De Vega Theatre

Opening date 11 November 2004

Original principal cast
Donna: Nina
Sofi: Mariona Castilla
Sky: Alejandro Vera
Tania: Marta Valverde
Rosy: Paula Sebastian
Sam: Alberto Vazquez
Javi: Nando Gonzalez
Bruno: Bruno Squarcia
Edu: Jaime Zatarain
Chili: David Avila
Ali: Monica Vives
Lisa: Mamen Marquez

Translators
Book: Juan Martinez Moreno
Lyrics: Albert Mas Griera

OSAKA

Venue Shiki Theatre

Opening date 9 January 2005

Original principal cast
Donna: Chizu Hosaka
Sophie: Asami Higuchi
Sky: Ryota Suzuki
Tanya: Izumi Mori
Rosie: Yayoi Aoyama
Sam: Tadashi Watanabe
Harry: Shingo Akedo
Bill: Masuo Nonaka
Eddie: Hiroki Tange
Pepper: Michihito Otsuka
Ali: Yuki Morizane
Lisa: Kae Igarashi

Translators
Book: Hiromitsu Yukawa
Lyrics: Keita Asari

STOCKHOLM

Venue Cirkus Theatre

Opening date 12 February 2005

Original principal cast
Donna: Gunilla Backman
Sofie: Nina Lundseie
Tom: Niklas Riesbeck
Tanja: Charlott Strandberg
Karin: Sussie Eriksson
Sam: Reuben Sallmander
Harry: Bengt Bauler
Terje: Bill Hugg
Eddie: Martin Redhe Nord

Peppar: Henrik Orwander
Moa: Lisa Ostberg
Lisa: Jenny Miina

Translators
Book: Peter Dalle
Lyrics: Niklas Strömstedt

ANTWERP

Venue Stadsschouwberg

Opening date 12 March 2006

Closing date 2 July 2006

Original principal cast
Donna: Vera Mann
Sophie: Sasha Rosen
Sky: Davy Gilles
Tanja: Myriam Bronzwaar
Roos: Lulu Aertgeerts
Sam: Jan Schepens
Harrie: Mark Tijsmans
Bart: Marc Coessens
Eddie: Peter Fenwick
Pepper: Michael Macalintal
Ellie: Hannah Van Meurs
Lisa: Lokke Dieltiens

Translators
Book: Daniel Cohen
Lyrics: Coot Van Doesburgh

MOSCOW

Venue The MDM Theatre

Opening date 14 October 2006

Original principal cast
Donna: Elena Charkviani
Sophie: Natalia Bystrova
Sky: Andrey Kozhan
Tanya: Natalia Koretskaya
Rosie: Elena Kazarinova
Sam: Andrey Klyuev
Harry: Nikolay Stotsky
Bill: Vladimir Khalturin
Eddie: Denis Yasik
Pepper: Dmitry Bunin
Ali: Anna Guchenkova
Lisa: Victoria Kanatkina

Translators
Book: Natalia Federova
Lyrics: Alexey Kortnev

DRAMATIS PERSONAE

Benny Andersson and Björn Ulvaeus need no introduction, but here are brief notes on the other voices who have contributed to this book.

Bobby Aitken, sound designer, was a Led Zeppelin and prog rock fan in 1974, an 'uncool age' to be liking ABBA – especially in Glasgow. He was always interested in music and mixing bands, and still doesn't consider himself to be an especially technical sound designer. He joined Coventry's Belgrade Theatre as an assistant electrician, met Martin Koch on a production of *Cabaret* and joined him in London on *Chicago*. After more than ten years with the sound company Autograph, he set up Bobby Aitken Sound Designs, and as well as *MAMMA MIA!* has designed shows including *We Will Rock You* and several large-scale opera productions.

Adrian Bryan-Brown, US press representative, was born in Oxford, but has worked in the States for many years. He set up Boneau/Bryan-Brown Inc with Chris Boneau in 1991: it is now one of the leading PR firms in New York – specialising in promoting Broadway shows, from *Disney's The Lion King* to *Jersey Boys* and *Monty Python's Spamalot*. Adrian started working on *MAMMA MIA!* shortly after it opened in London and has overseen the press in North America ever since, as well as consulting on productions all over the world.

Nancy Coyne, US advertising director, saw the first London production of *MAMMA MIA!* with an American friend and her British husband. She remembers 'this dignified British gentleman jumping up and down with his umbrella in his hand. I said, "Mike you're going to hit somebody!"' Nancy worked on the Broadway production of *Chess* in 1988, by which time her company Serino Coyne – the biggest ad and marketing agency in US entertainment – was ten years old. They have handled most of the longest-running Broadway shows, including *Cats*, *Les Misérables*, *Phantom*, *Miss Saigon* and Disney's *The Lion King*, *Beauty And The Beast*, *Aida* and *Tarzan*.

Judy Craymer, MBE, global producer and creator of *MAMMA MIA!*, remembers watching ABBA win Eurovision, though in 1974 she was more interested in Led Zeppelin, Cream and Focus. She grew up in north London, passionate about horses, but also fascinated with theatre. After studying stage management at the Guildhall School of Music, Judy was a Stage Manager at the Haymarket Theatre, Leicester, the Actors Company and the Old Vic. She cut her musical theatre teeth on the original production of *Cats* before going on to join Tim Rice's production company, where she worked with Benny and Björn on *Chess*. She then moved into film and TV production and project development, producing the TV movie of Tim Firth's *Neville's Island* before giving up that career to concentrate on *MAMMA MIA!*. Judy was presented with a Woman of the Year award in 2002.

Jenny Galloway, the original Rosie, was more a Bob Dylan and Joni Mitchell fan, but she does have one ABBA memory: in the Green Room, a drinking club in Bristol where she was at the Old Vic, 'Dancing Queen' was always N9 on the jukebox. After working as an actress throughout the UK, her crossover to musical theatre came when she played Luce in the New Shakespeare Company's production of *The Boys From Syracuse* at Regent's Park Open Air Theatre, a performance which won her a Laurence Oliver Award in 1992 (she won another in 2000 for her role as Rosie in *MAMMA MIA!*). She has played Mme Thénardier in *Les Misérables*, Widow Corney in

Oliver! and Harriet Davernport in the BBC's *Grange Hill*, and also appeared in the movies *About A Boy*, *Johnny English* and *Mary Shelley's Frankenstein*.

Paul Garrington, associate director, was only a nipper when ABBA won Eurovision. He studied piano and cello and took a combined music and English degree, followed by a Masters in drama at Royal Holloway College, London. He has directed plays, operas and musicals in all sorts of places, from a National Tour of *Picasso's Women* with Jerry Hall for ATG to *The Maids* in a disused shop in Paris, and has enjoyed a long association with the RSC, including directing *La Nuit de Valognes* at Stratford-upon-Avon and leading the world tour of *A Midsummer Night's Dream*. He was resident director for the Really Useful Group on *Whistle Down The Wind* and the Pet Shop Boys' *Closer To Heaven* before joining *MAMMA MIA!* in 2001 to work on all the European and Asian productions of the show.

Nick Gilpin, synthesizer programmer, remembers as a young lad seeing the video for 'Super Trouper', which included some footage of ABBA in the studio. He was fascinated by all the recording gear, and thought, 'I want to do that'. He started out in 1986 working for Autograph Sound Recording, running their recording studio and working as a sound designer on many West End shows. His heart was really in the studio work, so in 1999 he joined forces with Martin Koch to found Koch & Gilpin, specialising in music production. As well as working on *MAMMA MIA!*, the company has composed and produced music for the opening titles of the UK Eurovision Song Contest and the Olivier and BAFTA Awards. Nick was co-producer, with Martin, of the London cast album of *MAMMA MIA!*, a role they have also undertaken for *Jerry Springer: The Opera* and *Billy Elliot*.

David Grindrod, casting consultant, co-founded David Grindrod Associates in 1998 after twenty years' experience in the theatre, including stints with the RSC and at the Aldwych Theatre and various West End plays and musicals. While working for the Really Useful Group on *Sunset Boulevard*, he was encouraged by Andrew Lloyd Webber to get into casting, and since then he has become one of the UK's most respected casting consultants, working especially, but not exclusively, on stage musicals.

Howard Harrison, lighting designer, remembers ABBA in Eurovision very clearly as a major cultural reference point. He had an aspiration to work in the theatre and entertainment industry, but was not sure in what capacity. After performing in the National Youth Theatre, he went to drama school and then got into stage management. He met Judy Craymer while working on Tim Rice's musical *Blondel*, and then did a stint as associate producer for Cameron Mackintosh before moving across into lighting design – what he calls his 'mid-life crisis' – specialising in opera and musicals. Howard's work includes *Mary Poppins* and the London 2005 revival of *Guys & Dolls*.

Catherine Johnson, who wrote the 'book' (script) for *MAMMA MIA!*, wasn't watching Eurovision in 1974: she was into soul and disco at that time. She hails from Suffolk, but has spent most of her life in the West Country, and started writing at five or six years old, seeing it as a potential career even though school careers officers told her no one makes any money out of being a writer. Catherine won the Bristol Old Vic/HTV Playwriting Award in 1988 with *Rag Doll*, which was later filmed by HTV. Her plays include *Renegades*, *Too Much Too Young* and *Shang-A-Lang*; she wrote the Channel 4 series *Love In The 21st Century*, and has written for

Casualty, *Byker Grove*, *Love Hurts* and *Gold*, as well as penning the screenplay for the film version of *MAMMA MIA!*. She was nominated for a Tony Award in 2002 for Best Musical Book for *MAMMA MIA!*.

John Kennedy, former head of Polygram, the original and principal investors in *MAMMA MIA!*, was at university in Leicester in 1974, and later spent part of his career at CBS, the label ABBA were with at the time, though his tastes were more Van Morrison, Roger Daltrey, Neil Young and 10cc. He always wanted to work in the music business, but trained as a solicitor and spent some time in shipping law before moving to Phonogram and then CBS. In 1984 he set up J P Kennedy & Co, a private legal practice specialising in music industry clients. He then acted as legal adviser and trustee for Band Aid, for which he received an OBE. John became CEO of Polygram UK in 1996, and of Universal Music UK in 1999. After three years as President of Universal Music International he became Chairman/CEO of IFPI, which promotes the interests of the recording industry worldwide.

Martin Koch, musical supervisor, remembers watching ABBA singing 'Waterloo' and particularly recalls being struck by the sight of Benny and Björn's platform boots. A trombonist and pianist, he studied at the Royal College of Music in London, and broke into conducting and writing with a job as assistant musical director on a London production of *Joseph And The Amazing Technicolor Dreamcoat*. His first major West End job was as MD on *Chicago*, and he has since worked as a musical supervisor on *Les Misérables*, *Miss Saigon*, *Cats*, *Martin Guerre*, *Billy Elliot* and all the productions of *MAMMA MIA!* worldwide. Martin set up Koch & Gilpin with Nick Gilpin in 1999, and received a Tony nomination in 2002 for his orchestration on *MAMMA MIA!* as well as a Grammy nomination the same year for his production of the show's cast album.

Nina Lannan, North American general manager and executive producer, didn't realise until she started work on *MAMMA MIA!* just how many ABBA songs she already knew. She began working in theatre management in 1980 and has been managing major musicals ever since, both on Broadway and on tour. Her credits include *Cats*, *Sunset Boulevard*, *Joseph And The Amazing Technicolor Dreamcoat*, *Thoroughly Modern Millie*, *Gypsy*, the Broadway staging of *Chess* and the Washington DC premiere of *Whistle Down The Wind*. She is the president of Nina Lannan Associates.

Phyllida Lloyd, director, recalls the 'compulsive cheesiness' of Eurovision in 1974, but at the time she was not a particular ABBA fan. Hell-bent at sixteen on being an actress, she studied English and Drama at Birmingham University, where she shared a house with Mark Thompson and began directing. After that, she joined the BBC and then became a trainee director at the Wolsey Theatre, Ipswich. She has directed plays including *Six Degrees Of Separation* and Terry Johnson's *Hysteria* at the Royal Court in London, *The Threepenny Opera* at the Donmar Warehouse, *Mary Stuart* at the Donmar and the Apollo, *The Duchess of Malfi* at the National Theatre, and operas for Opera North, the Royal Opera House, English National Opera and the Paris Opera. She received an International Emmy for the film version of *Gloriana* and was nominated for the Olivier Award for best director for *Mary Stuart*, for which she won the South Bank Theatre Award in 2006.

Siobhán McCarthy, the original Donna, was born in Dublin, where she once auditioned for a part in an ABBA tribute band. She came to London to create the role of the Mistress in the original stage production of *Evita*, later playing the title role. She was Mary Magdalene in *Jesus Christ Superstar*, Frankie Frayne in *On Your Toes*, and Fantine in *Les Misérables*. She created the role of Svetlana in the original production of *Chess*, had her first straight acting role in *Dancing At Lughnasa*, was

Mrs Johnstone in Willy Russell's *Blood Brothers*, and has appeared on TV in *Bad Girls* and *Lovejoy*.

Louise Pitre, the original Donna in Toronto, on the first US tour and on Broadway, remembers dancing to 'Waterloo' and 'Dancing Queen' at the University of Western Ontario, where she was studying music education, wearing 'the most outrageous pair of platform shoes, in green leather with gold and brown straps. I wish I still had them, I'd have worn them to the opening party.' She became a favourite on the Toronto theatre scene, working in musicals there and across North America, playing Fantine in *Les Misérables* in Montreal, Toronto and Paris and taking the title role in *Piaf*. When Louise auditioned for *Napoleon* in New York, the show's director recommended her to Phyllida Lloyd as Donna, a role for which she received a Tony nomination. She has released three CDs, most recently *Shattered* in 2005.

Louise Plowright, the original Tanya and London's second Donna, was a huge ABBA fan, doing the full hairbrush routines with her sister. She trained as an actress at the Bristol Old Vic theatre school, moving on to pay her dues on the provincial theatre circuit, and touring the UK in the Michael Rose production of *Hot Shoe Shuffle*. Louise was the feisty hairdresser Julie Cooper in the BBC soap *EastEnders*, subsequently appearing in *London's Burning*, *Families* and *Footballers' Wives: Extra Time*.

Tim Rice's first published song, 'That's My Story', was recorded in 1965 by the Nightshift and re-released in 2006 as the title track of an album featuring his totally unsuccessful work as a pop/rock writer and producer in the 1960s. In 1965 he met Andrew Lloyd Webber and by the end of the decade they had embarked on a run of theatrical success with the musicals *Joseph And The Amazing Technicolor Dreamcoat*, *Jesus Christ Superstar* and *Evita*. He created *Chess* in the mid 1980s with Benny and Björn, and in the 1990s worked primarily with the Disney studios, writing lyrics for *Beauty And The Beast* and *Aladdin* (music by Alan Menken), and for *The Lion King* and *Aida* (music by Elton John). Tim, who was knighted in 1994, has three Oscars and still occasionally appears as lead vocalist for the band Whang and the Cheviots.

Michael Simkins, Sam in the London show, was 200 yards away when ABBA triumphed at Eurovision: his parents ran a sweet shop in Brighton. The young Michael, an enthusiast for amateur operatics, was more into Gilbert & Sullivan and jazz, but ABBA provided the soundtrack to his love life. After RADA Michael was in rep for four or five years before making it to the National Theatre, where he played opposite Michael Gambon in *A View From the Bridge*. His first musical was *Company* for Sam Mendes, and then he played Sam in year two of *MAMMA MIA!*'s London production. He returned for another run in year five, and has also appeared as Billy Flynn in *Chicago*. Michael is the author of the best-selling *What's My Motivation*, a wry look at the life of an actor.

Lisa Stokke, the original Sophie, born in Tromsø, Norway in 1975, and grew up dancing to ABBA. She went to a local music college and from there to the Liverpool Institute of Performing Arts: the role of Sophie in the original production of *MAMMA MIA!* was her professional debut, and she calls it 'the best start anyone could wish for in their career'. She's appeared on TV in *Jonathan Creek*, co-presented and performed at the 46664 Arctic concert for Nelson Mandela's AIDS charity, and in 2006 EMI released *A Piece Of Lisa*, a collection of her favourite songs from musical theatre and film – including her own version of 'The Winner Takes It All'.

Mark Thompson, production designer, was never into rock – more Shirley Bassey and Streisand; ABBA definitely struck a chord. He was often taken to the theatre as a child and would go back home and draw little scenes.

He studied theatre at Birmingham University, sharing a house there with Phyllida Lloyd, who describes him as 'one of the greatest cooks any student house could possibly have had gracing their kitchen'. He started at the Swan Theatre, Worcester, and moved to the Leeds Playhouse, Royal Exchange, Chichester and the RSC. He carved out his award-winning reputation (four Olivier awards) designing shows including *The Wind In The Willows* at the National, *Joseph And The Amazing Technicolor Dreamcoat* at the Palladium, *Art* at Wyndham's and Terry Johnson's *Hysteria*, directed by Phyllida Lloyd, at the Royal Court. Mark's other work includes *Doctor Dolittle*, *Company* and *Bombay Dreams*.

Andrew Treagus, executive producer, started as a stage manager in rep then became technical manager at the RSC and Royal Court, working on plays by David Storey, Christopher Hampton and David Hare (*Teeth'n'Smiles* with Helen Mirren). His 'Damascus moment' as far as musical theatre was concerned was working for the producer Michael White on *A Chorus Line*, watching Michael Bennett directing the show. He worked for Michael White for five years, on shows including *Annie* and *Ain't Misbehavin'*, and then set up Andrew Treagus Associates, managing *Starlight Express* for Andrew Lloyd-Webber and *Grease* for Robert Stigwood. He was the general manager for the London production of *MAMMA MIA!* and is the executive producer of the international productions.

Nichola Treherne, associate choreographer, has worked with Anthony Van Laast for twenty years. She has associate choreographed shows ranging from *Hair* to *Jesus Christ Superstar*, *Bombay Dreams* and *Whistle Down The Wind*, was responsible for the musical staging of *Romeo And Juliet* at the Chichester Festival and *Music Of Andrew Lloyd-Webber*, and has been a resident and associate director for *Joseph And The Amazing Technicolor Dreamcoat* and artistic supervisor for *Starlight Express*.

Anthony Van Laast, choreographer, trained at the London School of Contemporary Dance, later joining the Company as a performer and choreographer. From there he moved into entertainment, working with Kate Bush, creating dance routines for *The Two Ronnies*, *The Hot Shoe Show*, *Abbacadabra* and several Royal Variety Show performances, a dance spectacle for the Eurovision Song Contest, and choreographing shows including *Joseph And The Amazing Technicolor Dreamcoat*, *Hair* and *Jesus Christ Superstar*. Anthony's range of activities meant he was able to work simultaneously with the RSC and the Chippendales. He has worked with Jonathan Miller on the ENO's production of *The Mikado* and with Michael Crawford and Siegfried & Roy in Las Vegas. His production received an Oliver award for *Candide* at the Old Vic, a Tony nomination for *Bombay Dreams* and an MBE for services to dance and choreography.

PICTURE CREDITS

The Publishers would like to thank the following people for their kind permission to reproduce the photographs and illustrations in this book. Every effort has been made to trace the copyright holders and the artists shown in the production shots of *MAMMA MIA!*. Should there be any omissions or errors we would be happy to correct them in future editions.

Jacket
© 2008 Universal Studios, All Rights Reserved, © Lorenzo Agius.

Insides
Bobby Aitken (BA); Mats Andersson (MA); Catherine Ashmore (CA); Brinkhoff/Mögenburg (B/M); Andy Buchanan (AB); Serino Coyne (SC); Philip Dodd (PD); Robert Doyle (RD); Bruce Glikas (BG); David Grindrod (DG); Anders Hanser (AH); Kit Hawkins (KH); Wolfgang 'Bubi' Heilemann – www.rockphoto.de (WH); Lyn Hughes (LH); Catherine Johnson (CJ); Littlestar (L); Juno Lee (JL); Michael Le Poer Trench (MLPT); Emile Luider (EL); Joan Marcus (JM); James McCauley (JMcC); Liz McGinity (LMcG); Ian McRae (IMcR); Peter Mountain (PM); Fatimah Namdar (FN); Martin Norris (MN); Premium Publishing (PP) Photographers – Torbjörn Calvero, Anders Hanser, Ola Lager, Lars Larsson, Bengt H Malmqvist; John Reardon (JR) Redferns (R); Rex Features (RF); Atsutoshi Shimosaka (AS); Martin Skoog (MS); Peter Simpkin (PS); The Sunday Times (ST); Claire Teare (CT); Ian Tilton (IT); Nichola Treherne (NT); Deen van Meer (DvM); Myfi Williams (MW); Robert Workman (RW).
From the movie: Meryl Streep; Pierce Brosnan; Colin Firth; Stellan Skarsgård; Julie Walters; Dominic Cooper; Amanda Seyfried; Christine Baranski, © Peter Mountain

Key: t = top, c = centre, b = bottom, l = left, r = right

Front Endpaper PP, 1 WH, 2-3 MS, 4l JM, 4r WH, 5 AS, 7t MS, 7b AB, 9l ST, 9tr MW, 9br RF, 11 WH, 12-13 PP, 15tl, tr and br WH, 15bl PP, 16tl, cl and 16-17 WH, 16bl RF, 18 WH, 19t WH, 19b PP, 21-25 WH, 26 PP, 27t WH, 27b PP, 28-31 PP, 33-41 WH, 42-44 PP, 45 WH, 46 PP, 47 WH, 48t WH, 49 WH, 51t RF, 51b WH, 52-55 WH, 56-65 PP, 66-67 WH, 69t PP, 69b WH, 71 WH, 72-77 PP, 79t WH, 79cl, cr, bl and br PP, 80 tl, cl, bl R/Peter Still, 80-81 PP, 82-83 PP, 84 PP, 85tl WH, 85tr, cl, cr, bl and br PP, 86 PP, 87tl, tr, b PP, 87cr WH, 88-100 PP, 100-101t PP, 101bl WH, 101br PP, 102-127 PP, 128/129 AS, 130-131 WH, 132 Private Collection, 133 Private Collection, 134 PP, 135 MLPT, 136t and b RF, 137 Private Collection, 138-139 PP, 141 JM, 143 Private Collection, 145 CJ, 147 MS, 148 JM, 150l Private Collection, 150r RW, 151 RF, 152 Private Collection, 153 IT, 154 PD, 155 JM, 156 IMcR, 157 Private Collection, 158 MN, 159 KH, 161 Private Collection, 162tl Courtesy Siobhan McCarthy, 162acl PS, 162bcl PS, 162bl PS, 162tr FN, 162acr PS, 162bcr Courtesy Nicolas Colicos, 162br PS, 163 CA, 164 Private Collection, 165 L, 167 DG, 169-177 CA, 178 L, 179 Private Collection, 181-188 CA, 189 Private Collection, 190-191 CA, 192-3 MS, 194 PP, 195 CA, 197 Courtesy Koch & Gilpin, 199 CA, 200t L/Photography M+H, 200c L/Photography Dewynters, 200b L, 201 JM, 202-203 CA, 204-207t JM, 207b MP, 208-211 JM, 213 CA, 214 Private Collection, 215-217 JM, 218t JM, 218b SC, 219-222 JM, 223t JM, 223b BG, 224 LH, 225 JM, 227 NT, 228-231 JM, 232 EL, 233t DvM, 233b-235 B/M, 236 Private Collection, 237t Stage Entertainment/Stefan Malzkorn, 237c, bl and br B/M, 238t AS, 239 JL, 241tl JL, 241tr JM, 241cl RD, 241cr DvM, 241bl B/M, 241br MS, 242t L, 242b L, 243t B/M, 243b CT, 244-5 JM, 246 JMcC, 247 MS, 249 BA, 251 JR, 252 LMcG, 253 CT, 262 MS, Back Endpaper MS

ACKNOWLEDGEMENTS

Judy, Benny and Björn would like to thank Philip Dodd, whose task was particularly onerous. Firstly, for his patience in making himself available at short notice as all our schedules altered constantly and secondly for his brilliance in capturing the feeling of fun that defines *MAMMA MIA!* and for the many fresh insights into the perennially popular songs of ABBA, both sections of the book distilled from so many different voices. His dedication to ensuring that the mass of information he had to work with was as accurate as possible means the exhaustive record that is this book will stand the test of time. Thank you also to Michael Dover and his team at the publishers Weidenfeld & Nicolson, particularly Debbie Woska, David Rowley and Emily Hedges, for making the book happen. Thank you to the team at Littlestar, Claire Teare, Liz McGinity and Huw Williams for keeping us all on track and to Görel Hanser at Music & Artist Services. A thank you also to all those who contributed their voices to the book to help create this extraordinary record. We are very proud of the enormous amount of work that went into making the book. *MAMMA MIA!* certainly didn't happen overnight but when it did become a reality it subsequently broke all records. We hope the book will do the same!

Music and Lyrics: Benny Andersson and Björn Ulvaeus
With some songs by Stig Anderson

Book: Catherine Johnson

Creative Team: Phyllida Lloyd, Anthony Van Laast, Mark Thompson, Howard Harrison, Andrew Bruce, Bobby Aitken, Martin Koch

London Associate Team: Peter Addis, Nichola Treherne, Jonathan Allen, Lucy Gaiger, David Holmes, Andrew Voller, Nick Gilpin, Rodger Neate, David Grindrod

North American Associate Team: Robert McQueen, David Holcenberg, Tom Capps, Janet Rothermel, Martha Banta, Tom Caruso, Nancy Thun, Scott Traugott, Angie Kahler, Ed McCarthy, David Patridge, Edward G Robinson, Josh Marquette, Arthur Siccardi, Tara Rubin

Canadian Associate Team: Madeline Paul, Tracey Flye, Elizabeth Baird, Pat Thomas, Dianne Woodrow, Joanna Topp, Charles Chu, Stephanie Gorin, John Wilbur

Australian Associate Team: Gary Young, Stephen Amos, Darren Yap, Cass Jones, Richard Pacholski, Peter Grubb, Suzy Strout, Mark Rowe, Pat Boggs, Lynne Ruthven

International Tour & Foreign Language Productions Team: Paul Garrington, Andrew Wale, Stephen Palin, Nichola Treherne, Leah Sue Morland, Tim Stanley, Hans Johansson, Francis Chiappetta, Martin Lowe, Nick Finlow, Seann Alderking, Carlton Edwards, Jonathan Allen, Jane Slattery, Lucy Gaiger, Conchita Scott, Ruth McCorkindale, Rick Strickland, Brian Beasley, Richard Brooker, David Holmes, Andrew Voller, Pia Virolainen, Ros Evans, Marcus Kromer, Phillip Adams, Kim Robinson, Matt Towell, Stewart Crosbie, Simon Marlowe, Claire Whitfield, Stephen Crockett

Original Producers: Judy Craymer, Richard East and Björn Ulvaeus for Littlestar in association with Universal

Co-Producers Around the World: David Mirvish, Ed Mirvish, Brian Sewell (Canada); Paul Dainty, John Robertson, Louise Withers (Australia); Joop Van den Ende – Stage Entertainment (Holland, Germany, Spain, Belgium & Russia); Keita Asari – Shiki Theatrical Company (Japan); Myung Sung Park – The Seensee Musical Company (Korea); Benny Andersson, Björn Ulvaeus, Görel Hanser – Briggen Teaterproduktion (Sweden); Nick Grace – NGM (International Tour)

Management: Ashley Grisdale, Peter Austin, Katie Wolfryd, Claire Teare, Liz McGinity, Jo Reedman, Sheila Egbujie, Kerri Jordan, Matthew Willis, Kimberley Wallwork (Littlestar)

Press, Advertising & Marketing: Peter Thompson, Amanda Malpass, Michael McCabe, Anthony Pye-Jeary, Bob King, Jo Hutchison, Tom Littlechild, Jules Goddard, Mark Borkowski, Dee McCourt, Gavin Nugent, Claire Teare, Liz McGinity (London); Adrian Bryan-Brown, Nancy Coyne, David Kane, Greg Corradetti, Ruth Rosenberg, Caroline Lenher, Lance Williams, Tanya Grubich, Laura Matalon, David Kirvin, Susan Taylor (North America); John Karastamatis, Young In Turner, Randy Alldread, Sandra Iacobelli, Judi Pressman (Canada); Suzie Howie, Michele Bribosia (Australia)

Theatre Merchandise: Carlos Candal (GMG); Randi Grossman (Max Merchandising)

Professional Advisers: Howard Jones, Claire Lewis, Barry Shaw, Richard Walton, Scott Lazarus, Chris Cacace, Mark Devereux

And a special thank you to all the amazing actors, musicians, stage management, crews, theatre staff and creative teams that make *MAMMA MIA!* happen night after night around the world!

Philip Dodd would particularly like to thank Benny Andersson, Björn Ulvaeus, Judy Craymer, Catherine Johnson and Phyllida Lloyd for making themselves available for interview on numerous occasions, and all the interviewees for sharing their thoughts and memories: Bobby Aitken, Adrian Bryan-Brown, Nancy Coyne, Jenny Galloway, Paul Garrington, Nick Gilpin, David Grindrod, Howard Harrison, John Kennedy, Martin Koch, Nina Lannan, Siobhán McCarthy, Louise Pitre, Louise Plowright, Tim Rice, Michael Simkins, Lisa Stokke, Mark Thompson, Andrew Treagus, Nichola Treherne and Anthony Van Laast. Organising those interviews would not have been possible without the persistence and hard work of Claire Teare, Liz McGinity, Mel Bartram and Huw Williams at Littlestar, who also provided invaluable research support, and without the help of Görel Hanser, Annette Stone and Stefan Saager and the staff at the Hotel Rival. It was a pleasure to work again with so many former comrades-in-arms: Michael Dover, David Rowley, Jennie Condell and Debbie Woska at Weidenfeld & Nicolson; Sian Rance and Emil Dacanay at D.R. ink; Emily Hedges; Adèle Herson and her team at Adèle's Typing Works; Jez at Printhouse Notting Hill and his colleagues; and Ben Donald, who gave quick and efficient support. And thanks as ever to my family, Wan, Wan Mae and new arrival Mei Mae, especially for singing 'Money, Money, Money' and 'Dancing Queen' all the way home from Devon.

INDEX

First published in 2006 by Weidenfeld & Nicolson
This edition published in 2008 by Phoenix Illustrated
10 9 8 7 6 5 4 3 2 1

A CIP catalogue record for this book is available from the British Library.

ISBN-13: 978 0 7538 2101 5

Interviews by Philip Dodd
Design direction by David Rowley
Design style by Lippa Pearce
Design by D.R. ink
Design assistance by Justin Hunt
Picture research by Emily Hedges
Editorial by Debbie Woska and Jo Murray
Research by Brónagh Woods
Index by Alan Rutter

Colour reproduction by Coloursystems
Printed and bound in Italy by Printer Trento srl

Phoenix Illustrated
The Orion Publishing Group Ltd
Orion House
5 Upper St Martin's Lane
London WC2H 5EA

The Orion Publishing Group's policy is to use papers that are natural, renewable and
recyclable products and made from wood grown in sustainable forests.

Mixed Sources
Product group from well-managed
forests and other controlled sources
www.fsc.org Cert no. CQ-COC-000012
© 1996 Forest Stewardship Council
FSC

The dates given on the contents page relate to UK single releases, or UK album releases for
songs that were not released as singles.

MAMMA MIA! artists/casts are named on the relevant pages except:
Title page: Charlott Strandberg, Gunilla Backman and Sussie Eriksson with the original
Stockholm cast
Contents: Louise Pitre as Donna in the original Broadway show; Izumi Mori, Chizu Hosaka
and Yoyoi Aoyama from the original Tokyo cast
This page: Niklas Riesback and Nina Lundseie from the original Stockholm cast
Back endpaper: Gunilla Backman and the original Stockholm cast